COASTAL TRAILS OF THE CAROLINAS

COASTAL TRAILS OF THE CAROLINAS

Johnny Molloy

FALCONGUIDES

GUILFORD, CONNECTICUT

This is for those who love hiking and love the coastline of the Carolinas. May this book help you meld your two loves.

FALCONGUIDES®

An imprint of The Rowman & Littlefield Publishing Group, Inc.
4501 Forbes Blvd., Ste. 200
Lanham, MD 20706
www.rowman.com

Falcon and FalconGuides are registered trademarks and Make Adventure Your Story is a trademark of The Rowman & Littlefield Publishing Group, Inc.

Distributed by NATIONAL BOOK NETWORK

Photos by Johnny Molloy unless noted otherwise.
Maps by The Rowman & Littlefield Publishing Group, Inc.

British Library Cataloguing in Publication Information available

Library of Congress Cataloging-in-Publication Data available

ISBN 978-1-4930-4171-8 (paper: alk. paper)
ISBN 978-1-4930-4172-5 (electronic)

∞™ The paper used in this publication meets the minimum requirements of American National Standard for Information Sciences—Permanence of Paper for Printed Library Materials, ANSI/NISO Z39.48-1992.

CONTENTS

ACKNOWLEDGMENTS

Thanks to my wife, Keri Anne, for accompanying me on and off the trail. Thanks to Sierra Designs for providing excellent tents and sleeping bags in which to sleep. Thanks also to the land managers and trail builders and maintainers, otherwise we wouldn't have coastal trails to hike.

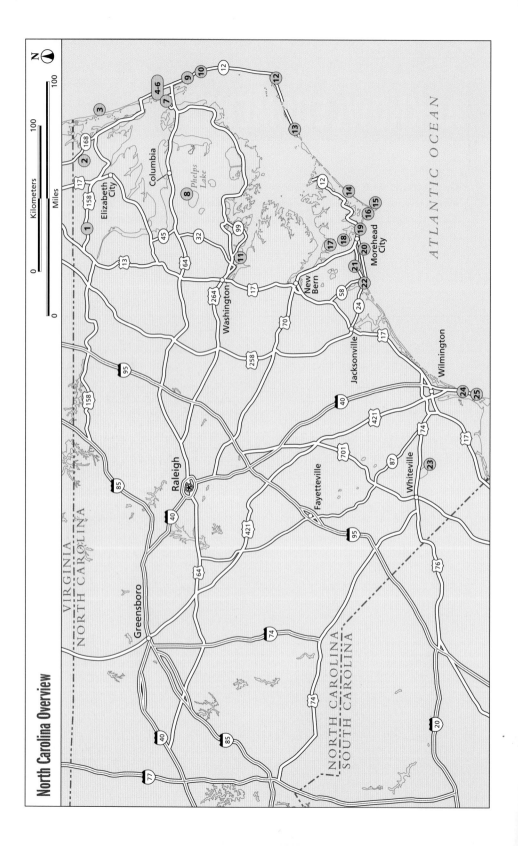

North Carolina Overview

South Carolina Overview

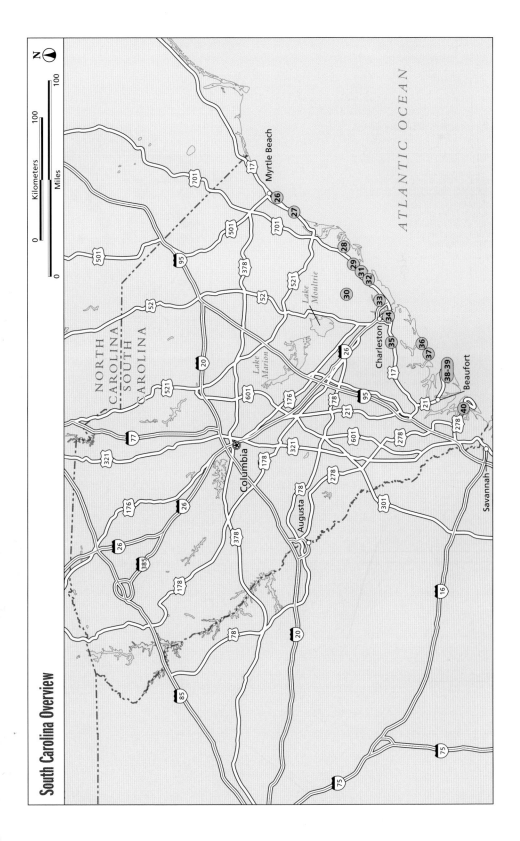

This hike traces dikes rising above
wildlife rich wetlands (hike 2).

MEET YOUR GUIDE

Native Southerner **Johnny Molloy** has been exploring the great outdoors and writing about them for three decades. The writer and adventurer has penned more than seventy outdoor hiking, camping, and paddling guides, as well as true outdoor-adventure stories. His outdoor passion started on a backpacking trip in Great Smoky Mountains National Park while attending the University of Tennessee. That first foray unleashed a love of the outdoors that has led Molloy to spend much of his time hiking, backpacking, canoe camping, and tent camping, averaging 150 nights per year under the stars for more than thirty consecutive years. Friends enjoyed his outdoor adventure stories, and one even suggested he write a book. He pursued his friend's idea and soon parlayed his love of the outdoors into a full-time occupation, that of outdoor

writer. Molloy has paddled, hiked, and camped throughout North Carolina and South Carolina, writing several other outdoor guides to these states in addition to *Coastal Trails of the Carolinas*. He continues writing and traveling extensively throughout the United States, engaging in a variety of outdoor pursuits. His non-outdoor interests include serving the Lord as a Gideon and University of Tennessee Volunteers sports. For the latest on Molloy, visit johnnymolloy.com.

Beach view of
Roanoke Sound
(hike 5).

HOW TO USE THIS GUIDE

This book covers trails along and adjacent to the coastline of North Carolina and South Carolina, from the Virginia state line in the north to the Georgia boundary in the south, including locales directly along the Atlantic Ocean, barrier islands, and the Atlantic Coastal Plain. The **Trail Finder** helps you sort these coastal hikes by seven categories—best hikes for beaches, views, children, dogs, solitude, history, photography. The Top Five Hikes are family friendly and sprinkled north to south as samples of coastal Carolina's most stunning scenery.

Before You Hit the Trail gives you an overview of North Carolina's and South Carolina's coastal ecology and history. It also includes sections that underline the area's highlights and hazards and information to help you prepare for your hike and enhance your excursion.

The hikes are categorized by state, moving from north to south within each state. The trails are chosen primarily for the close proximity to the shoreline and superlative scenery for the hiker's maximum enjoyment of a coastal experience. The hikes vary in distances from under 1 mile to 47 miles, though the vast majority of them are around 5 miles and make for excellent day hikes (only 1 hike is longer than 10 miles). The hikes were chosen for points of interest, appealing setting, and trail conditions. Recommended routes are both there-and-back as well as loops. Shuttles—where necessary—are indicated in the narratives. The hike distances were calculated using a handheld GPS unit, which the author personally carried on every single trek.

Each hike starts with a short **summary** of the hike's highlights. This is followed by **The Rundown.** These quick overviews give you a taste of the hiking adventure to follow. You'll learn about the trail terrain and the surprises each route has to offer.

Features below **The Rundown** include the following:

Distance gives the total distance of the recommended route—one-way for loops or round-trip for out-and-back sections of trail. Options detail alternate routes along the given hike. The options may shorten the route or describe spur trails to add more highlights to the hike.

Start describes the location of the trailhead.

Nearest town helps orient you to the location of the trail.

Hiking time gives the average time it will take to cover the route. This is based on the total distance as well as conditions and difficulty of the trail. Your personal fitness level will affect your time.

Fees and permits indicates whether you need to carry any money with you for park entrance fees and what permits are necessary for the hike.

Conveniences tells about trail amenities, including visitor centers, restrooms, and picnic areas.

Beach access lets you know if there is an accessible beach from the trail.

Trail users lists those with whom you may share the trail. This is most often bicyclists and occasionally equestrians. Birders, backpackers, and beachcombers are found along the paths as well.

Trail surface details general information about what to expect underfoot.

Difficulty offers information about the hike's level of difficulty. Each hike has been given a level of difficulty using a rating system developed from several sources and personal experience. These levels are meant to be a guideline only—hikes may prove easier or harder for different people depending on ability and physical fitness.

Easy: 4 miles or less total trip distance in one day, with minimal elevation gain and paved or smooth-surface dirt trail.

Moderate: Up to 8 miles total trip distance in one day, with moderate elevation gain and potentially rough terrain.

Difficult: More than 10 miles total trip distance in one day, with rough and/or rocky terrain.

Highlights focuses on natural attractions whether they be flora, fauna, geological, or historic.

Canine compatibility details trail regulations for your furry friends.

Schedule lists the opening and closing times of parks and preserves where the trails are located.

Managing agency lists the address, phone number, and website for the local land manager(s) in charge of the trails within the hike. Get trail access information before you head out, or contact the land manager after your visit if you see problems with trail erosion, damage, or misuse.

Finding the trailhead gives dependable driving directions to parking for each hike.

What to See is the meat of the chapter. Detailed and honest, it's a carefully researched impression of the trail. It also often includes lots of area history, both natural and human.

Miles and Directions is a concise summary of key junctions and significant landmarks along the trail. Mileage cues identify all turns and trail name changes, as well as points of interest.

Sidebars throughout the book include interesting information about the area or trail that doesn't necessarily pertain to the specific hike, but offers some human or natural tidbit that may pique your interest to explore beyond the simple mechanics of the trek.

Enjoy your time in the outdoors, and remember to pack out what you pack in.

TOP FIVE HIKES

1. SHACKLEFORD BANKS.
This family-friendly trek starts with a fun ferry ride, then you can walk the beach and scan for ponies. The shelling isn't bad either, and you can hike as long or short as you desire.

The wild ponies of Shackleford Banks (hike 16)

Scenes like this make the Charles Towne Landing State Historic Site hike a winner (hike 34)

2. CHARLES TOWNE LANDING STATE HISTORIC SITE.
Family fun abounds here as you delve into the first settlement in South Carolina. First view a wild animal park before stopping by re-created buildings of Old Charles Towne. Stop for a watery panorama and check out the wooden ship *Adventure*. View ancient live oaks and a restored home and gardens.

Admiring iconic Cape Lookout Lighthouse (hike 15)

A shell sample at Botany Bay (hike 36)

Hiking Elliott Coues Nature Trail (hike 19)

3. CAPE LOOKOUT LIGHTHOUSE HIKE.
This is one of the must-do trips. Take a ferry to see iconic Cape Lookout Lighthouse, then cruise the beach to visit historic Cape Lookout Village before looping back to the point of origin.

4. ELLIOTT COUES NATURE TRAIL.
Explore maritime woods, marsh, and tall dunes and walk along the rolling Atlantic Ocean while circling a Civil War fort that is worth a tour itself.

5. BOTANY BAY.
Leave a plantation turned wildlife management area, crossing islands to an Atlantic beach, and trek along remote shores of sand on a wild, protected Carolina coast.

BEFORE YOU HIT THE TRAIL

The Carolina coast is both scenic and historic. North Carolina boasts 301 miles of Atlantic Ocean shoreline between the Virginia border to the north and the South Carolina border to the south. South Carolina claims 187 miles of Atlantic frontage between its boundaries with North Carolina and Georgia. These two numbers, calculated by the Congressional Research Service, count direct miles of land bordering the Atlantic Ocean. However, when you add up the curving shorelines of individual barrier islands, tidal rivers, and estuaries, as does the National Oceanic and Atmospheric Administration (NOAA), you get a much higher figure for each state. North Carolina has 3,375 miles of coastline, and South Carolina features 2,876 miles. That is a lot of coast! No matter the method of reckoning, both North Carolina and South Carolina offer up a wealth of beautiful coastline and coastal trails upon which to explore these shores.

Both North Carolina and South Carolina were part of the original thirteen colonies established by the British. However, the stories of these two states start much earlier than that. Aboriginal natives populated both states in their entirety. In fact, they left their mark along the coast in the form of shell rings that date back 4,000 years as well as midden mounds. Coastal natives typically spent the warm season out on the islands and adjacent tidal lands harvesting shellfish and other treasures of the sea, enjoying the bug-relieving breezes, then working their way inland come fall, avoiding hurricane season as well as obtaining fresh meat and other foods in the woods. European explorers began working along the Carolina coastline as early as the mid-1500s. Sir Walter Raleigh, for whom the North Carolina capital is named, attempted to colonize the coast in 1585, sending a group of settlers to what is now Roanoke Island (Raleigh stayed back in England). Times were tough for the colonists, and they sent for more colonists from England (bringing along Virginia Dare, the first English child to be born in North America, on Roanoke Island on August 18, 1587; Dare County is named for her). When help finally arrived in 1590, however, the entire colony was gone, with only the word *Croatan* carved on the fort wall, leaving a great historical mystery. Later settlements were more successful, and North Carolina expanded from east to west. The coast of North Carolina is also known as the base for famed pirate Blackbeard. Of course you can't talk about Carolina coastal history without bringing up the world's first airplane flight by the Wright Brothers at Kitty Hawk.

You can actually go on a hike (detailed in this guide) at South Carolina's first European settlement—Charles Towne Landing State Historic Site. This was the precursor of the modern-day Charleston. The Civil War stands prominent along the South Carolina coast, as the conflict infamously began in April 1861 at Fort Sumter. Other parts of the Carolina coast were contested for during the War Between the States.

Later, both states began to realize the true beauty of their coastlines and sought to protect them. This protection has taken place in the form of national parks, state parks, state wildlife management areas, national wildlife refuges, national forests, and historic sites. These protected lands are the places upon which coastal trails have been lain, and they are the places where we can enjoy the combination of hiking and the coastline, from the forests of the Atlantic Coastal Plain to the shores of the strange Carolina bay lakes to the beaches of barrier islands.

Starting in North Carolina up near the Virginia state line, you have Merchants Millpond State Park, a protected swath of water and woods on the Atlantic Coastal Plain. Mackay Island National Wildlife Refuge is the first of a string of national wildlife refuges in the Tar Heel State. Following that is the historic Currituck Beach Lighthouse and the Wright Brothers National Memorial. Cape Hatteras National Seashore and Cape Lookout National Seashore protect the string of barrier islands fronting the Atlantic and provide a large parcel of protected shoreline where we can hike, camp, and beachcomb, as well as view historic lighthouses. Some of the adventures use ferries to reach islands where you can hike, explore, and even camp in a primitive setting. Lighthouses are a special part of the Carolina coast, and they are detailed when at or near a particular hike. Croatan National Forest includes the Neusiok Trail, a backwoods hiking adventure. Walk smaller protected parcels managed by the Nature Conservancy. Goose Creek State Park is located along tidal waters well back from the Atlantic. Preserved forts along the North Carolina coast provide additional hiking opportunities.

A variety of coastal trails await you down South Carolina way. Take a hike at venerated Myrtle Beach State Park. Walk the beach and the trails of Huntington Beach State Park. Explore preserved tidal wildlife management areas at Santee Coastal Reserve and South Tibwin. Walk through the vast wildlands of the Francis Marion National Forest on the Palmetto Trail and other pathways. Enjoy nature at Palmetto Islands Park, as well as at Caw Caw Interpretive Center. Take a trip back in time at Charles Towne Landing State Historic Site. Visit two beachfront destinations at Edisto Beach State Park and Hunting Island State Park, where you can walk to the top of the lighthouse there. Trek the wild beaches of Botany Bay and enjoy an extended island hike at Pinckney Island National Wildlife Refuge.

The Carolina coast is a wonderful world where the ocean meets the land, the place where rising and falling tides meet the surf, sandy beaches, extensive marshes, and waterways big and small. The coastline is your ticket to maritime forests, majestic pinelands, wetlands fresh and salt, wild islands, wildlife rich ponds, shell-laden beaches, and deep freshwater swamps where inland terrain invariably slopes to the sea.

Walking coastal trails and beaches of North Carolina and South Carolina presents a chance to engage in nature's beauty and biodiversity, as well as explore extensive human history overlain on the shores. Visitor centers and interpretive information at many of the hikes enhance your ability to learn about these special places. And as peoples have been drawn to the coast for time immemorial, so are we in this day and age drawn to walk these destinations with much appreciation for the experience as well as for the escape from the rush rush of our increasingly electronically chained lives.

A DYNAMIC COASTLINE

The coastline, where the land meets the sea, is a continually changing place, a dynamic interaction of solid and liquid. Wind and the ceaseless action of the tides untiringly shape the shoreline. These changes are usually slow but nonstop. Barrier islands move,

Visitors explore Bodie Island Lighthouse (hike 9)

water eats away at the land. Other changes are quick and drastic when hurricanes strike the shore with their powerful blows and deluges, flooding areas and creating new water channels. Winds can flatten groves of trees or move sands instantaneously. Of course we all know what hurricanes and tropical storms can do to man-made structures on the shoreline. The devastation can be sure and quick. But remember this: Disasters happen only where the works of man have been introduced. The Carolina coast wouldn't be the Carolina coast without the shaping force of hurricanes and tropical storms. Over time the barrier islands and tidal shores will be built back, sands gathering where they always have, and then another hurricane will come, resuming the cycle.

This shaping of the land speaks to another dynamic part of the coastline: dunes. Sand dunes are important to the overall ecosystem of barrier islands and other coastal lands. Winds blowing off the Atlantic build up these dunes, with a little help from such plants as sea oats. These plants and their roots form an infrastructure upon which the dunes can rise. The highest dunes are often the most vegetated. Barrier islands and their dunes are not only attractive but functional as well. They absorb impact from hurricanes, providing the first defense of bay waters and the mainland. It is strange to think of, but barrier islands migrate. Winds primarily come in from the southeast, pounding the shore and pushing sand westward. Sand builds on the western end of the islands, while it is being stripped away from the eastern ends of barrier islands. Hurricanes like 1989's Hugo, 2016's Matthew, and 2018's Florence make more sudden changes. Therefore, expect and appreciate an ever-changing coastline, altering as it does on nature's schedule.

There is yet one more important agent of change for beach ecosystems—humans. Condos and other developments flatten dunes and channelize marshes. Propellers damage the seafloor. Swimmers and sunbathers dump their trash on the sand and in the water. Let's be a positive agent for change, working with nature instead of against it.

Our shores are more precious now than ever, and it is our responsibility to take care of them. I believe if you go out and experience the natural wonders of the Carolina coast, if you build an appreciation for the beauty and biodiversity of our distinctive natural legacy, you will in turn develop a protective attitude toward the coast and all it preserves and nurtures.

SAFETY BY THE SEA

The seductive sea and the salt life can seem like an endless summer day on a beach lounger. However, hiking along the coast is not always a carefree vacation. The lure of a hiking trail in the woods or a walk along the beach brings many visitors to the Carolina coast, and the vast majority of them go home with nothing more than good memories. There are hazards to look out for, however, especially when you are walking along the beach. A little self-education can help ensure a positive outing. The warmer times of the year are the most popular beach times. This means hot days—and I mean hot—and not the best for hiking. If going during this time, drink plenty of nonalcoholic fluids, keep yourself shaded for a reasonable amount of time, and cool off in the water to prevent symptoms that could lead to heat exhaustion. Most important, the sun can do plenty of damage on its own. By all means wear a hat and use plenty of sunscreen. Of course shade and clothing are the most effective sunscreens around. I personally try to keep as much of my body covered in clothing as I can tolerate.

Beachcombing is a time-honored coastal hiking pastime. Unfortunately, especially in populated areas, trash sometimes washes up on the beach. Watch for nails on boards, glass, and other foot-puncturing items. Consider wearing sandals instead of hiking the beach in bare feet, especially after the sun starts to go down. After a hike there's nothing like a swim in the ocean. Beaches with lifeguards are ideal, but that is not always possible. Exercise caution when swimming and keep apprised of tide and surf conditions.

You are much more likely to get injured in a car wreck on the way to your coastal hike than to get bitten by a shark, but there are a few oceanic organisms that can ruin your day. Jellyfish can inflict damage. The most notable is the Portuguese man-of-war, whose tentacles can cause severe burns and blisters even if it is dead on the beach. Sea nettles and upside-down jellyfish cause rashes and itching. Not all jellyfish are toxic, of course, but stay away from all jellyfish as a rule of thumb.

Don't forget that threats run both ways. All of us who want to enjoy the beautiful Carolina coastline also pose a threat to them. When you interact with coastal environments, tread lightly. Picking sea oats destabilizes the dunes. Driving motorized vehicles in restricted areas tears up the landscape. Honor fishing regulations. You know what not to do. Think about what you *can* do. Be a steward of the land. Together we can make the Carolina coastline the bountiful beautiful place that we know it can be and should be in the future.

Here are some tips for a safe and happy coastal hike:

1. Use your smartphone to check the local tides to avoid being stranded or swept out.

2. Respect posted signs on water conditions and watch for high surf and wind advisories.

3. Never turn your back to the ocean. Rogue waves can sneak up on you any time.

4. Wet sand is easier but riskier to walk on. Walk and picnic on dry sand higher up from the surf line.

5. Keep children close.

6. When in doubt, leash your dog. Both dogs—and people—are vulnerable to dangerous surf conditions and hypothermia.

7. In a rescue situation, throw something the person can grab onto rather than go into the water. Many rescue attempts with someone going in after the distressed person result in double tragedies.

8. Watch the weather, especially for summertime thunderstorms that can sneak up on you.

WHAT'S OUT THERE?

The Carolina coast features long stretches of undeveloped coastline, barrier islands, and tidally influenced terrain. This means places where nature's creatures can be seen in the air; in, on, and under the water; and on land. Being along the Atlantic Flyway makes many of the coastal trails in this guide hotbeds for birders; there are way too many winged creatures to name. However, consider some species of note. Starting on the barrier islands are laughing gulls, the most likely shorebird you will see. Interestingly, the notorious food beggars' head changes from black in the summer to white in the winter.

Sunrise on Great Island (hike 14)

Don't feed them or any other animal in the wild. Piping plovers need wild undeveloped beaches to thrive. The American oystercatcher, known for its yellow eyes and bright-orange bill, is found in intertidal zones feeding on oysters. These birds are the canary in the coal mine of shorebirds—where they thrive, the general ecosystem is also doing well.

Moving inland, snowy egrets, ibis, and wood storks are found in both freshwater and coastal marshes, as well as in freshwater ponds of the Atlantic Coastal Plain. These species often are seen where the hikes in this book take place. These wetlands are also stopping points for scads of waterfowl, including teal, black scoter, and pintail ducks. Raptors find their place in the Carolinas, too, from osprey toward the salt water to bald eagles, hawks, and falcons farther inland. The coast of the Carolinas is truly paradise for birders, and that is why you often share the trails with them.

As the waters of the coast transition from fresh water to salt water, they create rich wild-life zones in and under the water, too. The daily fluctuations of the tides strongly affect this area back from the oceanfront, where energy is less and coastal marshes form, places where Spartina grass, needlerush, and cordgrass rise above crab-filled mudflats, where tidal creeks harbor varied stages of the food chain from plankton to fish to porpoises. Moving farther inland, the water transitions to primarily fresh and so transitions the wildlife. These freshwater wetlands are home to critters such as otters, turtles, and alligators.

And then there are elements of nature that make the Carolina coast unique. Carolina bays are freshwater, rain-filled wetlands of unknown and inexplicable origin with specific characteristics: They are elliptical or oval shape, have a northwest–southeast orientation with parallel axes, have raised sand rims and depressed interior surfaces, and are shallow. After filling with rainwater, they dry over the warm season and are often filled with vegetation. Although centered in the Carolinas, a few bays are found as far north as Delaware and as far south as Georgia.

The strange Venus flytrap plant is also of special note in coastal Carolina. Perhaps you have heard the catchy name of this unusual plant growing landward only within a 75-mile radius of Wilmington, North Carolina. The modified leaves of this plant close rapidly when an insect touches tiny hairs on the inside of the plant, trapping the insect, which the Venus flytrap then eats. The nutrition from the insects supplements the poor, sandy soils of the area. Other carnivorous plants found in coastal Carolina are sundew, bladderwort, and pitcher plants.

The ponies of the coast deserve a nod as well. More than one hundred wild ponies call Shackleford Banks, part of Cape Lookout National Seashore, home. They also are found on state-owned Rachael Carson Reserve. Ponies that were formerly wild are kept penned in a certain area of Ocracoke Island, and wild ponies still roam up near Currituck. These squat adaptive descendants of Spanish horses add a quaint touch to your coastal Carolina experience.

The forests of the coastal Carolinas change as they range from sea to shore. Maritime hardwood forests are found closest to the Atlantic. Here, palms, Atlantic white cedar, live oak, and loblolly pine rise in ranks, sometimes being sculpted by wind the closer they are to the sea. Palms and magnolias are found in South Carolina maritime woods but less so in North Carolina. Moving away from the coast, cypress/tupelo/red maple complexes dominate bottomlands and swamp forests, along with hickories, oaks, and sycamores in less wet situations. Higher ground sees longleaf pine–dominated forests, along with turkey oak, post oak, and live oaks, often draped in Spanish moss. Deer are the land animal you most often see while hiking, but also be on the lookout for armadillos, maybe an occasional black bear rumbling through, as well as turkeys and coyotes.

GEARING UP FOR COMFORT AND A GOOD TIME

The weather is one of the most variable factors for hiking coastal Carolina. Proper clothing for the proper situation can make the difference between an enjoyable hike and a miserable one. Along the coast you can have fog, sun, wind, cold, and heat all in one day. Conditions are usually more stable inland. However, during the warm season hikers need to be prepared for thunderstorms, which often arise in the afternoon. In cooler times, rains come in the form of continental fronts, followed by cold, clear weather. These occurrences are much easier to predict and plan for. Use your smartphone—when reception is available—to stay up on the latest weather radar.

Trail conditions change, especially after major weather events. To be sure the trail you want to hike is good to go, check the website listed with each hike or call the land management agency for each particular destination. Be smart and be prepared. That way you can focus on having a good time while hiking the coastal trails of the Carolinas. Now, get out there and hit the trail!

Trail Finder

HIKE NO.	HIKE NAME	BEST HIKES FOR BEACHES	BEST HIKES FOR GREAT VIEWS	BEST HIKES FOR CHILDREN	BEST HIKES FOR DOGS	BEST HIKES FOR SOLITUDE	BEST HIKES FOR HISTORY LOVERS	BEST HIKES FOR PHOTOGRAPHY
1	Lassiter Trail				•	•		
2	Mackay Island National Wildlife Refuge		•			•		
3	Currituck Banks Reserve	•	•	•				•
4	Hills of Nags Head Woods			•				•
5	Roanoke Trail	•	•		*		•	
6	Dunes of Jockeys Ridge	•	•	•	•			•
7	Fort Raleigh Nat'l Historic Site	•	•	•			•	
8	Somerset Place Historic Hike		•	•	*	•	•	•
9	Bodie Island Lighthouse & Beach Walk	•	•		•			•
10	Pea Island National Wildlife Refuge	•	•	•	•			•
11	Goose Creek Hike	•	•	•	•	•	•	
12	Open Ponds Trail		•	•	•	•	•	
13	Hammock Hills Trail		•	•	•		•	
14	Great Island	•	•	•	•	•		•
15	Cape Lookout Lighthouse Hike	•	•	•	•	•	•	•
16	Shackleford Banks	•	•		•	•		•
17	Middle Neusiok Trail							
18	Neusiok Trail near Newport		•	•	•			
19	Elliott Coues Nature Trail	*	•	•		•	•	•
20	T. Roosevelt Natural Area and Hoop Pole Creek		•	•	•		•	•

#	Trail							
21	Patsy Pond		●		●	●		
22	Cedar Point Tideland Trail	●			●	●	●	
23	Lakeshore Trail	●	●		●	●	●	
24	Sugarloaf Trail	●	●	●	●	●	●	
25	Fort Fisher Hike	●	●	●			●	●
26	Myrtle Beach State Park Hike Park		●		●	●	●	●
27	Huntington Beach Hike	●		●	●	●	●	●
28	Santee Coastal Reserve			●				
29	Trails of South Tibwin				●	●	●	
30	Swamp Fox Passage of the Palmetto Trail			●	●	●		
31	Awendaw Passage of the Palmetto Trail	●			●	●	●	
32	Interpretive Trails of Awendaw		●	●		●		
33	Palmetto Islands Hike	●			●		●	
34	Charles Towne Landing State Historic Site	●	●	●				
35	Caw Caw Interpretive Center		●					
36	Botany Bay				●	●	●	●
37	Edisto Beach State Park Hike		●					
38	Hunting Island State Park Beach Hike	●	●				●	●
39	Hunting Island State Park Nature Center Hike	●	●				●	
40	Pinckney Island National Wildlife Refuge	●			●		●	●

Map Legend

Municipal

≡⟨20⟩≡ Interstate Highway

≡⟨178⟩≡ US Highway

≡⟨107⟩≡ State Road

≡⟨263⟩≡ Local/County Road

⟨FR 356⟩ Forest Road

= = = = Unpaved Road

├──┼──┤ Railroad

— - - — State Boundary

•—•—• Utility/Pipe Line

Trails

- - - - - - Featured Trail

- - - - - - Trail

───── Bike Path

Water Features

Body of Water

Marsh

River/Creek

Intermittent Stream

Symbols

⏝⏝ Bridge

▲ Backcountry Campground

▥ Boardwalk/Steps

⬎ Boat Launch

■ Building/Point of Interest

⛺ Campground

⚲ Gate

☀ Lighthouse

🅿 Parking

▲ Peak/Elevation

⊞ Picnic Area

🔳 Ranger Station/Park Office

🚻 Restroom

◧ Scenic View

○ Town

⟨20⟩ Trailhead

❓ Visitor/Information Center

Land Management

National Park/Forest

National Monument/Wilderness Area

State/County Park

NORTH CAROLINA COASTAL TRAILS

The one and only Cape Hatteras Lighthouse.

1. LASSITER TRAIL

You'll be happily surprised by this hike, adjacent to a two-centuries-old scenic swamp pond bordered by undulating hills in continually scenic woodlands. The Lassiter Trail is your conduit for exploring Merchants Millpond State Park. It leads along Merchants Millpond, then winds past Lassiter Swamp before passing a backcountry campground. The path then loops back to the trailhead via more hilly terrain that will give you an additional appreciation for eastern North Carolina.

THE RUNDOWN

Distance: 5.7-mile balloon loop
Start: Picnic area
Nearest town: Gatesville
Hiking time: 3.0 hours
Fees and permits: None if day hiking; fee and permit required for overnight backpacking
Conveniences: Picnic shelter, picnic area, restrooms at trailhead, park visitor center/office nearby
Beach access: No
Trail users: Hikers, backpackers, bicyclers on portions of trail
Trail surface: Natural
Difficulty: Moderate, does have hills

Highlights: Merchants Millpond, Lassiter Swamp, backcountry camping
Canine compatibility: Leashed dogs permitted
Schedule: Nov through Feb from 8 a.m. to 6 p.m.; Mar and Oct from 8 a.m. to 8 p.m.; Apr, May, Sept from 8 a.m. to 8 p.m.; June through Aug from 8 a.m. to 9 p.m.; closed Christmas Day
Managing agency: Merchants State Park, 176 Millpond Rd., Gatesville, NC 27938; (252) 357-1191; www.ncparks .gov

FINDING THE TRAILHEAD

From the intersection of US 158 and NC 32 in Sunbury, head west on US 158 for 5.1 miles to a left turn on Mill Pond Road. Follow Mill Pond Road south for 0.9 mile, then turn left into the park. Quickly pass the visitor center/park office and continue to the road's end at the park picnic area at 0.5 mile. GPS trailhead coordinates: 36.438118, -76.694288

WHAT TO SEE

A wonderful resource for coastal Carolina is Merchants Millpond State Park, centered by a 200-year-old man-made millpond, where Bennetts Creek was dammed back in 1811 to create waterpower for operating a sawmill and other engagements. The subsequent impoundment created behind the dam has become a first-rate destination for paddlers, anglers, and nature lovers. Over 3,000 wild acres surround Merchants Millpond, where surprisingly hilly terrain rolls between steep–cut hollows, a real mix of swamp and hill flora and fauna blending into one fascinating and worthwhile place. Speaking of flora, the park is known for its stands of straight and regal beech trees, along with a host of other hardwoods, making it a fine fall color hike. This particular hike traces the Lassiter Trail as it cruises near and above Merchants Millpond before turning away and coming near Lassiter Swamp, another wet wildland. The trail rolls underneath more impressive stands of

The Lassiter Trail takes you through a swamp on a boardwalk.

beech before coming to the designated backcountry camping area found along the path. Here, those wishing an overnight stay can pitch their tent in woods lording over Lassiter Swamp. The balance of the hike then works back toward the trailhead, aiming westerly in flatwoods before resuming hilly terrain.

Hiking is just one activity at this highly recommended state park situated on the Atlantic coastal plain. Paddling Merchants Millpond is a time-honored tradition. The heavily wooded tarn can be navigationally challenging (bring a GPS), but luckily the park has created a marked water trail that leads you through the admirable cypress and tupelo trees rising from the depths of the brooding yet beautiful millpond. And those inclined can even camp out in the backcountry by the water, at the canoe/kayak-accessible backcountry campground on the millpond. Paddlers also have the option of overnighting on Bennetts Creek, downstream of the millpond. And if that isn't enough, campers also can use the auto-accessible camping area that features deep woods and private sites. All camping options are highly recommended. In addition to the Lassiter Trail, hikers can explore bottomland woods on the Bennetts Creek Trail or take the 2-mile Coleman Trail, the path named for A. B. Coleman, who bought the initial tract to preserve Merchants Millpond on his own, then later donated the property to the state. Coleman's parcel formed the heart of the park. Acreage was later added, and now the park comprises nearly 3,500 acres of fascinating flora and fauna, including alligators and black bears.

Lassiter Trail

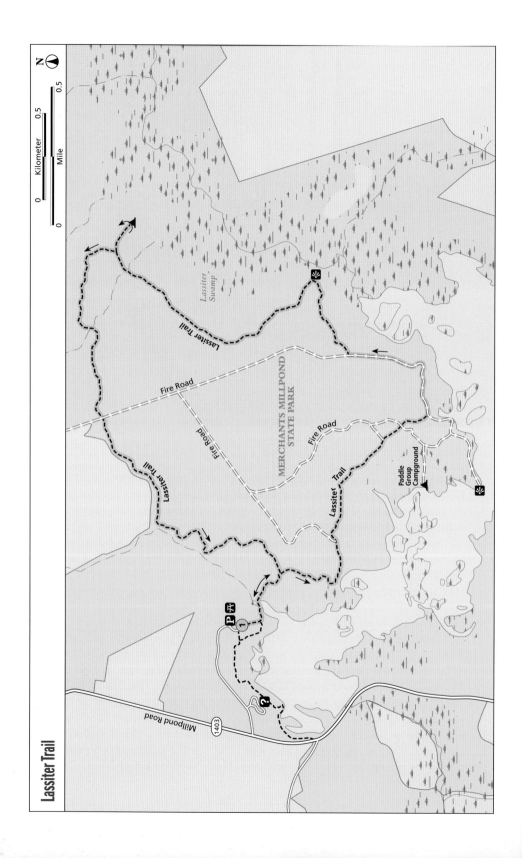

N

Kilometer
0   0.5

Mile
0   0.5

MERCHANTS MILLPOND
STATE PARK

Lassiter Swamp

Lassiter Trail

Fire Road

Fire Road

Fire Road

Lassiter Trail

Lassiter Trail

Lassiter Trail

Paddle Group
Campground

Millpond Road

1403

MILES AND DIRECTIONS

0.0 From the back of the picnic area, pick up the white-blazed Lassiter Trail and begin following a gravel track downhill. Quickly intersect a path leading right to the visitor center. Here, head left, descending to Merchants Millpond on a singletrack natural surface trail. Quickly reach a long boardwalk spanning a small cove of Merchants Millpond. Cypress and tupelo are scattered in the water, with duck moss on the pond surface.

0.2 Reach the end of the boardwalk and climb into wooded hollows bordered by steep hills under a mantle of sweetgum, beech, and beard cane. Look for a massive tulip tree to the right of the trail just after rising from the boardwalk.

0.3 Rise to a trailside kiosk and intersection. Here, you begin the loop portion of the Lassiter Trail. Head right, southerly, in rich forest, crossing hollows with trickling streams gurgling at their bases.

0.6 Once again, come near Merchants Millpond. Enjoy views from a high hill overlooking the impoundment.

0.7 Pass a trailside restroom and a fire road. Ahead, cross occasional boardwalks in the hollows on wooded slopes rife with beech trees.

1.2 Reach a trail intersection. Here, a fire road/bicycle trail crosses the Lassiter Trail. Keep straight. Shortly, reach a second intersection. Again, stay with the white blazes as a fire road leads right to a point and good view of Merchants Millpond. You are now on a doubletrack. Keep east then turn north, as the Lassiter Trail runs in conjunction with the fire road/bicycle trail.

1.6 Span a wooded swamp on a bridge. Obscured views open east toward Lassiter Swamp. Keep north on doubletrack trail.

1.8 Leave right with the Lassiter Trail, as the fire road/bicycle trail keeps straight, northbound. Resume a singletrack path wandering through rich woods. Roll through hill and hollow amid holly and cane.

2.2 Reach a bluff, bench, and view above wooded Lassiter Swamp. This is a good place to take a break. Turn away from the swamp and hike through mostly level forest of pine and hardwoods.

3.1 Drop into bottomland, bridging a narrow, deeper than average stream. Rise away from the hollow.

3.2 Intersect the signed spur trail leading to the backcountry campground, situated on a peninsula between two hollows. It is 0.1 mile to the backcountry campground. The camp features five separate campsites, each with a fire ring. Some of the sites border a hill overlooking Lassiter Swamp. The campground also features a common privy. Backtrack and continue the loop, now westbound in alluring flatwoods.

3.9 Dip into a hollow spanning the same stream you did at 3.1 miles, well upstream from the original crossing. Resume flatwoods after climbing from the hollow.

4.2 Meet and cross the fire road/bicycle trail, remaining on the singletrack path. Resume rolling terrain, cutting through some of the deepest hollows of the hike. Boardwalks span streamlets.

5.4 Complete the loop portion of the hike after rising to flatwoods. Backtrack toward the picnic area.

5.7 Arrive back at the picnic area, completing the hike.

The author treks through a beech grove on a spring afternoon.

BEECH TREES OF NORTH CAROLINA

Beech trees are prevalent on this hike, especially on the slopes and hillsides of the trailside hollows. This gray-trunked tree ranges throughout North Carolina. Beech trees are among the easiest trees to identify. First, the smooth gray trunk makes it stand out in the forest, as the man-made carvings common to this tree testify. Many woodland walkers simply can't resist the flat surface of the beech—it seems a tablet for a handy pocketknife. The smooth trunks contrast vividly with the knobby and fissured oaks elsewhere at Merchants Millpond State Park.

Pick up a beech leaf from the forest floor. The sunlight-absorbing leaves are generally 2 to 4 inches long. Note the sharply toothed edges of the leaves. They are a dark green on top and lighter underneath. During autumn the leaves turn a yellowish golden brown. Under ideal conditions, beech trees can reach 120 feet in height. However, the average mature trees, like those you will see along the trail, stretch 60 to 80 feet from the ground.

After the leaves fall from the beech, you will notice the buds of next year's leaves. They are just a half-inch in length but resemble a mini cigar. Come spring, these buds will unfurl to once again convert sunlight for the tree as it resumes growing during the warm season. Beechnuts are about the size of a thumbnail. They are an important food for wildlife, from mice to deer, and for birds, from ducks to blue jays. Critters break apart the burr-covered shell to reach the nutrient-rich treat. Humans use beech tree wood for everything from flooring to railroad ties to charcoal. And, of course, many people think of it as a carving tablet.

2. MACKAY ISLAND NATIONAL WILDLIFE REFUGE

This hike explores Mackay Island, a refuge just south of the Virginia state line. In fact, to get there you have to either take a ferry from Currituck, North Carolina, or drive through Virginia to reach Mackay Island. The hike starts at a fishing pier, then traces an elevated dike amid bird-rich marshes before looping around, opening to views of huge Currituck Sound. Expect year-round wildlife-viewing opportunities during your visit.

THE RUNDOWN

Distance: 2.8-mile loop
Start: Disabled fishing pier
Nearest town: Currituck
Hiking time: 1.3 hours
Fees and permits: None
Conveniences: None
Beach access: No
Trail users: Hikers, birders, bicyclers
Trail surface: Gravel and grass roads closed to public driving
Difficulty: Easy

Highlights: Wildlife, views of Currituck Sound
Canine compatibility: Leashed dogs permitted
Schedule: Sunrise to sunset year-round
Managing agency: Mackay Island National Wildlife Refuge, 316 Marsh Causeway, Knotts Island, NC 27950; (252) 429-3100; www.fws.gov/refuge/Mackay_Island/

FINDING THE TRAILHEAD

From the town of Currituck on NC 168, take the free Knotts Island Ferry (www.ncferry.org) to Knotts Island. From there, follow Ferry Dock Road for 0.3 mile, then turn left onto NC 615 and drive north for 2.2 miles to a left turn onto Mackay Island Road, following it to a dead end after 2 miles. Parking is very limited, so be considerate. GPS trailhead coordinates: 36.512954, -75.952574

WHAT TO SEE

One of the most northeasterly parcels of North Carolina, next to the quiet coastal community of Knotts Island, what became 9,500-acre Mackay Island National Wildlife Refuge has always been a backwater. North Carolina aboriginals seasonally used the island for fish and waterfowl subsistence. Later the island was named for John Mackie, about whom little is known except his island's name spelling was changed to Mackay. A later notable owner of the island was Joseph P. Knapp. The wealthy New Yorker come down here to spend time on the Carolina coast and was an avid hunter and conservationist. He knew the importance of islands such as this for waterfowl migration as well as for wintering locations. In the 1930s he came up with an idea to develop an organization committed to preserving places for waterfowl. This organization ultimately became Ducks Unlimited, the preeminent waterfowl conservation organization in the United States. Knapp used Mackay Island to experiment in waterfowl management, to improve the habitat for waterfowl from snow geese to ducks and swans. In 1960 the US Fish and Wildlife Service purchased the island, and to this day some of the waterfowl management

This hike traces dikes rising above wildlife-rich wetlands.

techniques developed by Knapp are used not only at Mackay Island but at wildlife refuges throughout the country.

The hike here, open to the sun in its entirety, makes a simple loop tracing elevated dikes above marshland and "dry land." In the distance cattails, black needlerush, and giant cordgrass stretch to the horizon, known as the Great Marsh. Most of the marshes are brackish; however, some impoundments are fresh water. This is one place where winter wildlife watching can be very rewarding. From November through January thousands of geese and swan inhabit the Great Marsh. In spring, neotropical birds migrate north from Central and South America to nest here. In summer, herons and egrets rule the roost. Fall sees waterfowl arriving for their wintering. Throughout the year, water levels are managed to create the best conditions for wildlife, from wood ducks to osprey to deer and amphibians. Refuge roads, overlooks, and lesser trails add to the wildlife viewing opportunities. By the way, check ahead to see if the area you want to visit is open, as portions of the refuge close seasonally to protect wildlife. Also, roads normally closed to the public are open certain days of the year for public use. During the warmer season, you will see anglers fishing in the canals along Mackay Island Road. Fishing the canals is a popular pastime on Mackay Island, though birders are well represented, often seeking the elusive king rail, breeding in the Great Marsh.

After carefully parking, you will join the Mackay Island Trail as it heads westerly on a dike. Marsh extends in the distance, while nearer dry areas will be forested. It isn't long before you cut left, south toward Little Bellows Bay. The Live Oak Point Trail can extend

HAVE YOU HEARD OF CHARLES KURALT?

Back in the days when television was confined to just a few networks (no cable or satellite) and the Internet didn't exist, gathering information about interesting out-of-the-way outdoor destinations was much more difficult than it is now. However, North Carolina native and outdoors lover Charles Kuralt created an innovative new show on the CBS network called "On the Road." During the program, Kuralt chronicled his travels, often to outdoor destinations, specifically our national wildlife refuges (which remain an under-visited outdoor resource for hikers). He died in 1997, and afterward the US Fish and Wildlife Service established the Kuralt Trail, a motor path ranging from the Virginia state line down to the lower end of the Outer Banks, encompassing twelve different national wildlife refuges, in honor of the North Carolina native who loved his home state. Mackay Island, the site of this hike, is one such refuge. Each of the refuges along the Kuralt Trail features a specific Kuralt Trail wildlife-viewing site designed to enhance your national wildlife refuge experience. So while you're exploring coastal Carolina, add the Kuralt Trail to your outdoor itinerary.

Coots gather in trailside ponds of the refuge.

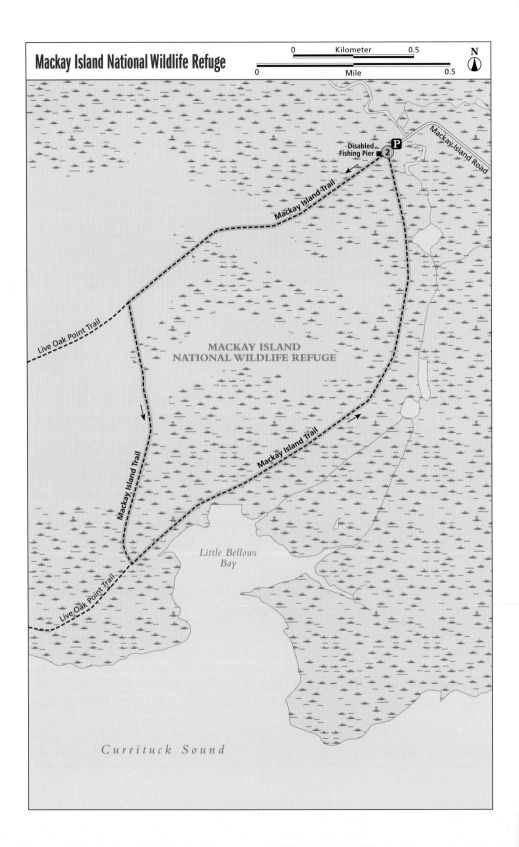

Mackay Island National Wildlife Refuge

Kilometer
0   0.5

Mile
0   0.5

N

MACKAY ISLAND
NATIONAL WILDLIFE REFUGE

Mackay Island Road

Disabled
Fishing Pier

P

2

Mackay Island Trail

Live Oak Point Trail

Mackay Island Trail

Mackay Island Trail

Live Oak Point Trail

Little Bellows
Bay

Currituck Sound

your loop, but it always seems to be closed, so don't count on it being open. If so, you could reach Live Oak Point and a small beach overlooking Currituck Sound.

The last part of the loop takes you past the open waters of Little Bellows Bay, an inlet on greater Currituck Sound. At this point you can scan the horizon toward the mainland and Currituck to the southwest as well as the islands in Currituck Sound. The trail curves back northeast, presenting more views of marsh lying between Mackay Island and Knotts Island before leaving the trailhead.

MILES AND DIRECTIONS

0.0 From the small parking area at the disabled fishing pier, walk around the pole gate, following the doubletrack aiming southwesterly, the Mackay Island Trail. Extensive panoramas open, showcasing the Great Marsh dotted with wooded islands near and far. Open-water impoundments are visible to your left, perhaps harboring avian wildlife, from ducks in the distance to red-winged blackbirds in the near.

0.4 The Mackay Island Trail reaches an island grown up with pine and wax myrtle.

0.8 Come to an intersection. Here, the seldom-open Live Oak Point Trail keeps straight while the Mackay Island Trail turns left. The hike also turns left, southbound, with partially open marshes on both sides of the grassy doubletrack. Look for wood duck boxes and nests of raptors on snags rising from the wetlands.

1.5 Turn left at the intersection, meeting the other end of the Live Oak Point Trail. Come alongside Little Bellows Bay. Far-reaching panoramas of Currituck Sound and the mainland stretch to the south. Open water stretches on both sides here. As you curve northeast, the water reverts to grassy marsh.

2.2 The trail turns more north than east. Views continue.

2.8 Return to the trailhead, arriving just east of the disabled fishing pier, completing the coastal trail.

3. CURRITUCK BANKS RESERVE

Combine this hike at an important preserve in the northern Outer Banks with a trip to the famed Currituck Beach Lighthouse along with a side sojourn to the attractive beach here. On the hike you will enter maritime woods and travel via boardwalk to a rewarding view of Currituck Sound. After backtracking a bit, take a natural surface path through wind-sheared woodland, where you might see one of the wild ponies that roam these parts, in addition to gaining a second panorama of Currituck Sound. After that, visit the nearby lighthouse, then take a stroll on the beach, making a day of it.

THE RUNDOWN

Distance: 2.1-mile out-and-back with spur
Start: NC 12 trailhead
Nearest town: Corolla
Hiking time: 1.1 hours
Fees and permits: None
Conveniences: None
Beach access: Very nearby
Trail users: Hikers
Trail surface: Boardwalk, natural surface
Difficulty: Easy

Highlights: Views of Currituck Sound, boardwalk, birds, ponies
Canine compatibility: Leashed dogs permitted
Schedule: Sunrise to sunset year-round
Managing agency: Coastal Reserve & National Estuarine Research Reserve, 983 W. Kitty Hawk Rd., Kitty Hawk, NC 27949; (252) 261-8891; www .nccoastalreserve.net

FINDING THE TRAILHEAD

From the intersection of NC 345, US 64 Bypass, and US 64 in Manteo, take US 64 East to join NC 12 North on the Outer Banks. Once on NC 12, drive north for 21.3 miles to the Currituck Banks Reserve trailhead on your left. Take note there is a strict two-hour parking time limit. GPS trailhead coordinates: 36.389566, -75.830804

WHAT TO SEE

Currituck Banks Reserve is an important natural parcel of the fast-developing Outer Banks. The popularity of the North Carolina beaches can sometimes be overwhelming, but here you can combine a nice little hike in preserved maritime woods enhanced by overlooks and then visit the Currituck Beach Lighthouse, which is less than a mile away from the hike's trailhead. Finally, top off your trip with a walk on Currituck Beach, either the beach part of the Currituck Banks Reserve or at the town of Corolla. Additionally, Historic Corolla Park, adjacent to the lighthouse, makes for a good base, as parking is very limited out here.

The high value of the land in these parts makes Currituck Banks Reserve even more valuable. Situated 10 miles south of the Virginia border on the Outer Banks, the reserve encompasses almost 1,000 acres from the Atlantic Ocean west across to Currituck Sound. Be apprised that vehicles can access and cross the beach part of the preserve. Furthermore, trailhead parking is tricky. A small lot is located at the trailhead, but there is a

Brick Currituck Lighthouse stands proud.

CURRITUCK BEACH LIGHTHOUSE

While at Corolla, a visit to the Currituck Beach Lighthouse is a must. Exploring the grounds of the lighthouse at Historic Corolla Park is free, but there is a fee to climb the beacon. The views are worth it. Currituck Beach Lighthouse was one of the last light stations built along the North Carolina coast, first shining its light on December 1, 1875. Interestingly, to distinguish this new lighthouse it was left unpainted, and the naked red brick exterior became the lighthouse's identifying characteristic. Along with the lighthouse, two keeper's quarters were built and still stand. Operating the lighthouse was a lot of work. The lightkeepers brought fuel to the lamp, lit it, kept the lens clean, and wound the mechanism that kept the light rotating. The 162-foot Currituck Beach Lighthouse features the largest of seven Fresnel lens sizes, making it a first-order lighthouse. It is still an important navigational aid, automatically coming on a dusk and off with the dawn. The lighthouse flashes for three seconds, then goes off for seventeen seconds, over and over and over (each lighthouse has its own distinctive on/off sequence). Currituck Lighthouse's beam extends 18 nautical miles out to sea. The lighthouse was eventually electrified in 1933, and by 1937 it was completely automated.

The keeper's quarters were left to deteriorate but were later restored along with the grounds and walkways. Today Currituck Beach Lighthouse is an attractive place to visit and is a popular attraction on the Outer Banks. While at the lighthouse, you might want to visit the nearby Outer Banks Center for Wildlife Education, where you can learn more about the nature of this area. Historic Corolla Park, 39 acres of beauty, also presents picnicking options near the lighthouse.

Ibis enjoy the view at boardwalk's end.

strict two-hour limit, and to park out on the beach you will need a four-wheel-drive vehicle—and a county permit during the summertime. The reserve comprises beach-front, sand dunes morphing to maritime forest and morphing yet again to coastal marsh. Interestingly, you have to go through a gate to start the hike—to keep the wild horses from heading south into the town of Corolla.

If you are lucky you may see a wild pony. You will certainly see pony manure. Another certain sight will be the boardwalk that leads you toward Currituck Sound. It travels under a mantle of twisted and sheared live oaks. The predominant shaping winds come from the northeast, when strong winter blows do their work. Like most wooded areas of the Outer Banks, the woods are riddled with small hills—old dune lines that became wooded after these continually shifting barrier islands moved. The forest is higher in the middle of the reserve, away from the ocean wind influence. In this area you will also see the rare freshwater maritime swamp forest dominated by red maple.

While on the boardwalk you will pass the natural surface trail to be hiked later. The recommended route, however, heads first to Currituck Sound. Here, the boardwalk opens to a marsh favorable for viewing birds as well as expansive panoramas of the sound. A bevy of benches allows you to hang out and watch wildlife. Sometimes it's best to just be still and let wildlife come to you. This area has a wealth of plant and animal species, with many northern species at the southern end of the range and southern species at the northern end of their range. The mixing of the warm Gulf Stream and the cool Labrador Current plays a part in this ecological intermingling.

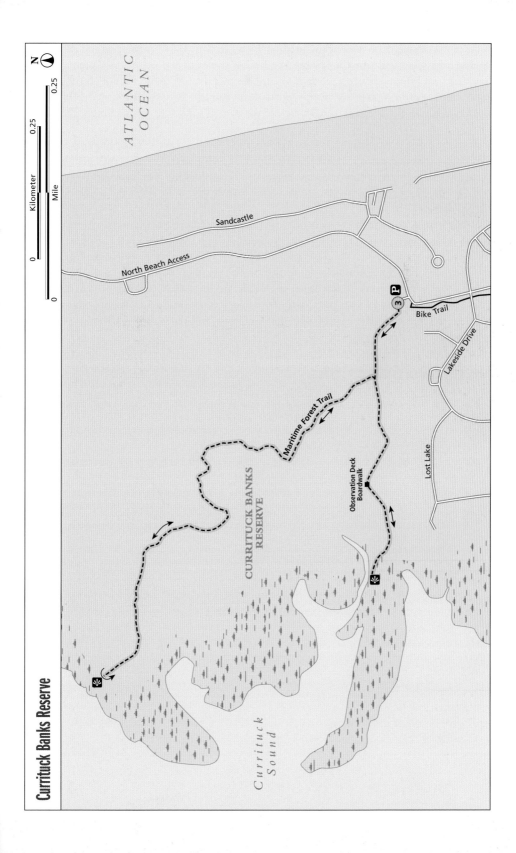

Currituck Banks Reserve

Atlantic Ocean

North Beach Access

Sandcastle

P
3
Bike Trail

Maritime Forest Trail

CURRITUCK BANKS
RESERVE

Observation Deck
Boardwalk

Lakeside Drive

Lost Lake

*Currituck
Sound*

N

0   0.25
Kilometer
0   0.25
Mile

Since the closing of an inlet near Currituck Banks back in 1828 (inlets open and close during hurricanes and tropical storms), the nearest outlet to the ocean for Currituck Sound is now 50 miles away at Oregon Inlet. Thus, Currituck Sound has a high freshwater content and is influenced mainly by the wind and less so by the tides.

After enjoying the boardwalk, backtrack to the natural surface Maritime Forest Trail. Here you will walk the ground among wind-sculpted woodlands, giving a near fairytale look to the forest. Loblolly pine, beech, and cedar add to the preponderance of live oaks. The trail winds and turns and turns again, but it is well marked so you can't get lost. Nevertheless, trails created by the feral horses can be misleading. The hike's end opens onto another look of Currituck Sound with a marsh stretching from the viewpoint toward open water.

While hiking, remember the two-hour parking limit. Afterward, if you have a four-wheel-drive vehicle, you can head out to the beach, which is but 100 yards distant, then find your oceanside nirvana and take a walk. If in a regular passenger vehicle, park near the Currituck Beach Lighthouse at Historic Corolla Park, then walk east from the lighthouse about a quarter mile to the beach at Corolla. Additionally, a walking/bicycle trail links Historic Corolla Park to the Currituck Banks Reserve trailhead, allowing you to connect all three destinations—the trail, the lighthouse, and the beach—by foot, if you so desire.

MILES AND DIRECTIONS

0.0 From the parking area, walk through the gate and join the boardwalk. Make sure to shut the gate behind you to keep in the feral ponies. Enter a maritime forest of pine, wax myrtle, and live oak sheared by winds blowing off the nearby Atlantic Ocean. Soon cross the rare maple freshwater maritime swamp.

0.1 The Maritime Forest Trail leaves right. For now, stay with the boardwalk, aiming for Currituck Sound under sun-dappled woodland, passing contemplation benches.

0.4 Reach the observation deck at boardwalk's end. A tidal creek enters to your right, bordered by marsh. An open view extends deep into Currituck Sound. Backtrack.

0.7 Join the signed, natural surface Maritime Forest Trail after dropping off the boardwalk. Begin winding through woods amid ancient wooded dunes. Look for feral ponies and their sign. The value of these woods is now incalculable with development throughout the Outer Banks. On a windy day you can hear waves crashing on the Atlantic.

1.3 Reach the overlook at trail's end. Marsh frames views of waters beyond. Backtrack.

2.0 Return to the boardwalk. Head left, still backtracking.

2.1 Arrive back at the traihead.

4. HILLS OF NAGS HEAD WOODS

You will be surprised at the steep hills divided by small freshwater ponds and swamps on this hike at Nags Head Woods Preserve, a Nature Conservancy property on the Outer Banks near the town of Nags Head. The hike leaves the visitor center to cruise by small ponds, then begins the nearly ceaseless undulations among thick, lush, and gorgeous woods with elevation changes of 50 feet or more. Ponds and swamps become common, and you are nearly always near water. The trek makes a pair of loops among the prominences and interdunal tarns before you backtrack to the trailhead.

THE RUNDOWN

Distance: 3.5-mile out-and-back with loops
Start: Visitor center
Nearest town: Nags Head
Hiking time: 1.7 hours
Fees and permits: None
Conveniences: Restrooms, water, information at visitor center
Beach access: No
Trail users: Hikers
Trail surface: Natural
Difficulty: Moderate

Highlights: Hilly maritime forest, wooded dunes, swamps and ponds
Canine compatibility: Dogs not permitted on preserve trails used during this hike
Schedule: Daily from dawn to dusk; office/visitor center open from 9 a.m. to 5 p.m.
Managing agency: Nags Head Woods Preserve, 701 West Ocean Acres Dr., Kill Devil Hills, NC 27948; (252) 441-2525; www.nature.org

FINDING THE TRAILHEAD

From the intersection of NC 345, US 64 Bypass, and US 64 in Manteo, take US 64 East to join US 158 West on the Outer Banks. Once on US 158 West, follow it for 6.9 miles to a left turn, west, at a traffic light, onto Ocean Acres Drive, a residential road. Follow the road for 0.8 mile and then it becomes gravel. Trace it a little bit farther and you will reach the Nags Head Woods Preserve parking area on your left. GPS trailhead coordinates: 35.99000214880, -75.66513792120

WHAT TO SEE

With the incredible popularity of and development pressure on the Outer Banks, it is hard to believe that a place like Nags Head Woods Preserve exists. A century back, when the Outer Banks were not seen as the vacation mecca they are today, the deservedly heralded beach destination of North Carolina was but a backwater of fishing villages and small communities with nary an inkling that millions of visitors would annually descend upon their area for rest and recreation. Back then, Nags Head Woods was—as its name implies—a forested area broken by a few cleared homesites on greater Bodie Island, just a few miles south of Kitty Hawk, the place put on the map by the Wright brothers as the location of the world's first successful flight.

And if the Wright brothers drew attention to the Outer Banks, it was still a while before the true vacation potential was realized. Nevertheless, by the 1970s visitors were thronging to the beaches of the Outer Banks. Beach homes and other getaways were

Looking down on one of the many ponds in Nags Head Woods

built, and now in this century the development has grown exponentially, yet Nags Head Woods remained relatively intact, especially compared to what was going on around it. The preservation story starts in 1974, when Nags Head Woods was designated a National Natural Landmark, and the Nature Conservancy aimed to play a part in preserving it. Using outright purchases along with donations of land and partnerships with local municipalities, the Nature Conservancy began to cobble together a tract containing a wide range of coastal habitat. Over the years other land was added to create a representative ecosystem that encompasses a variety of important habitats and a first-rate coastal hiking destination.

This hike at Nags Head Woods incorporates three trails to fashion a walk that shows off the preserve, especially the high forested dunes, interdune ponds, and wooded swamps.

The amount of vertical variation on this hike will surprise you, and the wetlands in the low areas are an added plus. The forest of Nags Head Woods has grown in part due to protection from direct Atlantic Ocean wind onslaught (being on the backside of the island), as well as being shielded by the big dunes of Run Hill and Jockeys Ridge. This geological arrangement has allowed the forest to thrive in an otherwise harsh environment of a coastal barrier island. Therefore, the tree makeup here is not merely the prototypical maritime woods of live oak, cedar, wax myrtle, and loblolly pine found in coastal Carolina. It also contains rather impressive hickory, beech, and dogwood trees, as well as a variety of oaks normally found in the central state and even the mountains of North Carolina.

The result is a barrier island preserve with rich woods and enough hills to make your legs quiver. The Nature Conservancy did right by protecting this terrain. You will find this out on your hike. The trek starts at the visitor center, where you can get trail maps and information. You then join the short Center Trail as it bridges the first of several ponds you will see. Next, you join the Sweetgum Swamp Trail and the undulations begin. Even though you may be expecting some hills here, you will nevertheless be surprised at their extent and height. Some of the climbs are in excess of 50 feet, and the

Duck moss covers a pond beside a hiker bridge.

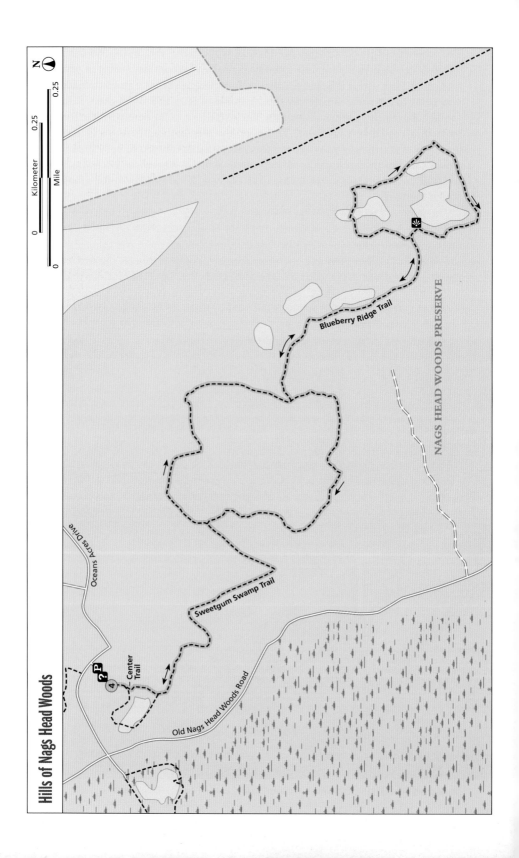

Hills of Nags Head Woods

N

Kilometer

0   0.25

0   0.25

Mile

Oceans Acres Drive

P 2
4

Center Trail

Sweetgum Swamp Trail

Blueberry Ridge Trail

NAGS HEAD WOODS PRESERVE

Old Nags Head Woods Road

ridges can be quite narrow. It would be hard to guess that you were a half a mile from saltwater judging by the hills through which you walk.

Spring and fall are great times to hike here. Springtime brings out the flowering dogwood, one of the big surprises here. Did you know the dogwood blossom is the official North Carolina state flower? More prominently found in the Piedmont and lower elevations in the mountains, the flowering dogwood is uncommon on the Outer Banks. The short tree with scaly brown bark and widespread crown is easy to identify. It is widely regarded as one of the most beautiful trees in the Southeast. Dogwoods range from east Texas north to Michigan, east to Massachusetts, and south to Florida. In the spring dogwoods offer showy white blooms that can also be pinkish. After greening up during the warm season, dogwoods produce a shiny red fruit in fall. These small berry-like fruits are bitter to humans but are an important food for birds. Dogwood is extremely hard and is used to make mallet heads, jewelers' blocks, and spools.

Downtrail, the Sweetgum Swamp Trail makes a loop as it wanders among more hills and swamps, most of them wooded. Then you reach the Blueberry Ridge Trail. It offers a combination of hill walking and flat trekking by open ponds and wooded swamps. Boardwalks span wetter areas. A final loop on the Blueberry Ridge Trail marks your return to the visitor center. No matter what time of year, you will be happily surprised with this coastal trail.

MILES AND DIRECTIONS

0.0   Leave the parking area and head toward the visitor center. From there, walk to the back deck of the visitor center and pick up the Center Trail, taking a short arched bridge over a small pond. Keep straight as part of the Center Trail goes right.

0.1   Meet the Sweetgum Swamp Trail and head left, immediately climbing a hill in deep woods. Hills abound. Rise to a high ridge.

0.3   Pass a gate and then come under a power line. Follow the power line.

0.5   Leave left from the power line and reenter lush woods rich with pine, holly, and bay trees.

0.6   Reach the loop portion of the Sweetgum Swamp Trail. Head left, cruising the margin between swamp and hill. Sweetgums abound on land, while tupelo and cypress dominate the swamps. Ahead, rise to piney dunes. Come near a police firing range.

1.1   Head left on the Blueberry Ridge Trail. Descend to walk among many a pond. Look for dogwoods in these parts.

1.4   Come to the loop portion of the Blueberry Ridge Trail. Head left, still among swamps and ponds divided by low hills of oak and pine.

1.7   An illegal bootleg trail leaves left toward an adjacent neighborhood. Ahead a boardwalk leads across an arm of a pond. There is next to no level land here. Contemplation benches provide resting spots.

2.1   Complete the loop portion of the Blueberry Ridge Trail, just after passing a bench and a view high on a high ridge overlooking some interdunal ponds of the preserve. Begin backtracking on the Blueberry Ridge Trail.

2.4   Return to the loop portion of the Sweetgum Swamp Trail. Head left, finishing the loop portion of the Sweetgum Swamp Trail, still winding among hills.

2.9   Complete the loop portion of the Sweetgum Swamp Trail. From here, it's a backtrack to the visitor center and trailhead.

3.5   Arrive back at the visitor center, completing the hilly coastal hike.

5. ROANOKE TRAIL

Explore a series of rewarding, pet-friendly trails at Nags Head Woods Preserve. The Discovery Trail leads you past a backwoods pond, then you join the historic Roanoke Trail, first passing a cemetery then a homesite of subsistence dwellers in what was the back of beyond. The hike leads out to a small beach on Roanoke Sound, where you can peer out to the water and onward to Roanoke Island, site of the first English colony in what became the United States. Finally, circle around a pond on an ADA-accessible trail, gaining extensive marsh views before returning to the trailhead.

THE RUNDOWN

Distance: 2.2-mile loop with an out-and-back
Start: Visitor center
Nearest town: Nags Head
Hiking time: 1.3 hours
Fees and permits: None
Conveniences: Restrooms, water, information at visitor center
Beach access: Yes, at trail's end
Trail users: Hikers
Trail surface: Natural, concrete on ADA Trail
Difficulty: Easy

Highlights: Small remote beach, history, views of Roanoke Sound and Roanoke Island
Canine compatibility: Leashed dogs permitted
Schedule: Daily from dawn to dusk; office/visitor center open from 9 a.m. to 5 p.m.
Managing agency: Nags Head Woods Preserve, 701 West Ocean Acres Dr., Kill Devil Hills, NC 27948; (252) 441-2525; www.nature.org

FINDING THE TRAILHEAD

From the intersection of NC 345, US 64 Bypass, and US 64 in Manteo, take US 64 East to join US 158 West on the Outer Banks. Once on US 158 West, follow it for 6.9 miles to a left turn, west, at a traffic light, onto Ocean Acres Drive, a residential road. Follow the road for 0.8 mile and then it becomes gravel. Trace it a little bit farther and you will reach the Nags Head Woods Preserve parking area on your left. GPS trailhead coordinates: 35.99000214880, -75.66513792120

WHAT TO SEE

Nags Head Woods Preserve encompasses over 1,400 acres of precious coastal land allowed to remain undeveloped, preserving not only the natural attributes of the land but also the history of days gone by. In the mid–1800s just over a dozen homes were scattered in the small community, consisting mostly of subsistence farmers getting what they could from the land and sea. A pair of churches served the spiritual needs of the Nags Head Woods community. A lone store availed dry good and supplies. On this hike you will see evidence of that time gone by, as much of the greater Nags Head Woods has been protected by the Nature Conservancy. Today you can enjoy over 8 miles of trails on this Outer Banks destination.

This particular hike first visits an intriguing pond, one of many interdunal wetlands found here. This particular pond is home to the rare water violet, blooming in April and May. From there you will travel west among hilly, now forested dunes before dropping

Beach view of Roanoke Sound

to cross historic Old Nags Head Woods Road, still a backwoods gravel path despite the exceptional development throughout this area of the Outer Banks. At the road you will find the cemetery of the nearby Tillett clan. At this point the hike joins the Roanoke Trail and you continue traversing tall woods that devolve into more typical maritime forests, along with lesser pockets of freshwater swamp forest. This is where you also will find the site where the Tilletts lived. You will march by some rusty buckets, brick home foundations, and a few other forgotten relics. A century ago no one would have traded places with the Tilletts. Nowadays they could've sold their property for amounts they couldn't even comprehend. Yet here they lived in a simpler, quieter time, where the land meets coastal marsh, where the Nags Head Woods give way to the marshes of Roanoke Sound, where to the west on Roanoke Island, the first English colony settled in America.

The hike follows the woods to its western edge. At this point you will find a small beach beside scattered woods. This is not only a fine place to experience a sunset, it is also where you can look on Roanoke Island and contemplate half a millennium back to the Roanoke Colony, the settlement founded by Sir Walter Raleigh that mysteriously disappeared. Today, on Roanoke Island, the National Park Service maintains a historic tableau—Fort Raleigh National Historic Site—where they believe the colony existed. Stop by when leaving the Outer Banks and delve deeper into this mystery swirling about England's first new home in the world, and the birthplace of the first English child in America, Virginia Dare.

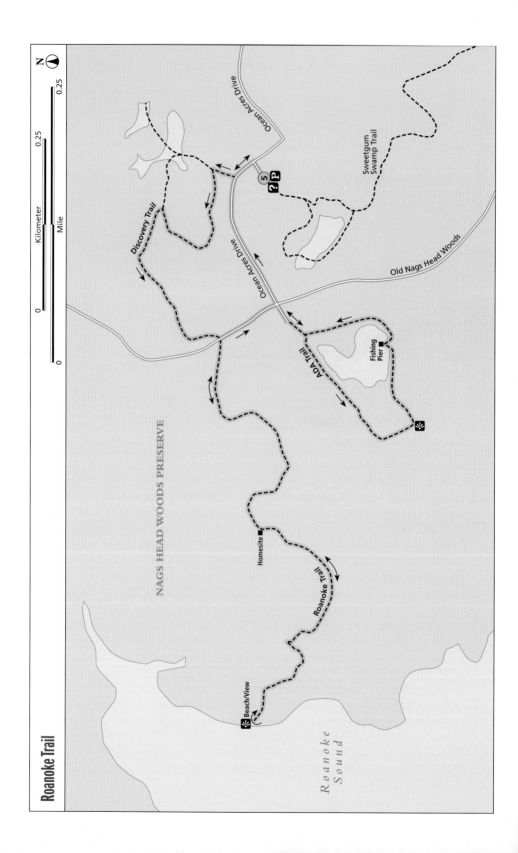

Roanoke Trail

N

Kilometer
0   0.25   0.25
Mile
0   0.25

Discovery Trail

Ocean Acres Drive

Sweetgum Swamp Trail

Old Nags Head Woods

ADA Trail

Fishing Pier

5 ? P

NAGS HEAD WOODS PRESERVE

Homesite

Roanoke Trail

Beach/View

Roanoke Sound

After contemplating such things from the Roanoke Sound beach, the hike backtracks to Old Nags Head Woods Road. Here you follow the quaint gravel track a short distance to join the ADA Trail. The name stands for American Disability Association, for the trail was spearheaded in 2011 by the president of the ADA. It circles an old interdunal pond on a site that was once the water plant for the town of Nags Head. The site has been reclaimed, and the forest is regrowing. Today you would hardly know a water treatment plant was here, save for the interpretive information detailing this. The concrete ADA Trail passes by the reclaimed site, then rolls through woods to reach an overlook. Here you can gaze across brackish marshlands into the waters of Roanoke Sound. The path then curves around the interdunal pond to reach a fishing pier, where anglers can vie for bluegill, crappie, and bass. All fishing here is catch and release. You will then continue circling the pond to complete the ADA Trail. From here it is a short road walk on Ocean Acres Drive back to the visitor center. Remember: The trails used on this hike are pet-friendly, whereas other trails at Nags Head Woods don't allow pets.

MILES AND DIRECTIONS

0.0 Leave the parking area and head away from the visitor center. Turn left, westerly, on Ocean Acres Drive for about 50 yards and then leave the road right, joining the Discovery Trail. Ahead, split left as the Discovery Trail becomes a loop. Begin rolling in tall woods, passing a pond on your right

0.2 Pass the other end of the Discovery Trail. Stay left. You are on a high ridge.

0.3 Descend from the high ridge to reach and cross Old Nags Had Woods Road. The Tillett Cemetery stands across the road, encircled in a fence. The place of interment has graves dating back to the 1800s. Head just a few feet south on Old Nags Head Woods Road, then pick up the Roanoke Trail. The natural-surface path wanders westerly under pines, bay, and holly, as well as dogwoods, magnolia, and live oak.

0.5 Pick up a boardwalk. The trees become bigger.

0.6 Circle around, then come to the old Herb and Maggie Tillett homesite. You can view brick home foundations and metal relics. Some of the biggest trees in Nags Head Woods are in the vicinity of the dwelling site, now growing over with brush, vines, and lesser trees. The home was abandoned in the 1940s. Contemplate the pace of life back then and what the Outer Banks were like at that time.

0.7 Reach a bridge crossing the marsh. Good views open in both directions.

0.9 Reach the trail's end and a small beach, with marsh melding into the nearby woods. Grab a view to the west of Roanoke Sound and the lands beyond. Backtrack to Old Nags Head Woods Road.

1.5 Head right, southbound on Old Nags Head Woods Road.

1.6 Turn right at the intersection with Ocean Acres Drive and descend west, coming to the parking area for the ADA Trail (disabled permit parking only). Pick up the level concrete ADA Trail, making a counterclockwise loop. Absorb the trailside interpretive information. Just ahead, pass the almost indiscernible site of the Nags Head water treatment plant.

1.8 Come to the wooden deck of the marsh overlook. Gaze southwest across grasses with the open waters of Roanoke Sound in the distance. The trail continues, then reaches the fishing pier. It offers angling and a good view of the pond.

2.1 Complete the ADA Trail. From here, head east down Ocean Acres Drive.

2.2 Arrive back at the visitor center, completing the coastal hike.

6. DUNES OF JOCKEYS RIDGE

This is a truly unique coastal trail adventure. From the visitor center at Jockeys Ridge State Park, you trace a boardwalk over lesser sand hills to open onto gigantic dunes. Here, follow posts in the sand across the massive mountains of grain. Then you cruise along Currituck Sound before returning to the big dunes. From here, freestyle hike to the top of Jockeys Ridge, soaking in distant 360-degree views. Finally, return to the visitor center. Next you drive a short way to an alternate trailhead to do a second hike among partly wooded older dunes, coming near the big ones of Jockeys Ridge before turning back along Currituck Sound.

THE RUNDOWN

Distance: 1.3-mile and 0.8-mile loop, respectively
Start: State park visitor center and West Soundside Road
Nearest town: Nags Head
Hiking time: 1.5 hours
Fees and permits: None
Conveniences: Restrooms, water, information at visitor center
Beach access: Yes, on sound side of park
Trail users: Hikers
Trail surface: A little boardwalk, open sand dunes
Difficulty: Easy, but sand can be slow going

Highlights: Huge sand dunes, views from Jockeys Ridge, beach on Roanoke Sound
Canine compatibility: Leashed dogs permitted
Schedule: Nov through Feb from 8:00 a.m. to 6:00 p.m.; Mar and Apr from 8:00 a.m. to 8:00 p.m.; May through Sept from 8:00 a.m. to 9:00 p.m.; Oct from 8:00 a.m. to 8:00 p.m.; closed Christmas Day
Managing agency: Jockeys Ridge State Park, 300 W. Carolista Dr.; Nags Head, NC 27959; (252) 441-7132; www.ncparks.gov/jockeys-ridge-state-park

FINDING THE TRAILHEAD

From the intersection of NC 345, US 64 Bypass, and US 64 in Manteo, take US 64 East to join US 158 West on the Outer Banks. Once on US 158 West, drive for 4.5 miles to a left turn on Carolista Drive and the state park. Follow it to a dead end at the visitor center after 0.3 mile. The boardwalk leading to the dunes starts at the rear of the visitor center. GPS trailhead coordinates: 35.963953, -75.632407

WHAT TO SEE

Jockeys Ridge State Park is one of those places that needs to be seen and experienced to be believed. A 400-acre parcel dominated by the largest sand dunes on the Atlantic coast, the park preserves ever-shifting ridges extending in mountainous heaps where you can gain 360-degree views. These particular dunes are known as medano, shifting sands that have no vegetation on them; they are pure sand mounds. The park also has a coastal marsh ecosystem along Roanoke Sound, as well as pockets of maritime forest. These dunes have been here a long time and have been a landmark for mariners passing by the Outer Banks. Dunes such as this once extended north all the way to the Virginia state

Viewing platform opens on Jockeys Ridge

line, but most were flattened for human use. However, in 1973 a woman named Carolista Baum literally stood in front of the bulldozers that were about to take down Jockeys Ridge. The dunes were saved, and the next year the National Park Service declared the dunes a National Natural Landmark. By 1975, the North Carolina legislature appropriated money to purchase the land that is now expanded to 426 acres and is practically encircled by development or ocean, so the terrain is quite extraordinary.

The name Jockeys Ridge comes from the practice of early residents capturing local feral ponies and racing them along the base of the dunes while spectators watched from the adjacent dune hills. Whether that is true or not, the dunes have always been an attraction and remain so today. Ironically, in most coastal destinations, visitors are constantly encouraged to stay off the dunes to allow vegetation to grow and stabilize the shoreline, yet here at Jockeys Ridge State Park, visitors are encouraged to traipse all over the sand, taking just about any route they please. In fact not only are walkers encouraged, but also kite flyers, model plane enthusiasts, and even hang gliders. In fact, an on-site outfitter offers hang gliding lessons for visitors during the warm season.

Known as an active dune system, storms and incessant winds constantly shift the sands, although wet sand underneath the dried top layer helps stabilize the dunes, estimated to be 3,000 to 4,000 years old. Interestingly, the prevailing northeast winds of winter shift the dunes one way and then the prevailing southwest winds of summer push the sands back again. Hurricanes and tropical storms can make instantaneous changes.

Climbing the open sands of Jockeys Ridge

You will know the dunes intimately before your adventure is over. From the park visitor center, a boardwalk leads you through maritime woods back to the dune system. After scaling a couple of lesser hills, you open onto the heights of Jockeys Ridge. A marked path leads through the dunes and over sand peaks where you can view Roanoke Sound and historic Roanoke Island beyond. The posts lead you down to the waters of the sound, where you can walk along the shore before the trail signposts lead through more woods and back to the bigger dunes. At this point, aim for the highest dune you can see, scaling the shifting yellow grains. Once atop Jockeys Ridge you can revel in panoramas extending every direction from the Atlantic Ocean, north and south along the land that is the Outer Banks, then east to Roanoke Sound. It's quite an inspiring panorama.

After returning to the visitor center, enjoy a second hike, after a short drive to the second trailhead on Soundside Drive. Here, a loop trail complemented with interpretive information leads through partly wooded older dunes, then out to Roanoke Sound, where you walk a sandy track. Spur trails leave from the second part of the loop over to the sound, where sunbathing and beachcombing are common pastimes. Thus you can get your hikes in and then relax at the beach, marveling in these massive preserved dunes that make for a unique hiking experience in coastal Carolina.

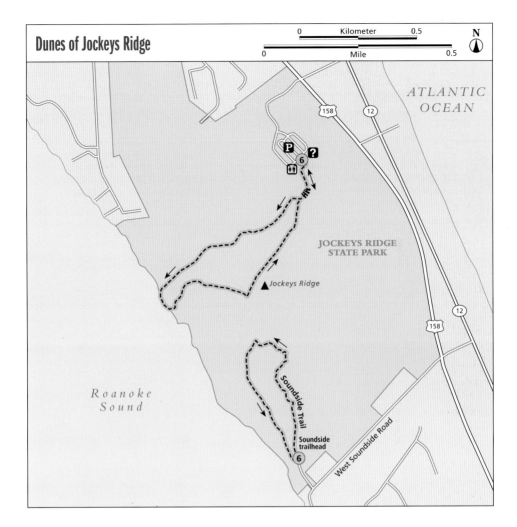

Dunes of Jockeys Ridge

ATLANTIC OCEAN

JOCKEYS RIDGE STATE PARK

▲ Jockeys Ridge

Roanoke Sound

Soundside Trail

Soundside trailhead

West Soundside Road

MILES AND DIRECTIONS

0.0 Leave from the back of the visitor center, joining an elevated boardwalk above hilly forest mixed with sands. Enjoy the interpretive information.

0.1 Reach the end of the boardwalk and come to an observation deck. Here, on a busy day, you can see hikers trekking all over the dunes near and far, some looking like ants. Drop to the sands and begin following the brown posts with arrows, heading generally westerly. Top over some partly vegetated dunes, then rise to naked pure sand dunes.

0.5 Top out and gain views of Roanoke Sound and Roanoke Island. Bigger dunes stand to your south. Continue following the posts downward.

0.6 Reach Roanoke Sound. Here, curve left, southerly snaking between the shoreline and partly vegetated smaller dunes. The trail leads you into woods of oak, pine, and cedar. Open to climb a steep dune, soon reaching the shoulder of the larger dunes.

0.8 Reach the end of the posts, then freewheel it toward the peak of the biggest dune you observe, walking over pure sand. You may have to drop some before climbing to the biggest dune atop Jockeys Ridge. After walking a bit, you will be able to identify by sight the more stable, less shifting sands.

1.0 Top out and gain incredible vistas of the water and land around you—sand in the near; other hikers, the nearby town of Nags Head, and of course the Atlantic Ocean to the east; and Roanoke Sound and historic Roanoke Island to the west. Spot the visitor center to the northeast and begin heading for it.

1.3/0.0 Return to the visitor center. From here, get in your car and head back out to US 158 and turn right, southbound, and follow it for 0.8 mile to Soundside Road and a traffic light. Turn right and follow Soundside Road for 0.4 mile to the signed trailhead on your right. After parking your car, join the Soundside Trail from the back of the parking lot and head north among lower, partly wooded dunes, passing by a small interdunal wetland.

0.4 Come near some of the huge dunes, then turn left toward the sound. Soon curve back south. The track is wider and sandier here, making for slower travel. Trail posts keep you in the right direction.

0.8 Return to the trailhead, completing the hike. However, in the vicinity of the trailhead, several paths cross over to reach the beach on Roanoke Sound. Beachcombers and beach lovers visit this area either during or after the hike. This is a good place to relax after a day of dune climbing at Jockeys Ridge State Park.

7. FORT RALEIGH NATIONAL HISTORIC SITE

This historical hike explores the site of England's first settlement attempt in the New World, as well as later periods of history on Roanoke Island, part of the Outer Banks. Leave the visitor center to see a reconstructed earthen fort. Next head out through woods to a beach on Albemarle Sound. From there, aim for the Freedom Trail and follow it west to end at another beach on Croatan Sound. The final part of the adventure is a backtrack to the trailhead.

THE RUNDOWN

Distance: 3.1-mile loop with spur
Start: Fort Raleigh visitor center on NC 12
Nearest town: Manteo
Hiking time: 1.6 hours
Fees and permits: None
Conveniences: Restrooms, water, information at visitor center
Beach access: Yes
Trail users: History buffs

Trail surface: Concrete, pavement, mostly natural surface
Difficulty: Easy
Highlights: History, beaches, woods
Canine compatibility: Leashed dogs permitted
Schedule: Daily from 9 a.m. to 5 p.m.
Managing agency: Fort Raleigh National Historic Site, 1401 National Park Dr., Manteo, NC 27954; (252) 473-2111; www.nps.gov/fora

FINDING THE TRAILHEAD

From the intersection of NC 345, US 64 Bypass, and US 64 in Manteo, take US 64 West toward Manteo and follow it for 4.4 miles to a right turn onto Fort Raleigh Road. Follow Fort Raleigh Road 0.2 mile to a left turn onto National Park Drive. Stay with National Park Drive to reach a large parking area. Make your way to the visitor center next to the parking area and start your hike there. GPS trailhead coordinates: 35.936920, -75.708356

WHAT TO SEE

Right here on Roanoke Island in the Outer Banks, back in 1584, there landed a reconnaissance boat from England, scouting to find a place to start the first British colony in what would become the United States. A second colonizing expedition failed in 1585 when much of the supplies were ruined en route to the New World. And thus, in the year 1587, a group of 118 men, women, and children landed on Roanoke Island to begin the first English colony. They were simply to land on Roanoke Island then move on to an ideal colonization point up Chesapeake Bay, but the ship's captain refused to take them any farther. The colonists worked hard to repair a fortification from previous expeditions and build houses. Relationships with local Indians were tenuous at best due to previous misunderstandings. However, during that time, Virginia Dare was born, the first English child born in the New World. It gave the colonists hope, but unreliable food sources and the approaching winter combined with Indian troubles left the colonists on edge. One John White and a company of men left for England for more supplies and hopefully more colonists. The remaining settlers on Roanoke Island were to divide

This beach abuts Albemarle Sound.

into two groups—one to stay on Roanoke Island and the other to find a more suitable colonization locale.

What happened after that is one of the great mysteries of history. See, John White fully expected to get supplies and more colonists and immediately turn back around to Roanoke Island. However, an impending war between Spain and England disrupted those plans and the mastermind behind the entire colonization effort—the famed Sir Walter Raleigh—lost interest in colonizing America, leaving John White to search for another way back to the New World. It wasn't until 1590, almost three years later, that White was back on Roanoke Island. And there he found no one—not one person was left. Yet there were no signs of violence or struggles, simply on abandoned settlement. White did find "CRO" carved onto a tree and the word "Croatan" carved onto the palisade wall. White immediately sailed toward the mainland, where the Croatan Indians were, but a tropical storm sidelined his efforts. Eventually he made his way back to England without ever knowing the fate of his fellow colonists.

And since that time no one has ever solved this mystery of the Lost Colony.

On this hike you will be treading the ground where the colonists once lived. After exploring the visitor center, you can cruise by the very location of the defensive earthen fort built by the colonists. Next, you will join the Thomas Hariot Trail, named for one of England's leading scientists of the sixteenth century. Hariot came over in 1585 and documented as much as he could about the people, flora, and fauna of the area in the

This hike features a second beach vista on Croatan Sound

short time he was here before returning to England. You will go through rolling maritime forest along old dunes before popping out on a white beach along Albemarle Sound. Beyond there, the hike leads back through woods, then by the park administration building before opening onto a large parking area used for the Elizabethan Gardens. Then you join the Freedom Trail as it heads westerly through level maritime woods to reach Croatan Sound. This part of the hike gives the illusion of remoteness in the deep, rich woods. A final backtrack returns you to the trailhead.

While here you can also explore the Elizabethan Gardens and see the Lost Colony drama at the Waterside Theatre, overlooking Albemarle Sound. Both activities require a fee. The Lost Colony drama has been playing for over eighty years. Through dialogue, music, and dance you will hear the story of the English colonists. During its inaugural 1937 season—when it was only supposed to run through the summer—President Franklin D. Roosevelt attended a performance and the rest is history. With the exception of the World War II years, the Lost Colony production has been in play, despite the theater being torn down by storms a few times. The drama runs every summer from late May through mid-August, bringing history to life.

The Elizabethton Gardens are the product of visitors to Fort Raleigh in the 1950s. They thought a garden would enhance the overall Fort Raleigh National Historic Site experience. The garden was established and has since grown to include not only fine plantings, but sculptures and artwork too, much of it pertaining to the Lost Colony. You

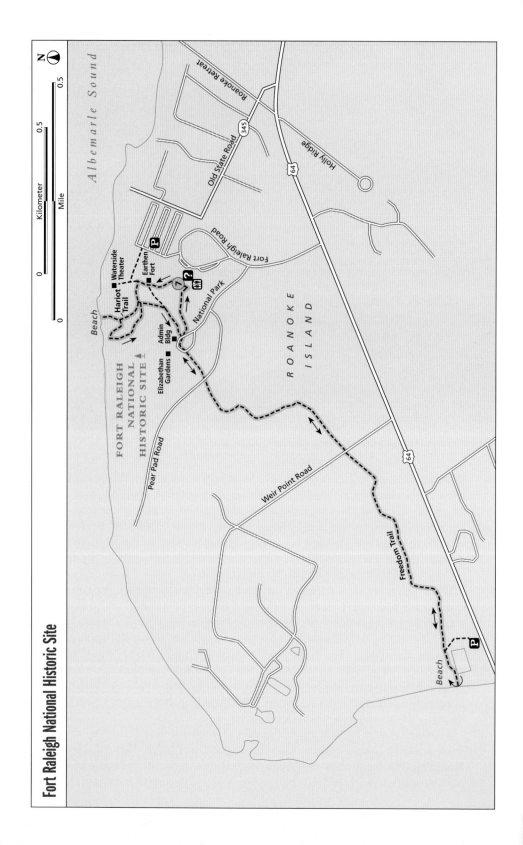

Fort Raleigh National Historic Site

will walk by the garden entrance on this hike. For more information about the gardens, visit www.elizabethangardens.org.

MILES AND DIRECTIONS

0.0 With your back to the visitor center entrance, facing the restrooms, head right, passing the Freedmen's Colony Monument, then turn right again toward the earthen fort on a concrete path.

0.1 Come to the re-created earthen fort. Interpretive information further explains the historic reconstruction. Also a path leads acutely left toward the Elizabethan Gardens. This will be your return route. But for now continue straight just a few feet beyond the earthen fort, then turn left on the Thomas Hariot Trail, a natural surface path. (The path you are on keeps straight toward the Waterside Theatre.) Head west under live oaks and magnolias, among other trees.

0.2 Join a spur trail going right. Here you drop off to a white sand beach. The Waterside Theatre is to your right. Walk around the beach, then backtrack, continuing the loop of the Thomas Hariot Trail.

0.4 Come to another overlook of Albemarle Sound on a little bluff, complete with interpretive information. Continue the loop.

0.5 Finish the Thomas Hariot Trail. Go right on a natural surface path, soon to intersect a sidewalk. Stay right here, soon reaching the park administration building.

0.6 Emerge onto the circular parking lot of the Elizabethan Gardens parking area. Cut directly across the parking area, picking up the natural surface Freedom Trail. Enter a rich forest. Quickly cross a paved park administration road.

1.2 Cross Weir Point Road, then immediately reenter woods, still westbound. The trail seems surprisingly remote.

1.7 A spur trail goes left by a pond and out to US 64. Keep straight.

1.8 Emerge onto a beach overlooking Croatan Sound. The US 64 bridge over the sound is to your left. Backtrack.

3.0 Return to the Elizabethan Gardens parking area. Now join a concrete path heading back to the visitor center.

3.1 Arrive back at the visitor center, completing the historic coastal hike.

8. SOMERSET PLACE HISTORIC HIKE

This coastal hike takes place at history-filled Pettigrew State Park, on the shores of Lake Phelps, one of the largest of the Carolina bay lakes, those waters of unknown formation. Here, walk the Moccasin Trail near farms then under tall trees to find a boardwalk and Moccasin Overlook, an aquatic vista. After backtracking, take a series of shorter yet interesting paths, following a boardwalk to historic Somerset Place State Historic Site, with its restored buildings and living history. Continue on to visit the Pettigrew Cemetery, then pass huge trees en route to Bee Tree Overlook, another panoramic place on the shores of Lake Phelps.

THE RUNDOWN

Distance: 9.8 miles in two out-and-back hikes from the same trailhead; can be separate hikes of 5.6 and 4.2 miles

Start: Near park boat ramp

Nearest town: Creswell

Hiking time: 3.5 hours

Fees and permits: None

Conveniences: Picnic area adjacent to trailhead, restrooms, water nearby at campground

Beach access: No

Trail users: Bicyclers, history buffs

Trail surface: Natural

Difficulty: Moderate due to distance

Highlights: Moccasin Overlook, Somerset Place State Historic Site, Pettigrew Cemetery, Bee Tree Overlook

Canine compatibility: Leashed dogs permitted

Schedule: Nov through Feb from 8 a.m. to 6 p.m.; Mar, Apr, May, Sept, Oct from 8 a.m. to 8 p.m.; June through Aug from 8 a.m. to 9 p.m.; closed Christmas Day

Managing agency: Pettigrew State Park, 2252 Lake Shore Rd., Creswell, NC 27928; (252) 797-4475; www.ncparks.gov/pettigrew-state-park

FINDING THE TRAILHEAD

From exit 558 on US 64 near Creswell, head south on 6th Street and follow it 0.4 mile to a left turn onto East Main Street. Follow East Main Street for 1.9 miles, then turn right onto Thirty Foot Canal Road and follow it for 4.5 miles to a left turn onto Lake Shore Road and then turn right into Pettigrew State Park. Curve right past the park office, then keep straight for the boat ramp, and the trailhead is on the left. GPS trailhead coordinates: 35.791545, -76.410073

WHAT TO SEE

Pettigrew State Park stands on a vast peninsula of eastern North Carolina, bordered by Albemarle Sound to the north and the Pamlico River to the south. Here you will find Lake Phelps, North Carolina's second largest natural lake and one of the mysterious–origin Carolina bay lakes. Stretching 7 miles by 5 miles, Lake Phelps is the focal point of Pettigrew State Park. It is along these shores where you can take a historic and scenic hike.

Well before North Carolina became a state, Algonquin Indians visited clear Lake Phelps. We know this because over two dozen of their dugout canoes have been found

Looking out on Lake Phelps, one of the unexplained-origin Carolina bay lakes

at the lake bottom. They hid them here for use year to year. Among this collection of canoes is one over 35 feet in length! Later, colonial settlers moved in from the coast. In 1787 a man named Josiah Collins established a plantation on the shores of Lake Phelps, called Somerset Place. Nearby wooded swampland was cut down and canals were dug to drain the land, making it arable. Eventually the plantation grew into a regular self-sustaining village of its own; hundreds of people were living on the site when the Civil War came. However, the end of the war spelled freedom for the 850 slaves and the end of Somerset Place as a plantation. At one time over fifty buildings were scattered on the shores of the complex, with stables, gristmills, churches, laundry facilities, and more. The plantation fell to ruin, but was incorporated into brand-new Pettigrew State Park in 1939. Since then the site has been restored and you can visit several original buildings and other re-created structures, as well as enjoy living history tours and demonstrations. Visitors are encouraged to explore the buildings and history of Somerset Place. Check https://historicsites.nc.gov/all-sites/somerset-place for details.

Josiah Collins's next-door neighbors were the Pettigrew family, for whom the park is named. They had established a farm of their own, known as Bonarva. The Pettigrews also grew rice and corn using cutting-edge agricultural practices for the time period. On this hike you can visit the Pettigrew Cemetery and the grave of General James Johnston Pettigrew, a Confederate general of note who led what became known as Pickett's Charge during the battle of Gettysburg. General Pettigrew was wounded while retreating from the battle and died at age thirty-five. Unfortunately the Pettigrew family farm is now but rubble, save for the elevated cemetery, raised because of the extremely low water table in this part of North Carolina.

Top: The author poses in front of a big tulip tree.
Bottom: Inside one of the many historic buildings at Somerset Place

Even with the expansive historic aspects of Pettigrew State Park, there is also a natural side of the preserve to enjoy. You will first take the Moccasin Trail, heading northwesterly along the north shore of Lake Phelps. The path initially presents views of farmland to the north outside the park and of swamp woods to the south. However, the path delves deeper into woods and reaches an area of tall trees all around. Next thing you know you are walking the boardwalk out to Moccasin Overlook. Here you can gaze 5 miles south to a faint and distant shoreline. Nearer, Big Point juts out into the water.

After backtracking the Moccasin Trail, you join the Lake Shore Trail, a cool boardwalk that winds among swamp woods and along the shoreline. The costly path uses enough lumber to build two houses and extends for

Swamp lilies brighten the hike.

0.4 mile before returning to dry land. From here you are just a short distance from Somerset Place. At this point you can either explore the grounds or continue the hike and explore the structures of Somerset Place on your return. Continuing on you will pass the Bonarva Trail, delivering yet another spectacular view of Lake Phelps. After that, the Bee Tree Trail takes you by some massive trees. Make sure to take the detour to the Pettigrew Cemetery. Here you can look out on farmland and woods—and Carolina coastal history. Finally, head to Bee Tree Overlook. There you can look westerly and not see the far end of Lake Phelps, due to Earth's curvature. That's how big Lake Phelps is!

Finally, visit the quaint park campground. It offers a mix of shaded and open sites and exudes a relaxing atmosphere. Hot showers and water spigots enhance the experience. Most of the wooded campsites offer good privacy. Even if you're not into camping, try a picnic here. The park picnic area is adjacent to the trailhead and offers wooded picnic sites as well as a picnic shelter. While here you can also enjoy the Morotoc Trail, a path open to hikers and bicyclists that also skirts the shoreline of Lake Phelps. It extends 4.2 miles one way.

MILES AND DIRECTIONS

0.0 From the parking area at the Lake Shore Trail almost to the park boat ramp, walk back north a bit toward the park office and join the Moccasin Trail. Immediately cross 30 Foot Canal, heading west. Quiet Lake Shore Road and fields, along with a few houses, lie to your right, while a forest of tupelo, cypress, sycamore, and sweet-gum rise to your left, with Lake Phelps visible through the trees. Vines form a brushy understory.

0.3 Pass the foundations of an old building. Ahead, a break in the forest allows views of the big body of water.

1.2 More lake views open near where Mountain Canal Road meets Lake Shore Road to your right. Look for mayapples in spring as well as white Atamasco lilies, also known as swamp lilies.

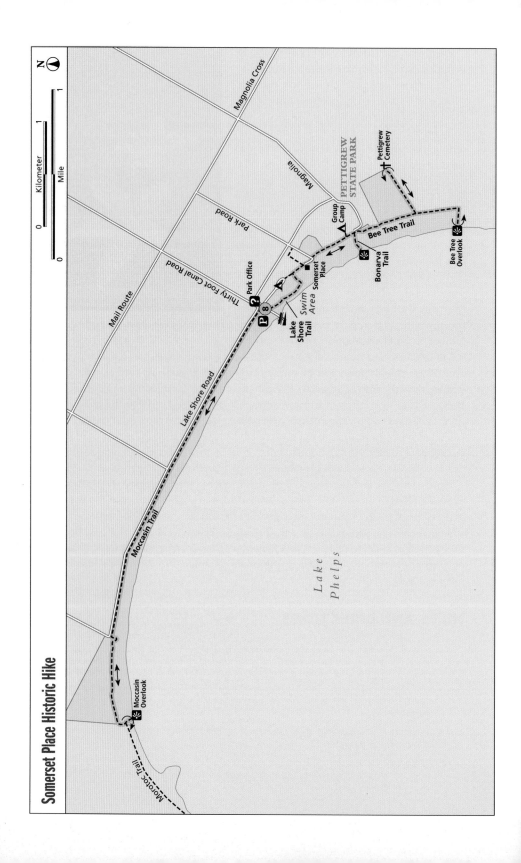

Somerset Place Historic Hike

2.3 Come to Weston Canal. Turn left here, entering more remote big woods after bridging the canal. Sweetgums tower above.

2.7 Come to Moccasin Canal. Here, head left and shortly join a long boardwalk extending through cypress woods.

2.8 Reach the Moccasin Overlook. Spyglass extensive vistas of the lake in the distance and Big Point to your right. Backtrack.

5.6 Return to the Lake Shore Trail parking area. Now join the boardwalk of the Lake Shore Trail winding above swampy maple forest. Ferns rise from the forest floor.

5.8 A spur boardwalk splits right to the lake. This is the park swimming area. Continue on the Lake Shore Trail.

6.0 Return to dry land. A spur trail heads left to the campground, but turn right to quickly reach Somerset Place State Historic Site. Explore now or on your return trip. Continue along the trail beyond the last structure.

6.4 A spur trail leads left to the park's group camp. Keep straight and quickly reach the Bonarva Trail. Follow the boardwalk out to yet another rewarding view of Lake Phelps. Backtrack, then continue the Bee Tree Trail, nearing the group camping parking area and a ranger residence.

7.2 Head left toward the Pettigrew Cemetery in forest.

7.5 Reach the well-tended Pettigrew Cemetery, an elevated locale with but a few graves. View adjacent fields. Backtrack.

7.8 Return to the Bee Tree Trail and head left, southerly, under big, big trees including one massive tulip tree.

8.2 Turn right toward Lake Phelps at the Bee Tree Canal.

8.3 Reach Bee Tree Overlook. Scan west toward the horizon and nearer to the wooded swampy shores. It is one big lake. Backtrack.

9.8 Arrive back at the trailhead near the park boat ramp, completing the hike.

9. BODIE ISLAND LIGHTHOUSE & BEACH WALK

On this two-prong hiking adventure, first visit iconic Bodie Island Lighthouse and walk the boardwalk here to an elevated viewing platform, where you can see the lighthouse and grounds and surrounding seashore, and even climb the lighthouse in season. From there, drive just a short distance to Coquina Beach, where you take a boardwalk over the dunes then walk north on Cape Hatteras National Seashore beach bordered by dunes on one side and the Atlantic Ocean on the other.

THE RUNDOWN

Distance: 0.6-mile and 2.2-mile there-and-back, respectively
Start: Bodie Island Lighthouse parking area
Nearest town: Manteo
Hiking time: 1.5 hours
Fees and permits: None
Conveniences: Restrooms, water, information at Bodie Island Lighthouse; restrooms, changing area, cold outdoor showers at Coquina Beach
Beach access: Yes
Trail users: Hikers, beachcombers, lighthouse buffs

Trail surface: Boardwalk, sand
Difficulty: Easy; slower going on the beach
Highlights: Historic lighthouse, views from observation platform, Coquina Beach
Canine compatibility: Leashed dogs permitted
Schedule: Daily dawn to dusk
Managing agency: Cape Hatteras National Seashore, 1401 National Park Dr., Manteo, NC 27954; (252) 473-2111; www.nps.gov/caha

FINDING THE TRAILHEAD

From the intersection of NC 345, US 64 Bypass, and US 64 in Manteo, take US 64 East to join NC 12 South on the Outer Banks. Once on NC 12 South, follow it for 5.9 miles to a right turn onto Bodie Island Lighthouse Road. Follow it 0.3 mile to a dead end at the lighthouse. GPS trailhead coordinates: 35.818334, -75.564523

WHAT TO SEE

The shallows and shoals of the Carolina coast had been dangerous for mariners since the days of North Carolina's own favorite pirate Blackbeard in the early 1700s. The danger was not necessarily from pirates, rather from the irregular depths and shifting sands of yon ocean. It became incumbent upon a young United States to establish a series of lighthouses on those lonely and perilous Outer Banks. By 1837, the Cape Hatteras Lighthouse was already emitting its helpful beacon, but still more aid was needed. The area around Bodie Island seemed a good choice for a light station, as more ships were foundering in that area than anywhere else along the Carolina coast. Thus, the spot was picked on Pea Island, just north of Bodie Island, but unfortunately the man in charge of building the original 54-foot tower failed to stabilize its foundation, and that first Bodie

The lightkeeper's quarters fronts Bodie Island Lighthouse.

Island lighthouse began to lean in similar fashion to that famous tower in the Italian city of Pisa. Postconstruction repairs failed to straighten the lighthouse, and it was eventually abandoned in 1859. Another lighthouse—this one 80 feet high and straight as an arrow—rose to warn shippers of aquatic navigational hazards.

However, the second lighthouse was very short-lived, a victim of the rising conflagration between North and South. As the Civil War became a reality in 1861, the Confederates decided that it would be better to blow up the beacon rather than let the Union use it to their advantage. And down it went.

For six years no lights guided mariners from the area. Civil War reconstruction lowered the lighthouse down the priority list. Ships continued to founder off the Outer Banks. Washington heard the cry and another lighthouse was to be built. The site was picked on Bodie Island, 15 acres of fine land purchased for $150 from a man named John Etheridge. (Can you imagine the value of those 15 acres today?) Experienced hands of those who had built the sturdy Cape Hatteras Lighthouse joined forces for the new project. And they did it right. The steel-reinforced brick lighthouse was outfitted with a first order Fresnel lens (still in use today) and came online the first day of October in 1872, sporting its alternating black-and-white stripes to distinguish it from other lighthouses.

Originally lit by oil, the beacon was tended by lighthouse keepers who lived in the on-site keeper's quarters (as well as Manteo in later years), a duplex that now serves as the lighthouse visitor center managed by the National Park Service. The run of lighthouse keepers lasted sixty years, until the Bodie Island Lighthouse became an electric beacon. Today the light makes a new full rotation every 27½ seconds, sending its light 19 miles to the horizon, still aiding mariner's navigation of shoals dubbed "the graveyard of the Atlantic."

In 1953 the National Park Service took over the property (but not the lighthouse operation), establishing the national seashore and keeping the area open to the public. However, for decades the 214 steps to the top of the still-active 156-foot lighthouse were closed to climbing. In 2013, the renovated inner lighthouse was open to tours and now visitors can climb the tower for a fee. The lighthouse-climbing season starts on the third Friday in April and lasts until Columbus Day in October. Ticket sales begin at 9 a.m. daily, with tours running every twenty minutes until the last climb at 4:30 p.m. Ascending the lighthouse is a highlight of anyone's visit to Cape Hatteras National Seashore.

And you can hike here, too. The lighthouse is built well back from the Atlantic ocean-front, with marsh between it and the sea. Starting at the same parking lot as for the light-house, you can enjoy a boardwalk that takes you astride the grounds of the lighthouse then onto a marsh and up an elevated and shaded observation deck. At this point you can scope toward the Atlantic, down to the immediate marsh below, and back to the Bodie Island Lighthouse rising to the sky. Unfortunately the marsh walk is only 0.6 mile there and back, but coastal trail hikers can augment their experience with a walk at nearby Coquina Beach. The parking area for Coquina Beach is but a quarter-mile distant from the lighthouse. Here you can surmount the big dunes on a boardwalk, then descend to the beach, where heading north vehicles are not allowed. You can walk 1.1 miles of natural Cape Hatteras National Seashore before reaching private property and beach houses. And if that is not enough beach for you, you can walk south for more miles than your legs can handle, with the Bodie Island Lighthouse as your personal beacon.

This walkway leads to an overlook of wetlands astride the Atlantic Ocean.

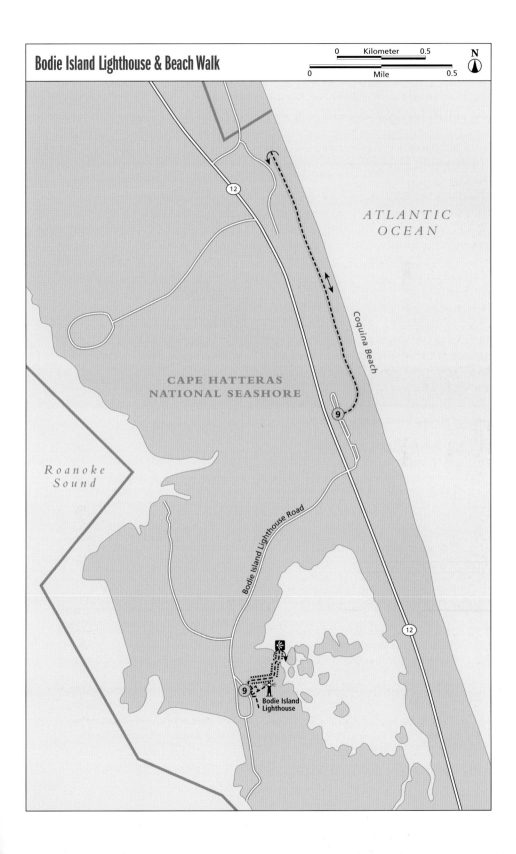

0   Kilometer   0.5

0   Mile   0.5

N

ATLANTIC
OCEAN

12

Coquina Beach

9

CAPE HATTERAS
NATIONAL SEASHORE

Roanoke
Sound

Bodie Island Lighthouse Road

9

Bodie Island
Lighthouse

12

Hike this Atlantic Beach next to Bodie Island

MILES AND DIRECTIONS

0.0 From the north side of the Bodie Island Lighthouse parking area, as you face the keeper's quarters and lighthouse, leave east past the restrooms on a boardwalk with a line of trees to your left and the grassy grounds of Bodie Island Lighthouse to your right.

0.1 Leave the grounds and turn left, northeast, into marsh. Don't forget to look back at the lighthouse. Continue deeper into the grassy marsh broken with open waters.

0.3 Reach the shaded and elevated observation deck. Gaze over to the dunes of the Atlantic Ocean, to the nearby marsh as well as pines and, of course, the lighthouse. You will spot birds in season. Backtrack.

0.6/0.0 Return to the lighthouse parking area. From there, drive the short distance back to NC 12 and cross NC 12 to reach the Coquina Beach parking area. Leave the parking area to find the bathhouse building, then take the boardwalk over the dunes to the Atlantic Ocean. To your right, Ramp 2 allows four-wheel-drive vehicles to access the beach heading south. However, the beach to the north is for people on foot only. Head left, north, with tall dunes to your left and the waves of the Atlantic to your right.

0.5 Pass an alternate beach access to your left. Note how the tall dunes completely block you from the traffic of NC 12.

1.1 Come to the north end of the Cape Hatteras National Seashore property. Beach houses begin. Backtrack.

2.1 Arrive back at the Coquina Beach parking area, completing the lighthouse hiking adventure.

10. PEA ISLAND NATIONAL WILDLIFE REFUGE

This view-laden hike at Pea Island National Wildlife Refuge explores a variety of environments on Hatteras Island. Leave the visitor center, then cruise by a series of ponds on elevated dikes where you can look out beyond the ponds to the dunes of the Atlantic and the waters of Pamlico Sound. Scan the region from an elevated tower, then head north between open waters. Next, join the beachfront of the Atlantic Ocean to hike unspoiled sands where no vehicles are allowed, returning to the visitor center. Bring your binoculars to spot birdlife.

THE RUNDOWN

Distance: 4.2-mile loop
Start: Refuge visitor center on NC 12
Nearest town: Rodanthe
Hiking time: 2.3 hours
Fees and permits: None
Conveniences: Restrooms, water, information at refuge visitor center
Beach access: Yes
Trail users: Hikers, Mountains-to-Sea Trail thru-hikers
Trail surface: Natural

Difficulty: Moderate
Highlights: Birds in ponds, views, primitive Atlantic beachfront
Canine compatibility: Leashed dogs permitted
Schedule: Daily dawn to dusk
Managing agency: Pea Island National Wildlife Refuge, 100 Conservation Way, Manteo, NC 27954; (252) 473-1131; www.fws.gov/refuge/Pea_Island

FINDING THE TRAILHEAD

From the intersection of NC 345, US 64 Bypass, and US 64 in Manteo, take US 64 East to join NC 12 South on the Outer Banks. Once on NC 12 South, follow it for 15 miles to reach the national wildlife refuge visitor center on your right. GPS trailhead coordinates: 35.717067, -75.493770

WHAT TO SEE

Pea Island National Wildlife Refuge is an unexpected jewel in the crown of nature that is the Outer Banks. Located on the northern tip of Hatteras Island, this refuge protects nearly 5,000 acres of coastal terrain, including direct Atlantic Ocean frontage as well as extensive wetlands and ponds used by waterfowl, with both fresh and brackish water ponds, as well as sand dunes, salt flats, and salt marsh. During the migration seasons you can see incredible concentrations of swans, geese, ducks, and lesser birds on the 790 acres of impoundments located on the refuge. The long and narrow refuge stretches for 13 miles from north to south, yet it is but 1 mile wide at its widest and as narrow as 0.25 mile in places. These narrowest parts are almost all sand, and this sand is constantly shifting and blowing and subject to tidal surges that in turn cause trouble on NC 12. The State of North Carolina is constantly battling the sand to keep this road open, since it is the only land connection to the coastal villages located south of here. Interestingly, the Civilian Conservation Corps created artificial dunes to protect NC 12 back in the 1930s. (This section of road was not paved until the 1950s.)

You circle these wetlands on this hike.

Pea Island is legendary among birders and receives over 2 million visitors annually (this figure must include people incidentally driving through the refuge on NC 12). Before its establishment in 1938, the refuge and adjacent waters of the Atlantic Ocean and Pamlico Sound were waterfowl hunting areas and farmland. Even livestock were run here. Commercial fishing was undertaken in the waters of what became the refuge.

After becoming a refuge, the US Fish and Wildlife Service has protected, maintained, and enhanced the population of fish, birds, and wildlife and has maintained the vegetational health and biodiversity of the refuge. The refuge ponds you see on this hike were created in the 1950s and 1960s to improve waterfowl habitat. The US Fish and Wildlife Service also provides the public with wildlife viewing places such as the overlooks on this hike. The refuge offers guided and educational activities as well. They also enhance opportunities for nesting birds such as piping plovers and provide nesting beaches for loggerhead sea turtles, among other creatures.

This hike starts at the visitor center. Interestingly, much of the trek follows the route used by the coastal portion of the Mountains-to-Sea Trail. You should take the time to check out the visitor center, as the volunteers in there will inform you of the latest wildlife sightings. Furthermore, you can enjoy the wildlife exhibits, for Pea Island National Wildlife Refuge is all about wildlife. You first join the North Pond Wildlife Trail, a heavily used track leading west along the south side of North Pond, an impoundment. To your south you can see New Field Pond, but it is closed to public entry, as it is a hatchery area. You will enjoy views both north and south before reaching an elevated viewing platform that presents spectacular views of the area both near and far, from Pamlico Sound to the Atlantic Ocean. This viewing platform marks the end of the North Pond Wildlife Trail.

Most visitors turn around at this point. However, to make the loop, curve right, north-bound, along North Pond on an elevated dike. Spectacular panoramas continue as you walk the berm. You will reach another elevated lookout and the handicap-accessible Salt Flats Wildlife Trail, a short trek from NC 12. Soon, pop out onto NC 12. From here cross the road and come to the beachfront of the Atlantic Ocean. Here you turn south and walk unspoiled sand where no vehicles are allowed. Pass along what is known as exposed overwash flats community, an almost all-sand environment created during storms. This will later evolve to vegetated dunes, then will once again be subject to storm. Parts of the beach may be closed for nesting, but the portion of beach closest to the Atlantic should be open. Look for American oystercatcher nests in the open sand areas that are closed. Use binoculars to avoid violating the closed areas. Enjoy this segment of beach hiking, with dunes separating you from the road, before returning to the visitor center. Even though the visitor center is on the far side of NC 12 from the beach, you will be able to spot the American flag flying above it from afar.

A dune crossing at Pea Island National Wildlife Refuge.

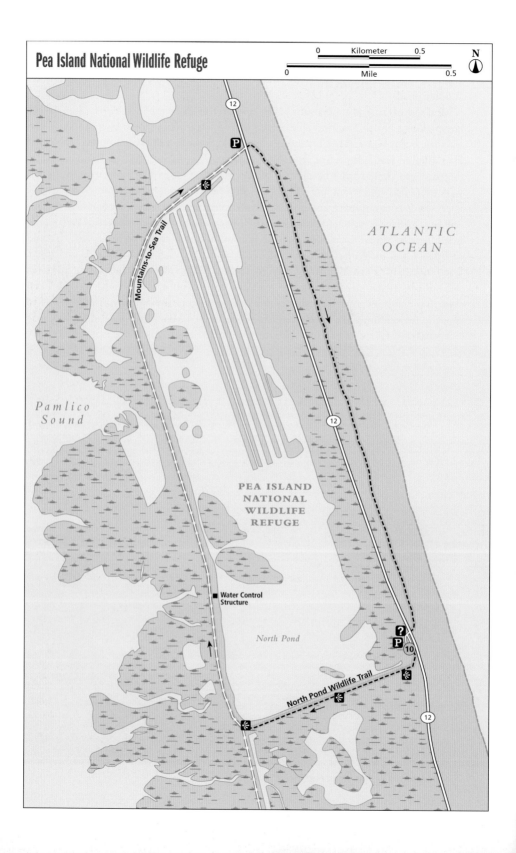

Pea Island National Wildlife Refuge

Kilometer 0 — 0.5

Mile 0 — 0.5

N

ATLANTIC OCEAN

Pamlico Sound

Mountains-to-Sea Trail

PEA ISLAND NATIONAL WILDLIFE REFUGE

Water Control Structure

North Pond

North Pond Wildlife Trail

12

10

The Atlantic Ocean beaches of the Outer Banks are both stark and beautiful.

MILES AND DIRECTIONS

0.0 Leave the south end of the Pea Island National Wildlife Refuge visitor center on the North Pond Wildlife Trail. Quickly pick up a boardwalk over a wetland. Shortly join an asphalt path westbound, away from NC 12, among low-slung pines and live oaks.

0.1 Reach an elevated overlook.

0.3 Reach another elevated overlook opening south to New Field Pond.

0.4 Come to another overlook. Note some overlooks are complete with viewing scopes for getting better looks at birdlife in the surrounding ponds.

0.6 Reach the elevated two-story viewing tower. Here you can climb steps to gain a princely panorama of the refuge and waters beyond in all four cardinal directions. This marks the official end of the North Pond Wildlife Trail. Most visitors turn around here, but our hike continues right, northbound, on an elevated berm much less used than the North Pond Wildlife Trail. The grass trail bed may be high. Rewarding views and wildlife viewing possibilities continue. This part of the hike is also part of the Mountains-to-Sea Trail.

1.0 Walk over a water control structure. Keep north atop the dike. Continue stellar views of marshes to your left and Pamlico Sound beyond, as well as ponds and dunes to your right.

1.9 The dike/trail begins curving right, northeast.

2.4 Come to the overlook and the official end of the wheelchair-accessible Salt Flats Wildlife Trail. Continue northeast.

2.6 The Salt Flats Wildlife Trail ends. Reach NC 12 and an alternate parking area in case the lot at the visitor center is full. Cross the road and reach the beach. Turn south, with the Atlantic Ocean to your left. Hear the waves roll. If it is a nice day, you will see people on this stretch of beach, but no cars, as this shoreline is part of the wildlife refuge.

4.2 Cut east away from the beach, crossing NC 12, and arrive back at the visitor center, completing the hike.

11. GOOSE CREEK HIKE

Situated on the northern shore of big, tidal Pamlico River, Goose Creek State Park presents a woodsy and rewarding coastal trek that takes you through the park by primitive footpath. Leave the worth-a-look environmental center to join the Palmetto Boardwalk, where you traverse a swamp. Then begin a circuit, cruising along Goose Creek, then pass a beach along the Pamlico River. Finally, turn up rush-bordered Mallard Creek before meandering through woods where you can see remnants of old tar kilns.

THE RUNDOWN

Distance: 7.4-mile balloon loop
Start: Environmental Center
Nearest town: Washington
Hiking time: 3.8 hours
Fees and permits: None
Conveniences: Restrooms, water, information at trailhead, swim beach en route
Beach access: Yes
Trail users: Hikers
Trail surface: Natural
Difficulty: Moderate

Highlights: Pamlico River beach, aquatic views, deep woods
Canine compatibility: Leashed dogs permitted
Schedule: Nov through Feb from 8 a.m. to 6 p.m.; Mar, Apr, May, Sept, Oct from 8 a.m. to 8 p.m.; June through Aug from 8 a.m. to 9 p.m.; closed Christmas Day
Managing agency: Goose Creek State Park, 2190 Camp Leach Rd., Washington, NC 27889; (252) 923-2191; www.ncparks.gov

FINDING THE TRAILHEAD

From Washington, NC, head east on US 264 for 9 miles to a right turn on Camp Leach Road, NC 1334, and follow it 2.2 miles to the park. After turning into the park, follow Main Road a short distance to the Environmental Center on your left. GPS trailhead coordinates: 35.478058, -76.901933

WHAT TO SEE

Goose Creek State Park occupies 1,672 acres and is bordered by three waterways: the massive tidal Pamlico River, Goose Creek, and Mallard Creek. The peninsula protects a melding of ecosystems, from brackish marshes to freshwater wooded swamps to upland hardwoods. You will appreciate the variety of vegetation offered in this eastern North Carolina preserve. And a great way to learn about the wilds of the park is at the informative environmental education center, where this hike starts. Here in these lowlands, the interplay between terra firma and water (both salt and fresh) creates the overlapping ecotones that make this park rich in both flora and fauna. The recommended hike at Goose Creek State Park takes you throughout the wilds here along Pamlico River.

Once the home of Tuscarora Indians who roamed this peninsula and later home to backwoods folk who scratched out a living with the plow, the axe, and the net (read: farming, timbering, and fishing), the park came to be in 1974 and was later expanded to its current size. The park trail system covers nearly 10 miles of pathways, and you walk most of them on this hike. You can complement your trek with an overnight stay at the

You will walk through fire-managed woods on this hike.

Looking out on a beach beside big and tidal Pamlico River

park's primitive tent campground. You will actually view some campsites during the hike. Situated on relatively elevated terrain between Flatty and Goose Creeks, the camp is stretched along a narrow tree-bordered road under tall oaks and pines. The campsites—each with tent pad, picnic table, lantern post, and fire ring—are very widespread, good for campers who love privacy. Some sites overlook Goose Creek and are the most popular.

Spring and fall are not only the best times to hike but also to camp at Goose Creek State Park. The campground fills on nice weekends during that time. Winter can be cool to cold, but you will find plenty of nice days to hike and camp here at this time of year too. Summer is too hot and buggy to walk or pitch your tent.

In addition to hikers, paddlers, anglers, and birders flock here. All three major waterways offer quality paddling experiences—Goose Creek, Mallard Creek, and the shoreline along Pamlico River present a natural shoreline by which to ply your canoe or kayak. Fishers vie for black drum, flounder, bream, and largemouth bass. The park also has a ramp for bigger boats. Finally, the swim beach on the Pamlico River is a draw, and you will hike by it.

Before you begin your hike, make sure to explore the Environmental Center. It is chock-full of displays about coastal North Carolina that will enhance your ecological understanding of this melding of land and water. Then you will leave the place of learning to quickly pick up the Palmetto Boardwalk, entering a swamp, locally known as a pocosin, Indian for "swamp on a hill." This swamp drains into both Goose Creek and Mallard Creek. This swamp is one of the most northerly locations of the palmetto bush. Cane, bay trees, cypress, myrtle, and other vegetation rise from the tannin-stained blackwater. The swamp is home of the fabled water moccasin, though you likely will not see one. Some areas of the marsh are more open than others due to storm damage.

Hiking beside a live oak along the Pamlico River

Pines grace this part of the hike.

After enjoying the swamp walk, you will return to dry land and begin your counterclockwise circuit, joining the Ivey Gut Trail under tall, fire-managed pines and oaks with a healthy understory of beard cane. You'll notice how well maintained the wide trails are. The Ivey Gut Trail leads west under sweetgum and evergreens, eventually to saddle alongside Goose Creek, where you can soak in watery views of the tidal tributary of the Pamlico River. The path then makes an additional secondary loop, which takes you alongside the waterway for a longer period before coming to the park's campground, where you can admire some of these attractive primitive tent sites for yourself.

The hike then turns easterly on the Goose Creek Trail. Enjoy the deep woods walk before joining the Live Oak Trail and the highlight of the hike. Here you walk along the

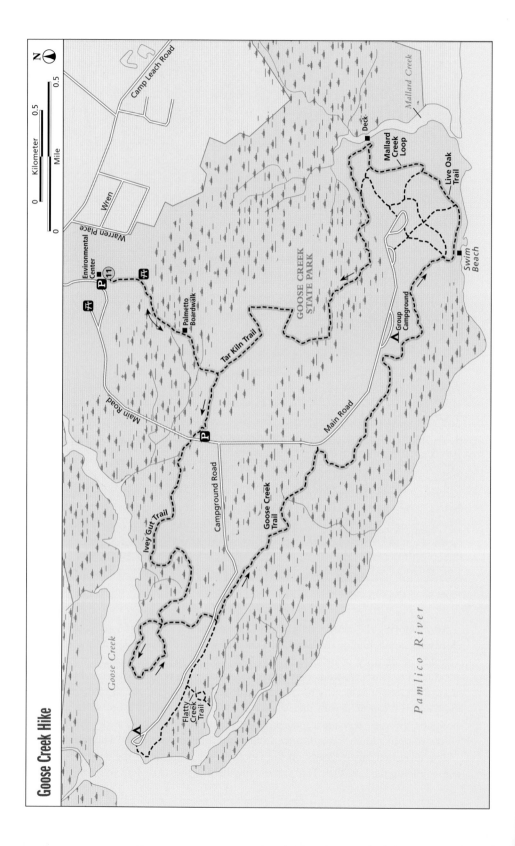

Goose Creek Hike

N

Kilometer
0   0.5   0.5

Mile
0   0.5

Camp Leach Road

Wren

Warren Place

Environmental
Center

P (1)

Main Road

Palmetto
Boardwalk

Tar Kiln Trail

Ivey Gut Trail

Campground Road

Goose Creek
Trail

Goose Creek

Flatty
Creek
Trail

GOOSE CREEK
STATE PARK

Main Road

Group
Campground

Deck

Mallard Creek Loop

Live Oak
Trail

Swim
Beach

Mallard Creek

Pamlico River

sandy shore at the park swim beach and enjoy distant views and beach while simultaneously walking under stately live oaks draped in Spanish moss. The hike continues among a series of shorter nature trails, visiting a viewing deck over Mallard Creek along the way. This brush-bordered tidal stream is dwarfed by the massive Pamlico River.

Next, you pick up the Tar Kiln Trail, exploring the early naval stores industry. In the days when ships were mostly made of wood, they had to be sealed tight and pitch was used to keep the wood waterproof. The trail traverses old woods roads in places that were used to access the tall pines used to make pitch. You will also circle around freshwater wooded swamps before returning to take the Palmetto Boardwalk a last time, finishing the coastal trail adventure.

MILES AND DIRECTIONS

0.0 As you face the Goose Creek State Park Environmental Center, leave right from a kiosk and circle around the building, heading toward the Palmetto Boardwalk. Traverse restored longleaf pine woods, passing a screened-in picnic shelter.

0.1 Begin crossing a swamp dry footed using the Palmetto Boardwalk. Enjoy viewing this heavily vegetated ecosystem, passing a sitting area ahead, while aiming southward.

0.6 Leave the boardwalk and return to dry ground, quickly coming to an intersection. Begin the loop portion of your hike. Head right on the Ivey Gut Trail, the route coming in from your left; the Tar Kiln Trail will be your return route.

0.9 Bisect Main Road after passing an alternate parking area, still on the Ivey Gut Trail, heading westerly toward Goose Creek. Cross shorter boardwalks over wetlands.

1.3 Come alongside Goose Creek, then turn away, circling around a drainage.

1.8 Reach a trail intersection. Head right on the loop portion of the Ivey Gut Trail and return to Goose Creek, where aquatic vistas open.

2.4 Complete the loop portion of the Ivey Gut Trail. Continue south.

2.6 Cross Campground Road, then reach another trail intersection. Head left, easterly, on the Goose Creek Trail, bordered in attractive woods with occasional boardwalks rising above seasonal wetlands.

3.4 Pass a short spur leading left to Main Road.

4.0 A short spur leads left to the group campground.

4.4 Come to a wide path, the Live Oak Trail, and head right, immediately coming to the park's foot-only accessible swim beach. Continue along the sandy shore of the Pamlico River under live oaks. Great views abound. Parts of the trail here can be slow and sandy.

4.6 Keep straight as the Huckleberry Trail goes left. Pull away from the shoreline.

4.9 Split right at a junction, picking up the Mallard Creek Loop. Ahead, pass a shortcut to the Huckleberry Trail, then come to the observation deck overlooking Mallard Creek.

5.4 Pick up the Tar Kiln Trail. Meander westerly in deep woods, coming to occasional interpretive signage explaining the process of making pitch from pines. The pitch was primarily used as naval stores to make ships watertight.

6.8 Complete the Tar Kiln Trail after winding in seemingly all directions through alternating pinewoods and swamp forests, sometimes on old roads. Turn right here, walking the Palmetto Boardwalk a second time.

7.4 Arrive back at the Environmental Center, completing the hike.

12. OPEN PONDS TRAIL

This hike at Cape Hatteras National Seashore travels through gorgeous maritime woods where live oaks form a canopy and through a rolling dune forest that provides a vertical challenge. Situated on a wide part of Hatteras Island, the trek starts near the graves of British seamen, then heads west through the attractive forest to end at Frisco Campground. A backtrack is in order, making this a 9-mile endeavor, the longest woods hike on the Outer Banks. Also, fabled Cape Hatteras Lighthouse is located very near the trailhead and is a must visit while here. You can even climb the beacon after your hike—if you have enough energy!

THE RUNDOWN

Distance: 9.0-mile there-and-back
Start: Lighthouse Road
Nearest town: Buxton
Hiking time: 4.5 hours
Fees and permits: None
Conveniences: Restrooms, water, information at nearby Cape Hatteras Lighthouse
Beach access: Nearby
Trail users: Hikers, Mountains-to-Sea Trail thru-hikers
Trail surface: Natural

Difficulty: Difficult due to distance and sandy sections
Highlights: Gorgeous live oak woods, British soldier graves, rolling forests, long woods hike
Canine compatibility: Leashed dogs permitted
Schedule: Daily from dawn to dusk
Managing agency: Cape Hatteras National Seashore, 1401 National Park Dr., Manteo, NC 27954; (252) 473-2111; www.nps.gov/caha

FINDING THE TRAILHEAD

From the intersection of NC 345, US 64 Bypass, and US 64 in Manteo, take US 64 East to join NC 12 South on the Outer Banks. Once on NC 12 South, follow it for 47 miles to Buxton and then turn left on Lighthouse Road. Follow Lighthouse Road for 1.5 miles to reach the trailhead on your right, after the left turn to the Cape Hatteras Lighthouse. GPS trailhead coordinates: 35.248005, -75.532705

WHAT TO SEE

The Open Ponds Trail is easily the longest woods trail hike on the Outer Banks. A portion of North Carolina's master path—the Mountains-to-Sea Trail—this hike takes place in an interesting parcel of Cape Hatteras National Seashore. Nearby stands iconic Cape Hatteras Lighthouse. This was the one that was moved in 1999 and further raised its profile to being one of the world's most renowned lighthouses. Also nearby is Cape Point Campground, Frisco Campground, and the fishing magnet that is the actual Cape Hatteras. Furthermore, the beach towns of Buxton and Frisco are close, adding more adventure possibilities to this already rewarding trek.

The hike takes you from the Cape Hatteras Lighthouse area west on a doubletrack trail. The first sight is nearly immediate, the graves of two British sailors, circled by a low white picket fence. Back in May 1942 the United States had just entered World War II. American merchant ships off the coast—including the Outer Banks—were being

Top: Hiking under a canopy of live oaks
Bottom: The graves of English seamen from World War II

sunk by the Germans. Protecting over 2,000 miles of coastline wasn't easy, and the British came over to help. One British ship, the *San Delfino*, was sunk and two deceased sailors washed ashore. One sailor, who gave his life defending the United States, remains unidentified.

Beyond the graves you enter tall maritime woods, reflecting the big swath of forest on this part of the Outer Banks. Pines rise straight, while live oaks form an arched canopy above the trail, lending a tunnel-like effect. Note palmetto in the understory, as well as ferns in the wetter margins. The Open Ponds Trail is marked in mile increments, keeping you apprised of your whereabouts. The hike terrain changes as you enter an area of ponds, coming along a sizeable tarn to the right of the trail and an open aquatic view. You then leave the pond area and enter old dunes, now covered in forest. Here the trail bed becomes sandy and combined with hills, and the Open Ponds Trail becomes more challenging. After a couple of miles of scenic rolling trail, you drop off the dunes and briefly merge with a horse trail that can have loose sandy footing. However, beyond there you've got it made. The last mile follows a well-packed doubletrack to reach Frisco Campground, at the campground's eastern end. Theoretically you could leave a shuttle car at the campground entrance area, but you'd have the additional mileage of walking through the campground, about a half a mile to the entrance station. Backtracking is recommend, as this is the longest woods hike on the Outer Banks. After your hike, no matter how tired you are, make sure to visit the Cape Hatteras Lighthouse.

ABOUT THE CAPE HATTERAS LIGHTHOUSE

This hike begins about a quarter mile from one of the world's most famous lighthouses. At 198.5 feet, the Cape Hatteras Lighthouse is the tallest beacon in the United States. The lighthouse was moved in 1999 due to an eroding shoreline not far from where it is today. This beacon's striped black-and-white paint job helps it stand out as well. The reasons for the Cape Hatteras Lighthouse location are geographical. Cape Hatteras marks the point where North Carolina's Outer Banks shift from a north–south axis to a northeast–southwest axis and marks the widest and some of the highest land on the Outer Banks. The result is some of the richest forests in the region, and it is in these forests through which the Open Ponds Trail travels.

Mariners from days gone by used ocean currents along with wind to travel, and staying within sight of land aided navigation. Both the south-running Labrador Current and the north-running Gulf Stream travel near here, so ships frequently passed by Cape Hatteras. But these clashing currents, shifting shoals, and variable weather factors led to innumerable shipwrecks, bringing about the need for a lighthouse here on Cape Hatteras. At one time lighthouses were spread approximately 40 miles apart along the Carolina coast, allowing mariners to almost always keep a beacon within sight. Each lighthouse had its own light flash pattern and paint job in order to distinguish one lighthouse from another. Nobody knows why the Cape Hatteras Lighthouse got its distinctive striped paint job, but it makes the beacon all the more remarkable.

From the third Friday in April to Columbus Day in October, the Cape Hatteras Lighthouse is open for climbs. There is a fee to climb the lighthouse. Smart climbers undertake their ascent early in the morning, as climbing the lighthouse can get hot and stuffy in the afternoon. Enjoy the 360-degree panorama once atop the lighthouse. You can look down on the beaches of the Atlantic, the ocean, and Pamlico Sound, as well as the big swath of woods through which the Open Ponds Trail travels.

The famed Cape Hatteras Lighthouse

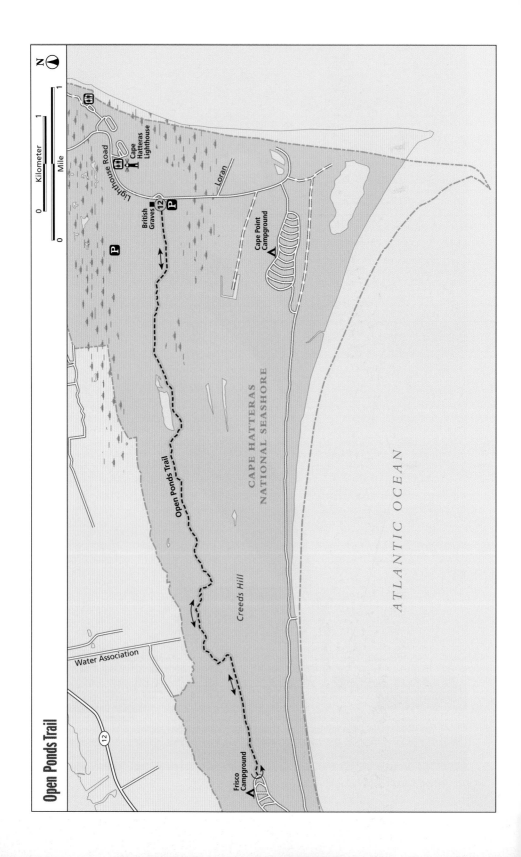

Open Ponds Trail

MILES AND DIRECTIONS

0.0 Leave the trailhead on Lighthouse Road west, passing around a pole gate. Just a few steps later you will see on your right the graves of the two British soldiers from World War II. Keep straight on a grassy doubletrack trail bordered by low-slung wind-pruned vegetation. Quickly pass a storage area on your right. Along the trail, note the white circles delineating this as a portion of the Mountains-to-Sea Trail. Ahead the forest rises in pines, cedar, laurel oak, and especially live oak.

0.2 Pass a closed park doubletrack leading right. Keep straight. In places, the trail bed is more pine needle than grass.

0.4 Pass another park doubletrack leading right. Keep straight again, still westerly.

0.7 Yet another closed road leads right. Keep straight in picturesque canopied woods of live oak alternating with stands of straight pine.

1.3 Cross an old canal by culvert. Begin looking for ponds in the vicinity.

1.5 Come directly beside an open pond to your right. This is the trail's best aquatic view and the closest the hike comes to water.

1.6 Enter hill country as you begin rolling through wooded dunes. The trail bed becomes sandy and the hiking slows.

2.0 Reach the 2-mile marker amid wooded rolling dunes. From the hilltops you can hear the Atlantic crashing on the shore.

2.9 Roll over the highest hills yet. Cedars grow in abundance.

3.3 Drop off a wooded hill into a big sand flat. Cross the flat and quickly reenter woods.

3.4 Merge with a horse trail used by park concessionaires. The trail bed sand is loose.

3.5 Leave right from the horse trail, back on singletrack.

3.6 The Open Ponds Trail makes a sharp right near a water tank. Begin tracing a flat and easy doubletrack, still aiming westerly. This is a pleasant section. The trail rises into piney hills. The ocean definitely sounds closer—and it is.

4.5 Emerge at Frisco Campground near site P38. Backtrack.

9.0 Arrive back at Lighthouse Road, completing the woodsy coastal trail.

13. HAMMOCK HILLS TRAIL

This hike takes place on Ocracoke Island, a scenic parcel of Cape Hatteras National seashore. Only accessible by auto ferry or plane, the island is home not only to this trail but also to miles of beachfront, a fine oceanside campground, and the eclectic historic village of Ocracoke (with its own lighthouse you can visit). Therefore, think of this hike as the lure to get you to Ocracoke with the village, beach, and campground the additional rewards for reaching the island. The Hammock Hills Trail starts near the ocean, then loops through wooded hills and former tall dunes and drops to a view of Pamlico Sound. From there you wander through maritime forest before returning to the trailhead.

THE RUNDOWN

Distance: 0.7-mile balloon loop
Start: NC 12 near Ocracoke Campground
Nearest town: Ocracoke
Hiking time: 0.5 hours
Fees and permits: None
Conveniences: Restrooms, water, information at nearby Ocracoke Campground
Beach access: Nearby
Trail users: Hikers

Trail surface: Natural
Difficulty: Easy
Highlights: Views of Pamlico Sound, other attractions nearby
Canine compatibility: Leashed dogs permitted
Schedule: Daily from dawn to dusk
Managing agency: Cape Hatteras National Seashore, 1401 National Park Dr., Manteo, NC 27954; (252) 473-2111; www.nps.gov/caha

FINDING THE TRAILHEAD

From the intersection of NC 345, US 64 Bypass, and US 64 in Manteo, take US 64 East to join NC 12 South on the Outer Banks. Once on NC 12 South, follow it for 58 miles to Hatteras. Take the free Hatteras ferry 45 minutes to Ocracoke Island. Once back on NC 12, follow it south for 9.5 miles. The trailhead is on the right, just after passing Ocracoke Campground on your left. GPS trailhead coordinates: 35.125428, -75.923843

WHAT TO SEE

You might say that Ocracoke is North Carolina's version of Key West—a relatively small town set on an island out in the Atlantic Ocean—except Ocracoke Island is only accessible by ferry or airplane, whereas you can drive to Key West. And if you are looking to visit Ocracoke Island, the Hammock Hills Trail can be your excuse. Once you get on the ferry aiming for Ocracoke, you are officially on "island time." Vehicle ferries run between Ocracoke and Cape Hatteras, as well as Cedar Island to Ocracoke and Swanquarter to Ocracoke, both mainland accesses.

It's a shame the Hammock Hills Trail isn't longer. But if you augment your hike with a beach walk, then even ardent exercisers and hike fans can be sated by the outdoors alone. The trail leaves NC 12, passing under a power line to enter maritime woods of wax myrtle, cedar, and yaupon. Interpretive information enhances the walk. It soon crosses a streamlet on a boardwalk. The trail splits and you make a counterclockwise loop to soon

Ocracoke Lighthouse was erected in 1823, and whitewashed in its iconic coloration.

enter tall pines. Then come lofty wooded dunes, and you are climbing a sandy, needle-covered track. Roll among the forested hills before dropping back to the lowlands, where a short spur opens to an elevated boardwalk. Here, look west across marsh grasses to Pamlico Sound. Now the path remains on level terrain, crossing boardwalks in wet places and through deep woods. You are suddenly finished with the loop and are backtracking to the parking lot, ready to explore more of Ocracoke.

Ocracoke Island runs on a southwest–northeast axis. The widest part of the narrow island is where the village of Ocracoke stands, a scant few miles from the Hammock Hills Trail. This wider part of the island supports the forest through which the trail travels. Pamlico Sound divides Ocracoke Island from the mainland, 15 or more miles distant as the crow flies. The vast majority of the island is part of Cape Hatteras National Seashore, leaving most of this barrier island on the Outer Banks in its natural state. The town of Ocracoke overlooks Pamlico Sound. The historic former fishing village, wreck salvaging station, and pirate headquarters has morphed into a tourist-friendly yet dignity-maintaining place to experience a different side of the Outer Banks. Its slow-moving traffic, narrow streets, and lack of franchise operations are a refreshing change from ordinary life. And to top it off, the funky town features one of the oldest operating lighthouses in the country.

Before or after your hike, you will have to visit the beaches of Ocracoke Island. The Atlantic Ocean fronts the south side of the island and offers miles of beachfront, with

Hammock Hills Trail climbs through evergreens.

a 2-mile stretch of Atlantic Ocean frontage closed to vehicles between ramp 68 and Ocracoke Beach Day Use Area near ramp 70. This makes for a great place for walking in solitude or simply planting yourself along the shore, staring at the waves and hopefully not at your phone or computer, as we are wont to do these days.

Wild ponies don't run free on Ocracoke as they do on some other Outer Banks islands. They once did, and they were here as early as 1735. Since then ponies have run wild and have also been domesticated. In 1957, NC 12 was extended onto Ocracoke Island and the remaining wild ponies were subject to auto accidents. Therefore, in 1959, the last wild ponies were rounded up and now reside in the Banker Pony Pens, a little north of the Hammock Hills trailhead. Seeing the ponies is also part of the greater Ocracoke adventure.

Ocracoke Campground is located directly across from the Hammock Hills Trail. The large campground is stretched along a paved loop broken by three crossroads and is located in a flat behind Atlantic Ocean dunes. A few wind-pruned cedars dot the mostly open grassy campground. Neither water nor electricity is available at campsites, but you do use common water spigots. The campground is served by three separate bathroom areas with cold showers. Spring and fall are the best times here, though families flock to the campground during summer, when the heat is on by day and the insects by night. Pray for winds during that time.

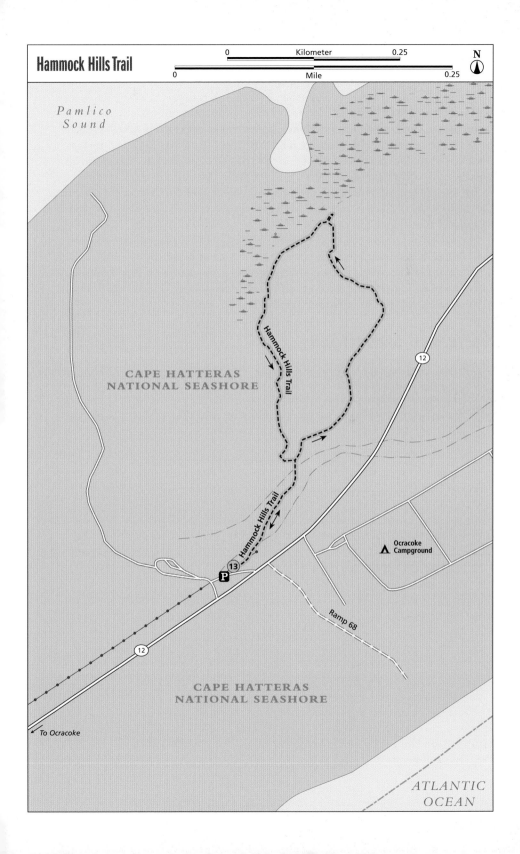

Kilometer
0   0.25

Mile
0   0.25

N

*Pamlico
Sound*

CAPE HATTERAS
NATIONAL SEASHORE

Hammock Hills Trail

12

Hammock Hills Trail

Ocracoke
Campground

13

P

Ramp 68

12

CAPE HATTERAS
NATIONAL SEASHORE

To Ocracoke

*ATLANTIC
OCEAN*

You've got to make a trip into the town of Ocracoke while out here hiking. First, make a quick visit to the Ocracoke Lighthouse, the second-oldest operating lighthouse in the nation, completed in 1823, and aiding mariners to this day. The solid white coloration distinguishes it from other lighthouses of the Outer Banks. These days the beacon is painted, but in days of yore it was whitewashed with a mixture of lime, salt, Spanish whiting, rice, glue, and boiling water and applied while hot! The 75-foot-high, solid-brick lighthouse is 25 feet in diameter at the base then narrows to 12 feet at the top. A small black roof tops the tower and protects the beacon. The original oil-burning light was changed to electrical signaling in the early 1900s. The light extends 14 miles out to sea, lesser miles than other taller lighthouses of the Outer Banks. You can also see the lighthouse keeper's quarters on-site. Climbing is not allowed. Note: Parking is limited to 15 minutes at the lighthouse.

The village of Ocracoke also offers dining and lodging and entertainment in season. Rent a bike and pedal around the town. Rent a boat or kayak and explore adjacent waters. No franchises are on the island, therefore every meal and every shop is an adventure unto itself. Just set your clock on island time, hike the Hammock Hills Trail, and explore the rest of what this Outer Banks island has to offer.

MILES AND DIRECTIONS

0.0 Leave from the Hammock Hills Trail parking area across the road from the Ocracoke Campground. Walk a few feet, then pass under a power line to enter maritime woods. Ahead, cross a creek on a boardwalk.

0.1 Reach the loop portion of the hike. Here, go right, making a counterclockwise loop. Shortly enter rolling pinewoods covering ancient dunes, some of the highest terrain on Ocracoke Island.

0.4 Come to the spur leaving right to an elevated deck overlooking marsh to Pamlico Sound.

0.6 Complete the loop portion of the hike. Backtrack.

0.7 Arrive back at the trailhead, completing the Hammock Hills Trail.

14. GREAT ISLAND

Take a ferry from the coastal village of Davis out to truly great Great Island and hike the beaches here. Known for its rustic oceanfront rental cabins, this part of Cape Lookout National Seashore presents a chance to overnight in the cabins, camp out, or just explore a parcel of the famed Outer Banks as a day trip. After landing, you walk through the cabin cluster and by the ranger station, then turn north, with the rolling Atlantic Ocean to your right and wide open Core Sound to your left. As you head north, the island flattens and becomes more sand than vegetation. This hike stops short of the north end of the island but ambitious hikers could tackle it in a day.

THE RUNDOWN

Distance: 5.2-mile there-and-back
Start: Great Island cabin cluster
Nearest town: Davis
Hiking time: 3.0 hours
Fees and permits: None to hike, fee for ferry ride to Great Island
Conveniences: Restrooms, water, showers at Great Island cabin cluster
Beach access: Yes
Trail users: Surf anglers, some beachcombers
Trail surface: Sand
Difficulty: Moderate to difficult due to continuous sand walking

Highlights: Barrier island, Atlantic Ocean
Canine compatibility: Leashed dogs permitted
Schedule: Year-round 24/7/365, access is ferry dependent unless you have your own boat; check Cape Lookout Cabins and Camps Ferry Service, https://cape-lookout-cabins -camps-ferry-davis-nc.com/
Managing agency: Cape Lookout National Seashore, 131 Charles St., Harkers Island, NC 28531; (252) 728-2250; www.nps.gov/calo

FINDING THE TRAILHEAD

From the intersection of US 70 and NC 101 in Havelock, take NC 101 East 16 miles; turn left onto Laurel Road and follow it for 2.3 miles; turn right onto Merrimon Road and follow it for 2.4 miles to a left turn onto US 70 East. Follow US 70 East for 13 miles, then at a four-way stop sign in Davis, keep straight to a dead end at Cape Lookout Cabins and Camps Ferry Service. GPS trailhead coordinates: Ferry service: 34.797040, -76.456326; Great Island ferry landing: 34.761286, -76.413339

WHAT TO SEE

Great Island, also known as South Core Banks as well as Davis Island, is one of the long barrier islands making up the Cape Lookout National Seashore portion of the Outer Banks. The island is only accessible by ferry and provides a throwback experience in visiting the coast of North Carolina. However, realize that vehicles are allowed on the island, driven primarily by surf anglers roving the beach looking for that perfect spot to toss a line. Nevertheless, it is a certain change from other areas of the Outer Banks crowded with beachfront homes, traffic-lined roads, and more stores than you can shop. Out here it is sun, surf, and sand—along with like-minded compadres who prefer simple oceanfront experiences. As far as hiking is concerned, the miles of beach provide as much Atlantic Ocean waterfront walking as a walker will desire.

Find your own Atlantic Ocean campsite on Great Island.

The twenty-four rustic cabins at Great Island are a big draw. The National Park Service–run and –operated primitive dwellings are open for rent from mid-March through the end of November. Sleeping anywhere from four to twelve people, the simple wooden affairs have bunkbeds, bathrooms with hot showers, and gas stoves. They do not have electricity, though some are wired to accommodate a generator. Bring your own bedding, cooking utensils, dishes, and so on. Water is available at a central location. Spring and fall are the most popular times to rent the cabins, yet a few hardy souls brave the heat of the summer. Cabin rates are discounted during the hot months of June, July, and August.

The cabins are rented out by surf anglers as well as families and vacationers who like a modest, basic experience. And if you want to rent an oceanfront dwelling on the Outer Banks, this is undoubtedly the cheapest option. Reservations can be made at www .recreation.gov. Tent camping on Great Island is free, but you must be at least 100 yards distant from the cabin complex. Be careful pitching your tent directly on the beach, as the winds can blow a tent down. Your best bet is to get behind the beachfront dunes. Be prepared for insects during the warm season.

The hike here has a busy beginning. After leaving the ferry dock, you immediately enter the cabin cluster. Make sure to stop by the park office for a map of the island with the beach access markers on it. You will work your way toward the ocean, passing the small bathhouse and emerging at foot-only beach access 30. Almost all other accesses are primarily for vehicles. By this point you may be concerned about the softness of the sand, but the shifting sugar sand is found only around the cabins where the tracks are heavily used both by foot and vehicle.

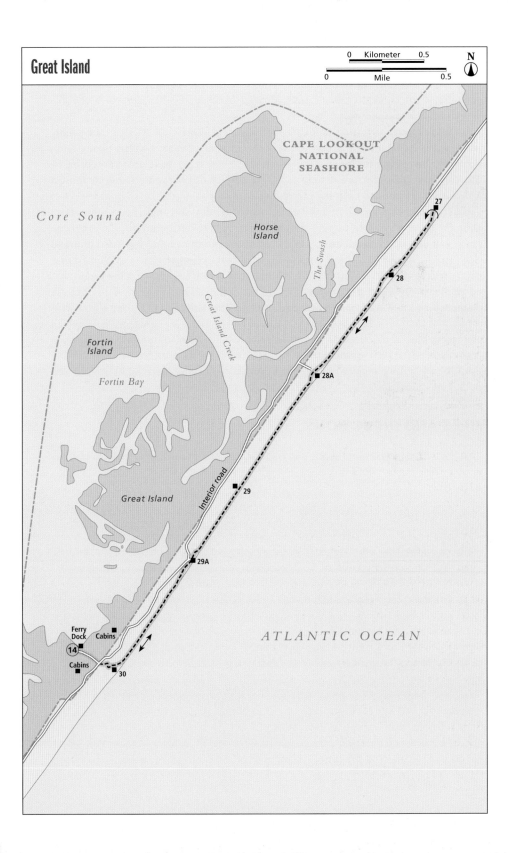

You open onto the great Atlantic Ocean extending to the edge of the horizon. Here, Great Island stretches 14 miles south to Cape Lookout Point. It is near the southern tip where the famed Cape Lookout Lighthouse is located. To your left, the island extends for 6 miles north, ending at Ophelia inlet. That's a lot of island—20 miles worth of walking—and that is just one way!

You will experience vehicle traffic on the beach and also lots of tracks. I have simply walked along the high tide line and wasn't bothered at all, even after setting up my camp and pulling out a chair for the beach. Remember: There is no shade unless you bring it. Also, you may encounter bird nesting areas where beach driving and walking are limited to a narrow corridor and camping is prohibited.

While walking you should find the shelling quite good, as surf anglers care more about fish in the water than shells on the sand. It's a good idea to head north for 2.6 miles one way, as you can see the northern tip of the island morph from more vegetated dunes to a sand spit. Also, you can check out the site of the old Carteret Rod and Gun Club if you are willing to extend your hike by 1.2 miles one way. It is located on the sound side, and you have to walk west a bit from the beach, but the old building—now in ruins—is still there for a look. Also, an interior sand road runs the length of the island if you want to execute a loop hike, but the interior road can be covered with very loose sand, which can make it slow going. But it is an option. From where our hike turns around, at beach access marker 27, it is 3+ more miles one way to the end of the island, potentially making your hike a 12+ mile endeavor. One good thing about having the vehicles around: You could bum a ride back!

MILES AND DIRECTIONS

- **0.0** Leave the ferry drop-off point and immediately enter the Great Island cabin cluster. Keep straight, passing the small park office on your right, and keep straight for the bathhouse and beach access marker 30. Emerge onto the Atlantic Ocean beach. Head left, the ocean to your right and cabins to your left.

- **0.2** Pass a cabin cluster road access.

- **0.5** Leave the last cabins at an access.

- **0.6** Walk past beach access marker 29A. From here on campers can pitch their tents.

- **1.6** Reach beach access marker 28A. Low dunes rise to your left, with marsh and the waters of Core Sound beyond and the mainland beyond that.

- **2.2** Pass beach access marker 28.

- **2.6** Come to beach access marker 27. Great Island extends 3+ more miles, but this is a good place to backtrack.

- **5.2** Arrive back at the Great Island ferry drop-off point, or your cabin, or your campsite, completing the great adventure on Great Island.

15. CAPE LOOKOUT LIGHTHOUSE HIKE

Take a ferry to one of North Carolina's iconic lighthouses at Cape Lookout National Seashore. After viewing the beacon and adjacent keeper's quarters, take a boardwalk to the wide Atlantic Ocean beach, where you can go shelling. Next, turn into the island to visit some standing buildings, part of the Cape Lookout Village Historic District. Complete this circuit with a walk along the sandy shoreline of Lookout Bight, enjoying more panoramas of Cape Lookout Lighthouse on your return.

THE RUNDOWN

Distance: 4.1-mile balloon loop
Start: Cape Lookout Lighthouse dock
Nearest town: Harkers Island
Hiking time: 2.3 hours
Fees and permits: None to hike, fee for ferry ride to Cape Lookout
Conveniences: Restrooms, water at island visitor center
Beach access: Yes
Trail users: Beachcombers, hikers
Trail surface: A little boardwalk, sand
Difficulty: Moderate
Highlights: Cape Lookout Lighthouse, Cape Lookout Village, beachcombing

Canine compatibility: Leashed dogs permitted
Schedule: Daily from dawn to dusk, access is ferry dependent unless you have your own boat; check Island Express Ferry Service, www.islandexpressferryservices.com; ferries leave hourly during the warm season
Managing agency: Cape Lookout National Seashore, 131 Charles St., Harkers Island, NC 28531; (252) 728-2250; www.nps.gov/calo

FINDING THE TRAILHEAD

At the intersection of US 70 and Harkers Island Road near Otway, take Harkers Island Road south for 8.7 miles to a dead end at the Cape Lookout National Seashore Visitor Center and the access for Island Express Ferry Service. GPS trailhead coordinates: Visitor center: 34.685528, -76.526942; Cape Lookout Island dock: 34.624725, -76.523526

WHAT TO SEE

This hike explores the area that became Cape Lookout Village Historic District, an 810-acre designated area that was once home to not only the tenders of Cape Lookout Lighthouse but also fishermen plying the waters of Lookout Bight and outward toward the open sea. Cape Lookout was largely uninhabited until residents of nearby Shackleford Banks had fallen prey to hurricanes and moved—leaving their storm-wrecked dwellings behind—and out to Cape Lookout south of the lighthouse but north of the actual point of the cape. What became Cape Lookout Village quickly grew to almost one hundred residents. At one point it had its own school and post office.

Debarking the passenger ferry to Cape Lookout

But technology was already at work to undo this newfound fishing village. Motorized boats were heard buzzing around Cape Lookout. It wasn't long before these fishermen realized that by using these newfangled "gasoline boats" they could live on the mainland and access the amenities of civilization while still being able to head out and fish for a living. One by one the families moved away.

Yet Cape Lookout Village was changing again, as those very motorboats that allowed the fishermen to live where they wanted also made accessing Cape Lookout Village easier for outsiders wanting to spend some time at the beach. Thus entered the first tourist and part-time residents of Cape Lookout, using some of the abandoned fishing shacks as well as building their own houses, or moving and reconstructing still others. You can view some of these houses on this hike.

Cape Lookout Village, like many other coastal communities, sprang to life during World War II, but this period was short-lived, and before the war was over no members of the Army were stationed at Cape Lookout. The seasonal tourists still came over, but the establishment of Cape Lookout National Seashore marked the end of Cape Lookout Village, except as a historic district to which visitors of the twenty-first century can gaze upon to imagine the way of life gone by.

Despite the village, Cape Lookout Lighthouse is the star of the show on this hike and the reason visitors flock to this part of the Carolina coast. The first lighthouse—100 feet high—was built in 1805, and despite its shortcomings with lesser light and a low tower,

This trail leads from the beach to Cape Lookout Lighthouse.

Cape Lookout Lighthouse and keepers quarters as seen from Lookout Bight

remained in operation until 1859, when the new—and current—lighthouse was constructed of red brick. This lighthouse quickly became a point of contention during the Civil War and was first rendered nonoperational by the Confederates, then occupied by the Union, who reinstalled the lens that the Rebels had removed. Even then, the Confederates tried to blow up the lighthouse without success. In 1873, the beacon was painted with its trademark diagonal black-and-white checkers and a new keeper's quarters was built. The lighthouse continued to operate. In the 1930s a radio beacon was established atop the lighthouse. Light keepers still remained on-site, operating the lighthouse until 1950, when the Cape Lookout light was automated.

By this time, the establishment of Cape Lookout National Seashore was attracting more and more visitors to the lighthouse area. Visitation rose through the decades. In 2003 the lighthouse tower and property were transferred to the National Park Service. It took a while, but since 2010 the lighthouse has been open for climbing. The climbing season lasts from mid-May to mid-September. A fee is charged. However, the views from up top are phenomenal, and climbing the lighthouse adds one more aspect to your hike should you be here during the climbing season.

Whether or not you climb the lighthouse, you will enjoy the hike out here in the shadow of the beacon. After embarking from the ferry, you trace a boardwalk to a small building cluster where the visitor center/gift shop, restrooms, and shelter are located. From there you take a boardwalk through woods, opening onto venerated Cape Lookout Lighthouse. Tour the grounds, the keeper's quarters, and ultimately the beacon itself, climbing the brick structure in season. On-site interpreters can answer your questions.

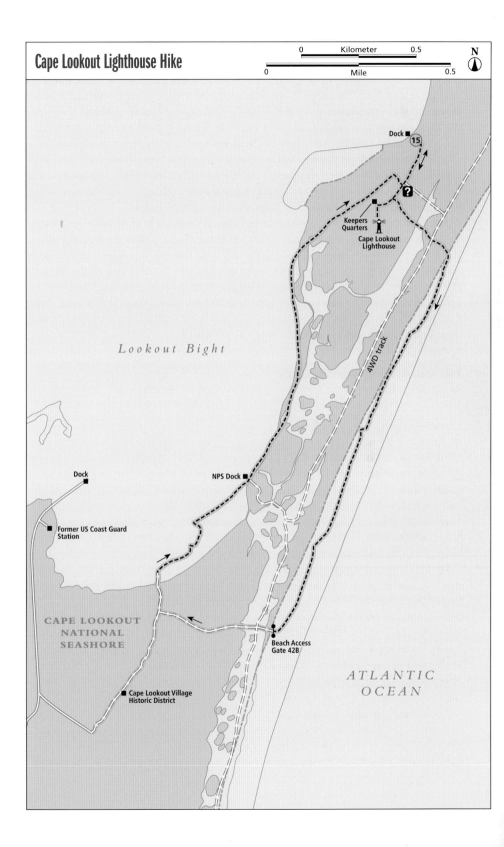

Cape Lookout Lighthouse Hike

0   Kilometer   0.5

0   Mile   0.5

N

Dock

15

Keepers
Quarters

Cape Lookout
Lighthouse

Lookout Bight

4WD track

Dock

NPS Dock

Former US Coast Guard
Station

CAPE LOOKOUT
NATIONAL
SEASHORE

Beach Access
Gate 42B

ATLANTIC
OCEAN

Cape Lookout Village
Historic District

Since most visitors take a ferry to the lighthouse, keep apprised of the time and keep up with your return time. Camping out here is also an option. Spring and fall are the best times for hiking or camping out here, though Cape Lookout receives the most visitors during high summer. From the lighthouse, a long boardwalk leads toward the Atlantic, where you cross the dunes to reach the beach. This is a productive shelling area despite the high summertime visitation. From here, walk the wide swath of sand southward to reach beach access marker 42B (these beach accesses are used by park personnel, off-road vehicles, and walkers on the national seashore). The access leads inland into pinewoods after bridging a marsh. Here you keep westerly to reach a road going left, southbound, beside which several dwellings of former Cape Lookout Village stand. Many of them have interpretive signage so you can learn more about their history.

After exploring the buildings, the hike leads to Lookout Bight and the sandy shoreline there. To your left you can see the former US Coast Guard station slowly collapsing in the distance. Our hike heads right, along the shore. At low tide this will be an easy sandy walk, but at high tide the strip of sand can be quite narrow. You will pass by the National Park Service park housing dock. Curve with the bight, exploring the sands and shallows for life in and near the water, as well as birds in the sky. The monolith that is the light-house looms closer, and soon you are back at the dock, with the memories of another coastal trail experience embedded in your memory bank.

MILES AND DIRECTIONS

0.0 Leave the ferry dock and follow the boardwalk to the building cluster, then continue on the boardwalk to reach an intersection. Here, stay straight for the remarkable Cape Lookout Lighthouse.

0.1 Reach the keeper's quarters and the Cape Lookout Lighthouse. Now, backtrack just a bit to reach the eastbound boardwalk for the beach, crossing a vehicle road then surmounting dunes using a designated access.

0.4 Come to the beach. It extends for miles in both directions. Head right, south, beach-combing and feeling the breeze and listening to the surf.

1.6 Leave right for beach access gate 42B, marked with a small brown sign. Leave the beach, cross a sand jeep trail, walk a wooden bridge, and enter pinewoods.

1.8 Pass a fading road leading left.

1.9 Come near the first building of Cape Lookout Village, the old lighthouse keeper's residence, which was moved to its current location. Head left, south, checking out other old structures.

2.1 Reach an old boathouse converted into a beach house. Backtrack, though other buildings can be explored to the south.

2.4 Come along Lookout Bight. The lower the tide the better the walking.

2.8 Pass by the National Park Service dock linking to park housing.

4.0 Come very near the lighthouse.

4.1 Arrive back at the dock, finishing the island hike. Hopefully you are back well in time to take your planned return ferry.

16. SHACKLEFORD BANKS

Here is your chance to hike along the island of Shackleford Banks, cruising the beach and perhaps seeing the famed wild ponies that live on this barrier island near Cape Lookout Lighthouse. First you have to take a passenger ferry or your own boat, then land on the island. Upon landing, it is a simple matter of walking westerly along gorgeous beach. In addition to the ponies, you will also enjoy birdlife as well as excellent views of Cape Lookout Lighthouse and south into the Atlantic Ocean. If taking a ferry, carefully time your hike with the coming and going of the landing schedule.

THE RUNDOWN

Distance: 6.0-mile there-and-back
Start: Shackleford Banks ferry drop-off point
Nearest town: Harkers Island
Hiking time: 3.3 hours
Fees and permits: None to hike, fee for ferry ride to Shackleford Banks
Conveniences: Restrooms, water at Harkers Island visitor center—the ferry departure point
Beach access: Yes
Trail users: Beachcombers, wild horse lovers
Trail surface: Sand
Difficulty: Moderate

Highlights: Wild ponies, beachcombing
Canine compatibility: Leashed dogs permitted
Schedule: Daily from dawn to dusk, access is ferry dependent unless you have your own boat; check Island Express Ferry Service, www.islandexpressferryservices.com; ferries leave hourly during the warm season
Managing agency: Cape Lookout National Seashore, 131 Charles St., Harkers Island, NC 28531; (252) 728-2250; www.nps.gov/calo

FINDING THE TRAILHEAD

At the intersection of US 70 and Harkers Island Road near Otway, take Harkers Island Road south for 8.7 miles to a dead end at the Cape Lookout National Seashore Visitor Center and the access for Island Express Ferry Service. GPS trailhead coordinates: Visitor center: 34.685528, -76.526942; Shackleford Banks ferry landing: 34.630772, -76.529742

WHAT TO SEE

The wild ponies are undoubtedly the star of the show here at Shackleford Banks. Reaching the point of legendary status, wild ponies have lived here for centuries, well before Shackleford Banks came under the auspices of Cape Lookout National Seashore. To this day visitors gasp with delight, breaking out their phones and cameras upon sighting a Shackleford Banks wild pony.

These wild ponies are subject to mythological mistruths. First and foremost is that they are survivors of a shipwreck. This is a remote possibility, as the horses are of Spanish origin and European ships coming to the New World did wreck on the Outer Banks. However, more likely it was simply a case of settlers and colonists bringing horses from Europe, then grazing them on the Outer Banks. We do know that the first horses arrived in this part of the world as early as the 1520s. So no one is 100 percent sure exactly how

Debarking onto Shackleford Banks

these horses arrived on Shackleford Banks. The second myth is that these wild horses drink salt water. That is simply absurd. These horses, like every other horse, have to have fresh water to drink. They do not drink brackish or salt water. Water is found on the islands in surface pools, seeps, and places where fresh water settles above heavier salt water. Another myth: Horses are swimming all over the Outer Banks from island to island. Horses do swim to very nearby adjacent islands, but they are not traveling by water throughout the Cape Lookout area.

These wild horses are on their own. They are not immunized against disease. They feed themselves; they find their own water; and they are not protected from the heat of the summer sun nor the wrath of tropical storms. However, the current herd is managed by Cape Lookout National Seashore and the Foundation for Shackleford Horses. Another herd of horses lives on nearby Rachel Carson Reserve, state land managed by the State of North Carolina and its coastal reserve program.

The herd on Shackleford Banks is kept to around 120 horses, scattered across the island, though they are commonly found in groups, either a dominant stallion and his

A wild pony catches the breeze with Cape Lookout Lighthouse in the background.

A flock returns inland at sunset.

mares, males together, and the occasional lone horse. To control the population, selected females are darted with a contraceptive. Still other wild horses are removed from the island and adopted out.

The horses are branded using a cold-branding technique, a way to remove color from hair follicles, leaving a brand, usually a number. The herds are the subject of scientific genetic studies. Managers keep up with births, deaths, body condition, parentage, and more. On the hike you can visit an old corral site where the horses were once gathered and worked over. However, nowadays individual horses are darted with an anesthesia, then worked over, including cold branding.

Over the centuries the wild ponies have evolved to be relatively short and stocky critters. Often referred to as Banker Ponies, they feed on grasses growing among the dunes and marshes, including smooth cordgrass, sea oats, and salt meadow cordgrass.

To keep the wild horses wild, come no closer than 50 feet, don't feed them, and let them be what they are—wild horses. If approached, they have been known to kick, bite, or even charge people. Keep your dog on a leash. By the way, these wild ponies are protected by federal law. Photographers will want to bring a long lens for those detailed close-up shots.

Wild ponies thrill us all because they symbolize the wildness and freedom of the Outer Banks. They are beautiful and remain a part the Outer Banks past and are a living cultural heritage. And Shackleford Banks is a wild and beautiful island, stretching almost 9 miles from one end to the other. The entirety of the land is given over to nature, although people can debark on the island to explore, hike, and camp. However, motorized vehicles are not allowed, in contrast to many other areas of the Outer Banks. Bordered with beaches, backed by dunes, mixed in with wooded hammocks and grassy marshes, the barrier island makes a fine place to visit—at the right time. Probably the best time to visit is from later winter through mid-spring, and during fall. In summertime, boats by the dozen land on Shackleford Banks, both on its westerly end as well as the easterly end, where this hike takes place. Do not come here then! You will be disappointed by the crowds, and the ponies are likely to be in remote areas of the island.

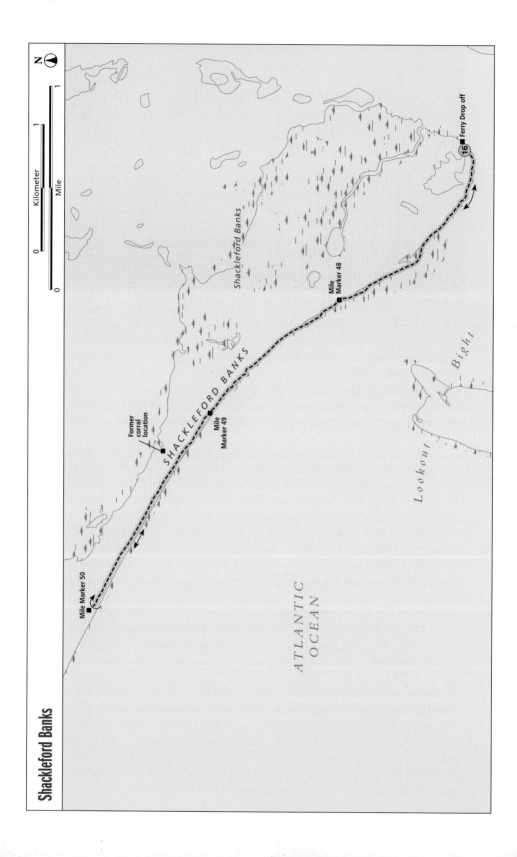

Shackleford Banks

N

0   Kilometer   1
0   Mile   1

Mile Marker 50

Former corral location

Mile Marker 49

SHACKLEFORD BANKS

Shackleford Banks

Mile Marker 48

Ferry Drop off

16

ATLANTIC OCEAN

Lookout Bight

The adventure does require some planning. First, you will have to arrange your transportation. Fortunately an official national park concessionaire operates out of the Cape Lookout National Seashore visitor center on Harkers Island. Island Express Ferry Service offers scheduled departures on its website, and you can reserve a spot on the ferry ahead of time. Furthermore, you can combine a visit to Shackleford Banks with a visit to Cape Lookout Lighthouse, within sight just across Barden Inlet. Finally, consider camping on Shackleford Banks. It is enjoyable to see the nighttime sky as well as the Cape Lookout Lighthouse beaming in the distance. And walking the beach around sunrise can be a most rewarding experience. Notes: Walking the beach can be slow going. The shelling is better than you may think, despite the heavy visitation. Mile markers are posted on the beach to help you know how far you have walked. Factor in return time and distance to your hike, as well as the ferry schedule.

A jellyfish lands on the shore during a falling tide.

MILES AND DIRECTIONS

0.0 Leave the ferry drop-off point on the east end of Shackleford Banks. Cape Lookout Lighthouse is just across the bay from this landing. Head away from the lighthouse, first going south then northwest. The immediate area around the ferry drop-off point can be busy, but then traffic tapers off. Cape Lookout is to your south and you can see relic buildings of historic Cape Lookout village. Low dunes fall away from the shore. At first the sand is softer, due to being partially blocked from direct Atlantic Ocean waves by Cape Lookout.

0.9 Get west of Cape Lookout. The sand becomes firmer and steeper, rising to low dunes.

1.0 Pass national seashore access marker 48. You can see the island making its gentle curve to the west in the distance.

1.6 The island has narrowed and you can look north of the dunes to marshes and beyond civilization on the mainland.

2.0 Reach access marker 49.

2.2 Pass the old road leading to the corral area. Here fence posts are visible, as are a small shelter and a dock on the landward side. The beach remains narrow and steep.

3.0 Come to access marker 50. The island goes on for many more miles, but this is a good place to backtrack.

6.0 Arrive back at the ferry drop-off point, completing the wild pony hike. Hopefully you have timed your return with the arrival of your ferry.

17. MIDDLE NEUSIOK TRAIL

This is a first-rate coastal woodlands hike, the centerpiece of which are numerous long and incredible boardwalks taking you through wetland woods that would otherwise be a rough slog. Instead you get to experience these wooded wetlands dry footed, as well as vast upland forest tracts, leading you to truly appreciate the sizeable acreage contained within the Croatan National Forest. The hike heads south under deep and tall pines amid lush undergrowth. Next come the remarkable boardwalks, so long some are named! The hike meanders south under mature evergreens to reach the Dogwood Shelter on a side trail. This makes a good overnight camp or simply a place to relax before backtracking to the trailhead.

THE RUNDOWN

Distance: 7.0-mile there-and-back
Start: NC 306 Neusiok trailhead
Nearest town: Havelock
Hiking time: 3.8 hours
Fees and permits: None
Conveniences: Trail shelter
Beach access: No
Trail users: Hikers, backpackers
Trail surface: Natural, lots of boardwalk

Difficulty: Moderate
Highlights: Long boardwalks, trail shelter
Canine compatibility: Leashed dogs permitted
Schedule: 24/7 year-round
Managing agency: Croatan National Forest, 141 E. Fisher Ave., New Bern, NC 28560; (252) 638-5628; www.fs .usda.gov/nfsnc

FINDING THE TRAILHEAD

From the intersection of NC 101 and US 70 in Havelock, take NC 101 East for 5.3 miles to NC 306. Turn left on NC 306 and follow it 1.9 miles to the Neusiok trailhead on your right. GPS trailhead coordinates: 34.901333, -76.818667

WHAT TO SEE

I admit it. I like being in the deep woods, in the back of beyond, in the middle of nowhere, because—in actuality—nowhere can be a great destination. And the Croatan National Forest has a lot of nowhere. In this case, nowhere is defined as over 150,000 acres of forests and wetlands, wilderness and recreation areas, and places in between. If you have a hankering for a coastal hike, the Croatan is a great place. And the Neusiok is a great trail. The name of the 22-mile end-to-end path is derived from the nearby Neuse River—it forms a boundary of the Croatan National Forest, and the northern terminus of the Neusiok Trail is on its banks.

The Neusiok Trail offers an overnight backpacking experience to those inclined, as three wooden Adirondack-style trail shelters are situated along the path. These shelters come in handy during winter. If the weather is warm and biting insects a possibility, bring along a tent or some kind of netting to string up in the shelter. No matter the season, these shelters will be a welcome sight when the rain starts falling.

This wooden boardwalk leads you over wooded wetlands.

One of the shelters—Dogwood Shelter—is the goal and turnaround point for this hike. Therefore, you will see one of these accommodations firsthand. The shelters also have a nearby pump well and a fire ring. The water from the wells is not the best, but it's better than nothing. Thoughtful hikers trekking the entire Neusiok Trail should consider caching their water at trail road crossings or toting it on their back.

This particular coastal trail adventure—from NC 306 to Dogwood Shelter—can be done as a day hike any time of year, but backpackers will be best served to overnight along the Neusiok Trail from late fall through early spring. The weather is cool and the bugs are few.

The Neusiok Trail was laid out and constructed by the Carteret Wildlife Club way back in 1971. They continue to maintain the trail to this day, along with help from local scouts and the US Forest Service, which manages the Croatan National Forest. And keeping up the trail here can be challenging, especially when hurricanes blow through, as did Hurricane Florence in the fall of 2018, roughing up the Neusiok Trail, especially along the Neuse River. The entire path was closed for a period after Florence pushed through.

You will cross your first boardwalk just a few steps into the adventure—albeit a short one. After walking awhile you will realize that just a few feet of elevation makes a big difference here in the lowland woods, the difference between dry pine forests mixed with dogwood, oak, and sweetgum or lowland woods of maple, titi, and bay. Titi is a shrubby green bush with darkish green leaves, always growing in wet margins such as along the boardwalks you will trek. It blooms in April here in North Carolina and is found in the eastern part of the state. Titi is best known for its tiny yet fragrant white blooms that fill the woods with a sweet perfume.

By the time you are through with this hike—going twice over the boardwalks—you will be surprised at the amount of wood and work needed to construct these walkways

Ferns border the trail.

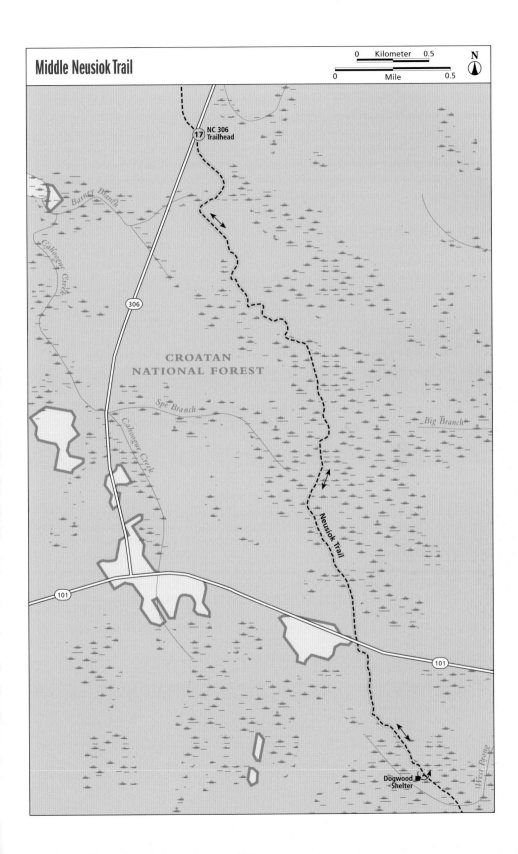

Middle Neusiok Trail

NC 306
Trailhead
17

Barney Branch

Cahoogue Creek

306

CROATAN
NATIONAL FOREST

Spe Branch

Big Branch

Cahoogue Creek

Neusiok Trail

101

101

Dogwood
Shelter

West Prong

Kilometer   0   0.5
Mile   0   0.5

N

over the seasonal wetlands, where the water raises and lowers with the seasons—and with the occasional tropical storm.

Additionally, the Neusiok Trail is part of the greater Mountains-to-Sea Trail, North Carolina's still-being-built master path that runs from Clingmans Dome, nestled in the Great Smoky Mountains at over 6,000 feet, easterly through the Piedmont all the way to the Outer Banks. Therefore, trail blazes on the Neusiok are the same circular white dot that signifies the Mountains-to-Sea Trail. Also, numbered posts with GPS coordinates stand trailside at each mile increment. Well marked, well maintained, and beautiful, a walk on the Neusiok is a sure-fire proposition. Enjoy your hike here on the Neusiok, one of my favorite coastal trails in the Carolinas.

MILES AND DIRECTIONS

0.0 Head southeast from NC 306 trailhead, with enough room for six or so vehicles, on the Neusiok Trail. The path immediately crosses a short boardwalk, the first of many on this trail segment. Hike roughly parallel to NC 306 under loblolly pines, beard cane, and maple. Watch your footing, as the trail bed can be irregular in places.

0.3 Traverse another boardwalk, this one a bit longer. Ahead, the trail nears the boundary line of the Croatan National Forest, marked with red painted trees.

0.7 Begin clacking your way across another boardwalk bordered by thickets of titi.

1.0 Circle around a swamp to the right of the trail.

1.1 Traverse another boardwalk.

1.7 Come to Cottonmouth Spa Boardwalk. This wooden walkway of wonderment makes a serpentine course for over 0.1 mile. Enter high pines after traversing the boardwalk.

1.9 Reach a wide grassy forest road. Note the boards and supplies for repairing the boardwalks stored here. Angle right at the road, then resume a slender footpath in the forest, leaving the road behind.

2.0 Join another boardwalk. Walk a brief spell of woods.

2.2 Begin the 0.5-mile-long Toad Wallow Boardwalk. This "eighth wonder" of the hiking world not only keeps your feet dry while hiking but also preserves the adjacent wetland vegetation. It has been reconstructed in places, as evidenced by differing building materials.

2.7 End the boardwalk, then emerge at NC 101. Cross the paved road, then reach the NC 101 parking area. Reenter the woods on the Neusiok Trail adjacent to the trail kiosk. Briefly run parallel to NC 101, then curve deeper into the pines.

2.8 Cross a shorter named boardwalk, Michael's Mire, built as a scout project. Rise from the boardwalk to enter widespread pinewoods. The walking is easy but decidedly different from the clacking of the boardwalks.

3.5 Come to a spur trail leading right a short distance to Dogwood Shelter. The shelter is close but not visible from the Neusiok Trail. Walk a few feet, then open onto the three-sided open-fronted Adirondack-style shelter, on a slight knoll above West Prong, a swamp stream. Look for dogwoods growing here, which gave the shelter a name. Backtrack.

7.0 Arrive back at the trailhead, completing the coastal trail.

18. NEUSIOK TRAIL NEAR NEWPORT

This hike traces the Neusiok Trail from its beginning at Oyster Point on the tidal Newport River. From there, the path skirts the bay of Mill Creek, where grassy marsh meets hillside maritime woods. Following Mill Creek upstream, the Neusiok Trail enters mature pines, heading deeper into the freshwater segment of Mill Creek. You will finally reach Blackjack Shelter, a trailside overnighting locale that makes a good turnaround point.

THE RUNDOWN

Distance: 4.8-mile there-and-back
Start: Oyster Point Campground
Nearest town: Newport
Hiking time: 2.2 hours
Fees and permits: None
Conveniences: Trail shelter, campground, restrooms at trailhead
Beach access: No
Trail users: Hikers, backpackers
Trail surface: Natural

Difficulty: Moderate
Highlights: Mill Creek bay, shelter, variety of ecosystems
Canine compatibility: Leashed dogs permitted
Schedule: 24/7 year-round
Managing agency: Croatan National Forest, 141 E. Fisher Ave., New Bern, NC 28560; (252) 638-5628; www.fs.usda.gov/nfsnc

FINDING THE TRAILHEAD

From the intersection of NC 101 and US 70 in Havelock, take NC 101 East for 11.6 miles to Old Newberry Road. Turn right and follow Old Newberry Road for 3.7 miles to reach a T intersection with Mill Creek Road. (You will hit Mill Creek Road at 1.7 miles a first time. Don't veer left at this first intersection.) Turn right on Mill Creek Road and follow it 0.2 mile and turn left onto FR 181 at the sign for Oyster Point Campground. Follow FR 181 for 1.0 mile to a dead end at the trailhead and Oyster Point Campground. GPS trailhead coordinates: 34.760667, -76.761667

WHAT TO SEE

This trail starts at Oyster Point Campground, a Croatan National Forest recreation destination. The campground avails fifteen reservable campsites nestled in maritime woods. Each campsite offers a tent pad, fire grill, picnic table, and lantern post. Bring your own water. More important for us hikers, Oyster Point Campground serves as the southern terminus of the Neusiok Trail and the beginning point for this hike.

The best part of this coastal trail adventure is experiencing the transition of habitats along the way. Starting the adventure on the shores of the wide and tidal Newport River, you see a large brackish body of water influenced by the tides, charging in and out just a few miles from the Atlantic Ocean. Next you look out on the grasses of the Mill Creek embayment, through which the tidal portion of Mill Creek ebbs and flows. While looking out on Mill Creek you are walking under the mantle of maritime forest, highlighted by cedar, live oak, and myrtle, as adjacent hills rise above you, where dogwood, hickory, and scrub oaks rule. Farther inland, longleaf pinewoods tower above the blackwaters of

Top: Drier portions of the hike traverse pinelands.
Bottom left: Wild iris rises near a small swamp stream.
Bottom right: The Blackjack Trail shelter can be your home for the night.

The Neusiok Trail leads along Mill Creek embayment.

upper Mill Creek, itself hemmed in by a corridor of freshwater vegetation of titi, ferns, and beard cane.

The vegetational variety and overlapping of ecotones is but one thing that makes this hike worthwhile. The Neusiok Trail is your conduit, a path stretching 22 miles from the Newport River to the Neuse River. It isn't long before you reach the Newport River and turn north. Soak in the view at the canoe/kayak launch across the water. Then you turn up Mill Creek valley, at this point a wide, tidal stream. Mill Creek is a common name throughout the Carolinas. In the early days of America, subsistence farmers would have to grind their own corn and wheat, commonly doing it at water-powered mills. Typically whoever owned the mill would charge a portion of the ground meal as a grinding fee. While gathering to grind their corn and wheat into meal and flour, locals would visit with the neighbors, and maybe do a little business as well. Mills often served as a combination trading post, community center, and gossip hotbed. Often a dam held back the creek to ensure a regular flow of water—thus power—to the mill.

There were several types of mills, the most common of which was a gristmill. Here, large circular stones were turned by waterpower to ground corn and wheat into meal for consumption. Oil mills squeezed linseed oil from flaxseeds. Sawmills turned trees into usable lumber. Paper mills transformed pulpwood into paper. A forge mill ran a hammer to bang and press metal into shape. A textile mill used waterpower to spin cotton and wool into yarn and run looms to weave the yarn into fabric.

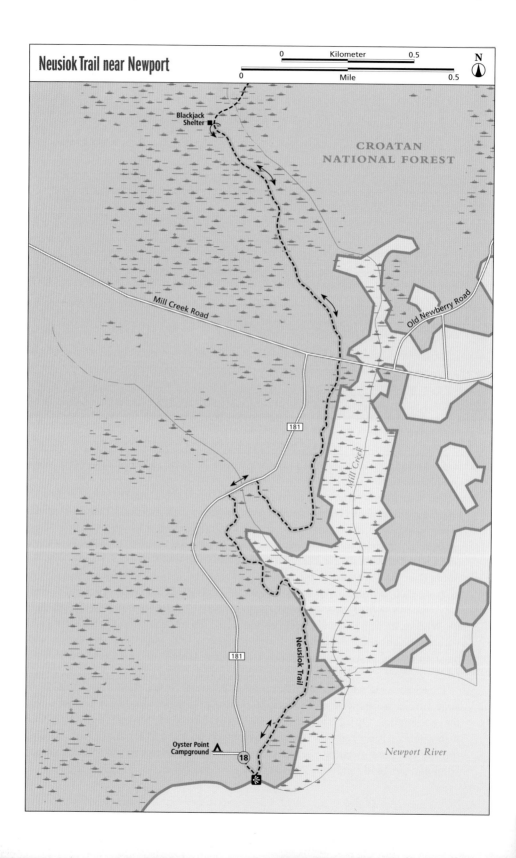

Neusiok Trail near Newport

CROATAN
NATIONAL FOREST

Mill Creek Road

Old Newberry Road

Blackjack
Shelter

181

Mill Creek

181

Neusiok Trail

Oyster Point
Campground

18

Newport River

Kilometer
0   0.5
0   0.5
Mile

N

While looking out on the tidal flats of lower Mill Creek, you can rest assured a mill wasn't located there. It would have been upstream in the freshwater segment of the creek, upstream of where Mill Creek Road crosses Mill Creek. For now, continue hiking a pine needle–covered track along the edge of the bay with a rising wooded hill to your left. The trail takes you away from Mill Creek and up the valley of a tributary stream, using FR 181 to cross the small watercourse. You then return to the edge of the marsh, while also passing through freshwater wetlands, where boardwalks make for easier footing.

You next reach and cross Mill Creek Road. Our hike keeps straight and enters pine-dominated woods with scattered wetlands all about. Mill Creek is silently flowing through swamp forest to your right, its dark tannic waters aiming for the Newport River, where our hike began.

Then you are at the Blackjack Shelter. The structure accommodates four or so campers and is first come, first served. However you should bring netting to prevent mosquitoes during the warm season. It also offers a fire ring and pump well. If you desire more hiking, the Neusiok Trail keeps northbound for nearly 20 miles before ending at the Neuse River.

MILES AND DIRECTIONS

0.0 Leave Oyster Point Campground entrance road, descending south to a small canoe/kayak launch overlooking the Newport River. Gain views to the south of the river aiming toward Beaufort. In the near, live oaks and cedar stand guard along the water. Follow the Neusiok Trail left, turning away from the Newport River and heading up the Mill Creek embayment, northbound.

0.4 Pass a clear view of the Mill Creek marsh. Continue walking the margin between the marsh to your right and the wooded low hills to your left.

0.8 Cross a boardwalk of a small stream as you head deeper up the valley of a tributary of Mill Creek, ensconced in a titi thicket. Pass a second boardwalk. Look for wild irises in spring. The woods become a bit hillier.

1.0 Pop out onto FR 181, the road you used to access the trailhead. Turn right here, using the forest road to bridge a stream by culvert. Note the wooded swamp lining the small waterway.

1.1 Leave right from the forest road, reentering forest on a singletrack footpath. Walk along wooded hillside terrain while looking out on the marsh of Mill Creek.

1.4 Cross a boardwalk over freshwater marsh.

1.7 The Neusiok Trail leads you over another boardwalk before reaching Mill Creek Road. Cross the two-lane paved road, then immediately rejoin the Neusiok Trail in piney woods divided by streamlets coursing through thickets of beard cane.

2.0 Cross a stream on a boardwalk.

2.3 Cross another boardwalk.

2.4 Come to a trail intersection. Here the Neusiok Trail keeps straight, while to your left a very short path leads to the Blackjack Shelter. Here you will find a three- sided open-fronted wooden refuge with a pump well and fire ring. This is a good place to relax before turning around. Backtrack.

4.8 Arrive back at the Oyster Point trailhead, completing the coastal trail.

19. ELLIOTT COUES NATURE TRAIL

Have a great hike here at Fort Macon State Park. First, leave the informative visitor center, then join the Elliott Coues Nature Trail. It leads along Bogue Sound under a canopy of gnarled live oaks before emerging near the Atlantic Ocean at a park beach access. From there, walk along the picturesque sands with stellar views of nearby waters and islands, following the sand to curve by Beaufort Inlet, completing a loop. While here, make sure to explore Fort Macon.

THE RUNDOWN

Distance: 3.5-mile loop
Start: Visitor center parking area
Nearest town: Atlantic Beach
Hiking time: 2.0 hours
Fees and permits: None
Conveniences: Restrooms, water, souvenirs inside visitor center
Beach access: Yes
Trail users: Hikers, runners, beachcombers
Trail surface: Pea gravel, natural, sand
Difficulty: Easy to moderate

Highlights: Views, live oaks, Atlantic Ocean beach, beachcombing, history
Canine compatibility: Leashed dogs permitted
Schedule: Oct through Mar from 8 a.m. to 6 p.m.; April, May, Sept from 8 a.m. to 7 p.m.; June through Aug from 8 a.m. to 8 p.m.; closed Christmas Day
Managing agency: Fort Macon State Park, 2303 East Fort Macon Rd., Atlantic Beach, NC 28512; (252) 726-3775; www.ncparks.gov/fort-macon-state-park

FINDING THE TRAILHEAD

From the intersection of the Atlantic Beach Causeway, linking Atlantic Beach to Morehead City, and NC 58 in Atlantic Beach, take NC 58 east for 3 miles to enter Fort Macon State Park. Stay with the main park road as it curves around the fort and ends in a large parking area north of the visitor center. GPS trailhead coordinates: 34.698174, -76.678787

WHAT TO SEE

The North Carolina coast is blessed with many fine harbors that ended up being places of settlement and trade during colonial English times. Beaufort, North Carolina, was one such place, founded in 1709. And just like that, Beaufort was susceptible to pirates and international raiders, and before the 1700s came to a close, the town was captured and occupied twice. The need was obvious to build a defense at the mouth of Beaufort Inlet, and the first fort was completed in 1808. Fort Hampton was built of bricks, but eventually the fledgling United States left it unoccupied. Perhaps that was a good thing since an 1825 hurricane washed the fort into the sea.

Construction began on a new fort the following year. Completed and garrisoned by 1834, this barricade, named Fort Macon, protected the passage through Beaufort Inlet. In the 1840s Robert E. Lee, future head of the Confederate Army, came here to build stone jetties to keep this bastion from washing away. Early in the Civil War the Rebels took and occupied Fort Macon. The Union knew they had to have Fort Macon to gain ship passage through Beaufort Inlet and undertook a siege. On April 25, 1862, an eleven-hour

Inside historic Fort Macon

pounding by cannons and from offshore naval boats shook Johnny Reb. The Confederates surrendered the next day. Thus, the Yankees controlled the fort and controlled the port of Beaufort, using it as a coaling station for their ships throughout the war. Later Fort Macon housed military and nonmilitary prisoners. During the Spanish-American War the fort was briefly recommissioned.

In 1923 the federal government sold Fort Macon to the state of North Carolina for one dollar, whereupon North Carolina established Fort Macon as its second state park. During the 1930s much of the fort was restored by the Civilian Conservation Corps. Fort Macon saw its last military life during World War II, when it was briefly reactivated. Ever since then, the bastion has remained a historical destination located in an incredibly scenic part of the Carolina coastline.

Today the 424-acre state park protects a stretch of Atlantic Ocean beach, the sands and dunes overlooking Beaufort Inlet, as well as marshland, and of course Fort Macon itself. Check out the visitor center, then explore the fort inside and out. This place is laced with historical information, and you can learn a lot on your own or take one of the park fort tours. And the views are excellent from the citadel itself. You can gaze down on the crashing surf of the Atlantic Ocean, outward to the Shackleford Banks on the far side of the inlet, as well as adjacent channels and islands. It is quite a scenic spot.

A soldier named Dr. Elliott Coues also realized the natural splendor of Fort Macon way back in 1870. Coues served the fort as a physician, but on the side he was a naturalist, specifically an ornithologist, a birder. And Fort Macon remains a birder's paradise to this day. While here, Coues wrote a guide titled *Key to North American Birds*. And to memorialize his passion for the nature of Fort Macon, the state park named a loop trail circling

Top: The Elliott Coues Nature Trail takes you along Atlantic dunes.
Bottom: A shell attracts a coastal hiker.

Elliott Coues Nature Trail

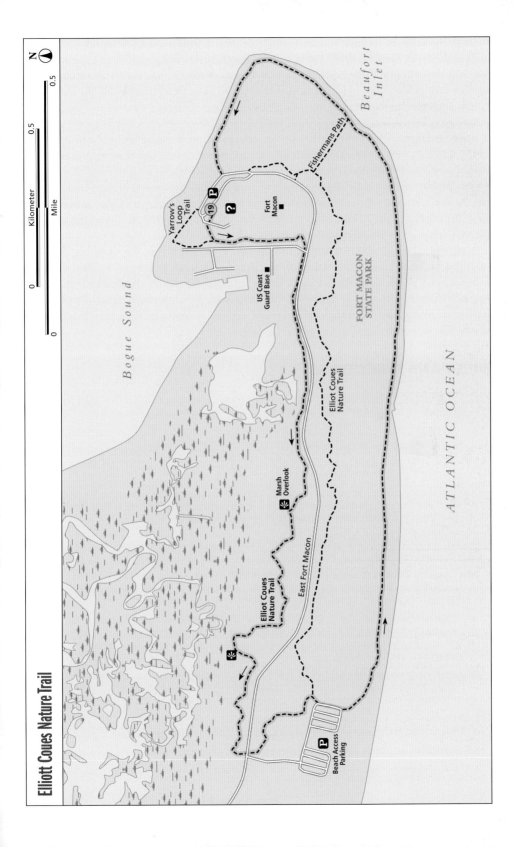

through the preserve for him. You start your hike on this path winding along the cord-grass marsh lying between Fort Macon and the mainland, traveling under wind-sheared live oaks and other trees that make for a scenic transition zone between maritime woods and brackish grasses. This overlapping of ecotones also makes it ideal for avian life, from herons and egrets along this side, to gulls and terns along the beach, to songbirds in the central wooded thickets.

After turning away from the marsh, you cross the park entrance road and reach an area of big dunes as well as the main beach access parking lot (which offers restrooms and shaded picnic tables). From there a boardwalk leads from the parking lot to the Atlantic Ocean beach, where a wide sloping swath of sand presents beachcombing opportunities. As you turn east, tall dunes partly covered in sea oats form a rampart. Upon nearing Beaufort Inlet, the guns of Fort Macon rise to your left, and across the shore you can see the wooded coast of Shackleford Banks, where wild ponies run free.

A stone jetty checks sand erosion at Beaufort Inlet. As you follow the shoreline, the waves become gentler away from the Atlantic. After completely curving away from the ocean, a beach overlooking shallow calm waters attracts families with children and other beachcombers. Finally you see the top of the visitor center over dunes. Access the parking lot via one of the designated walkways through the dunes, completing your sandy coastal trail adventure.

MILES AND DIRECTIONS

0.0   Pick up the signed Elliott Coues Nature Trail from the entrance walk to the park visitor center. Join a gravel track to soon cross a road used by park personnel.

0.1   Stay left as the Yarrow's Loop leaves right to return to the parking lot. Immediately curve left, walking along the boundary of the US Coast Guard base.

0.3   Reach the park access road. Turn right, walking along the grass beside the road, in front of the Coast Guard station.

0.4   Leave the base and reenter Fort Macon State Park. A boardwalk leads you over a wetland. Cross many boardwalks ahead among patches of woods rife with gnarled live oaks and cedars lending a fairy tale forest appearance.

0.9   Reach the marsh pond overlook.

1.3   Pass another quality marsh view and continue to traverse boardwalks.

1.6   Cross the park access road. Stay straight with the Elliott Coues Nature Trail as a spur path leads right toward the town of Atlantic Beach. Continue in taller live oak woods before opening onto dune scrub, with views of dunes ahead.

1.8   Reach the main park beach access lot and alternate trailhead. You are next to shaded picnic tables. The Elliott Coues Nature Trail continues straight, but our hike splits right, easterly, to a designated beach access, aiming for the Atlantic Ocean beach.

1.9   Come to the wide Atlantic Ocean and begin heading east along the continental edge. This is a popular relaxing and beachcombing spot. Dead ahead you can see the Shackleford Banks. In the distance look for the American flag atop Fort Macon.

3.0   Reach a rock jetty and the mouth of Beaufort Inlet. Ahead, the Fishing Trail leads left to the visitor center parking area. Continue curving along the inlet.

3.3   The sandy spit turns back toward the parking lot and visitor center.

3.5   Arrive back at the parking lot after cutting through a designated passage through the dunes, completing the coastal trail adventure.

20. THEODORE ROOSEVELT NATURAL AREA AND HOOP POLE CREEK

Indulge in two adjacent hikes on the barrier island of Bogue Banks. First, from the North Carolina Aquarium at Pine Knoll Shores, walk along Bogue Sound, past a small beach to ocean views (perhaps adding a trip to the aquarium), then drive a short way to tackle the nature trail at Hoop Pole Creek, presenting Civil War history, small beaches, and additional fine views of Bogue Sound.

THE RUNDOWN

Distance: 1.4-mile and 0.8-mile out-and-backs
Start: Parking area of North Carolina Aquarium at Pine Knoll Shores
Nearest town: Pine Knoll Shores
Hiking time: 1.4 hours combined hikes
Fees and permits: None, fee to enter North Carolina Aquarium
Conveniences: Restrooms, water inside North Carolina Aquarium
Beach access: Yes
Trail users: Hikers
Trail surface: Natural, some old pavement on Hoop Pole Creek Trail

Difficulty: Easy
Highlights: Maritime forest, small beaches, aquatic views
Canine compatibility: Leashed dogs permitted on Hoop Pole Creek Trail
Schedule: Theodore Roosevelt Nature Trail daily from 9 a.m. to 5 p.m.; Hoop Pole Creek Trail daily from dawn to dusk
Managing agency: North Carolina Aquarium Pine Knoll Shores, 1 Roosevelt Blvd., Pine Knoll Shores NC 28512; (252) 247-4003; www .ncaquariums.com/pine-knoll-shores

FINDING THE TRAILHEAD

From the intersection of NC 58 and NC 24 in Cape Carteret, take NC 58 South for 15.5 miles. Turn left onto Pine Knoll Boulevard and follow it 0.2 mile to a left turn on Roosevelt Boulevard. Follow Roosevelt Boulevard 0.5 mile to enter the North Carolina Aquarium parking area. Continue driving toward the back left parking area to find the signed trailhead. GPS trailhead coordinates: 34.698952, -76.830101

WHAT TO SEE

This part of the North Carolina Atlantic coast, specifically the barrier island that is Bogue Banks, has very little land remaining in its natural state. However, two special parcels have been preserved and both have trails we can hike. These two places are Theodore Roosevelt Natural Area and Hoop Pole Creek Preserve. Located just a few miles from one another among the condos and businesses of Atlantic Beach and Pine Knoll Shores, these preserves protect 265 and 31 acres, respectively. And both were preserved with the realization that coastal natural areas are limited and special.

Back in the early 1900s, the Bogue Banks were a forlorn part of the North Carolina coast, mostly still in its natural state. In 1917 Alice Hoffman bought a significant parcel on the Bogue Banks as an escape from crowded New York City. She fell in love with the scenic Carolina coastline and moved down here permanently in 1938. The spinster spent

Lookout out on Bogue Sound at Theodore Roosevelt Natural Area

the last fifteen years of her life in peace on the Carolina coast and was regularly visited by her niece Eleanor and Eleanor's husband, Theodore Roosevelt Jr. Upon her death, Alice Hoffman willed the land to her niece Eleanor. The Roosevelt family subsequently donated almost 300 acres of the tract to the state of North Carolina, stipulating that the land be kept in its natural state and maintained as a nature preserve and also to establish a marine resource center.

Thanks to the Roosevelt family, today we have the natural area upon which to hike and the North Carolina Aquarium—the marine resource center—to learn more about life on the coast, including underwater. The trail here is a good one. The path leaves the trailhead and immediately enters rolling maritime woods covering former dunes. Marshlands extend on both sides of a wooded peninsula. Views open of Bogue Sound, then you soon skirt along a small beach where you can access the shoreline. Birdlife is abundant along the sound and the adjacent marshes. The rest of the trail continues out the peninsula then curves back to end at a wetland.

There is another trail here, but you have to enter the aquarium and pay the fee to access it. This is the 0.5-mile boardwalk loop that is the Alice Hoffman Trail. So if you decide to explore the aquarium, make sure to hike the Alice Hoffman Trail.

Just a few miles away are the Bogue Banks's other premier wild area—Hoop Pole Creek Preserve. By the 1990s it was becoming obvious that significant natural parcels out here were rare. But there was one tract in the town of Atlantic Beach. In 1997 the North Carolina Coastal Federation bought the 31-acre parcel along Hoop Pole Creek for $2.5 million. The only thing on the tract was a crumbling asphalt road from a failed attempt at development back in the 1960s. (This road became a lover's lane for local high schoolers.) A trail was built on the tract using part of the old asphalt road. Now you can enjoy this often overlooked parcel.

The Hoop Pole Creek Trail begins at a shopping center parking lot. Then a boardwalk leads you through wooded wetlands to reach the erstwhile asphalt track. The hike then

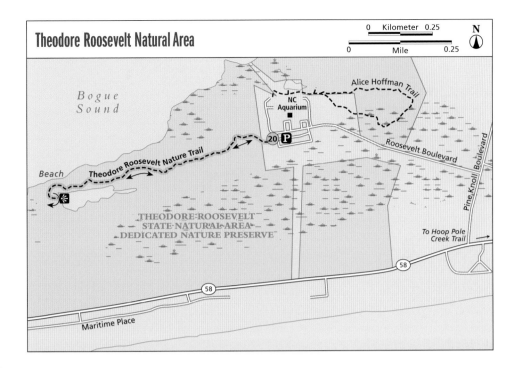

Theodore Roosevelt Natural Area

Bogue
Sound

Alice Hoffman Trail

NC
Aquarium

20

P

Roosevelt Boulevard

Theodore Roosevelt Nature Trail

Beach

Pine Knoll Boulevard

THEODORE ROOSEVELT
STATE NATURAL AREA
DEDICATED NATURE PRESERVE

To Hoop Pole
Creek Trail

58

58

Maritime Place

0   Kilometer 0.25

0   Mile   0.25

N

The mainland lies low across Bogue Sound.

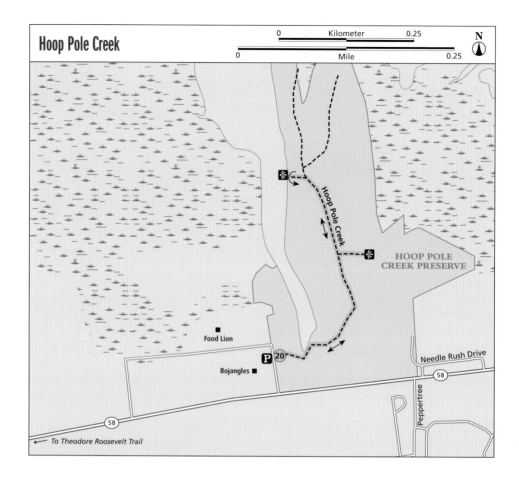

Hoop Pole Creek

HOOP POLE
CREEK PRESERVE

Food Lion

P 20

Bojangles

Needle Rush Drive

58

Peppertree

58

To Theodore Roosevelt Trail

leads through live oaks and other components of the maritime forest, taking a detour to a marsh overlook before ending at yet another overlook on Hoop Pole Creek. User-created trails lead to other points along the marsh and may be worth your exploration.

And while out there, contemplate the role of Hoop Pole Creek in the Civil War. Back in 1862 the Union had captured Carolina City, Morehead City, and Beaufort, yet the Confederates held the strategic water access of Beaufort Inlet on the Atlantic at Fort Macon. The Union tried to force a rebel surrender at Fort Macon, but the Southerners held on. The Union went into siege mode. Using any boats available, the Yankees began ferrying men, equipment, and cannons at high tide across Bogue Sound and up shallow Hoop Pole Creek, establishing a camp on the Bogue Banks roughly near the trailhead. The trials these men went through pulling the cannon through the marsh were rough! Next the men under General Ambrose E. Burnside (after whom sideburns are named) had to haul the cannons 4 miles east along the beach to set up against the Confederates ensconced at Fort Macon. Their efforts paid off and on April 25 the Rebels were bombed into surrendering the following day.

The efforts these soldiers underwent make our hikes the lightest of undertakings. Think about that when you trek here at Hoop Pole Creek Preserve and Theodore Roosevelt Natural Area.

Hoop Hole Creek is a tidal waterway.

MILES AND DIRECTIONS

0.0 Join the Theodore Roosevelt Natural Area at the large sign by the southwest end of the parking area. Walk a natural surface path into undulating wooded dunes covered in cedar, pine, wax myrtle, live oaks, red bay, holly, and magnolia.

0.1 Come alongside a marshy inlet leading into Bogue Sound. Roll over continual dunes leaving hardly a level spot. Contemplation benches are stationed along the path. A marsh develops to your left as well, leaving you a peninsula upon which to walk.

0.6 Come along a limited beach overlooking Bogue Sound. User-created paths lead down to the sand. The mainland is visible across Bogue Sound.

0.7 Reach an inland marsh overlook after turning away from the open waters of Bogue Sound. The trail dead ends. Backtrack to the trailhead

1.4 Arrive back at the trailhead. Then drive to the Hoop Pole Creek trailhead by returning to NC 58 and heading east for 4.0 miles to turn into the Food Lion shopping center and finding the signed path on the far east end of the shopping center, near Bojangles. The GPS trailhead coordinates: 34.701488, -76.751912.

0.0 Leave the shopping center on a boardwalk, immediately entering wind-sculpted live oaks and yaupon.

0.1 Reach the crumbling asphalt track from a failed attempt at development, now a canopied foot trail. Head left, north.

0.2 Leave right for a short out-and-back to a marsh overlook, then resume the main trail.

0.4 Reach an overlook of Hoop Pole Creek and a small beach. Other user-created trails lead farther out to the marsh and along a line of maritime woods. Backtrack.

0.8 Arrive back at the trailhead, completing the hike.

21. **PATSY POND**

Located near the community Cape Carteret, Patsy Pond Nature Trail takes you through coastal longleaf pinewoods, rare in these days of developed valuable coastal properties. Walk by dark ponds and beige grasses under the regal evergreens. Part of the Croatan National Forest, the fire-managed forest through which you walk, presents sweeping vistas of rolling wooded hills and close-up highlights such as carnivorous plants.

THE RUNDOWN

Distance: 1.7-mile loop
Start: NC 24 across from North Carolina Coastal Federation headquarters
Nearest town: Cape Carteret
Hiking time: 1.0 hour
Fees and permits: None
Conveniences: None
Beach access: No
Trail users: Hikers, daily exercisers
Trail surface: Natural

Difficulty: Easy
Highlights: Coastal longleaf pinewoods, ponds
Canine compatibility: Leashed dogs permitted
Schedule: Sunrise to sunset year-round
Managing agency: Croatan National Forest, 141 E. Fisher Ave., New Bern, NC 28560; (252) 638-5628; www.fs .usda.gov/nfsnc

FINDING THE TRAILHEAD

From the intersection of NC 58 and NC 24 in Cape Carteret, take NC 24 East for 6.4 miles to the Patsy Pond Nature Trail trailhead on your left. GPS trailhead coordinates: 34.718901, -76.963445

WHAT TO SEE

This is one of those hikes where you drive by the trailhead—usually seeing cars there—and vow to hike it one day. Do so. Located along the southeastern edge of the Croatan National Forest, the walk here is often passed up because it lacks a singular "wow" feature. However, when you consider how native coastal forests are becoming rarer by the day, the woods of Patsy Pond actually deserve more acclaim than they receive.

The longleaf ecosystem such as that here at Patsy Pond once covered more than 50 million acres in the Southeast and now grows in less than 3 million acres, with much less acreage near the ocean. These nearly level pinewoods are easy to develop or alter and thus have been cut over, changed, or allowed to evolve into other forest types due to fire suppression. Furthermore, these forests are fire dependent, with conflagrations occurring every three to five years on average. It is only natural when people move to an area that fire suppression takes place. That is why land managers of the Croatan National Forest now use controlled burning to replicate the lightning-caused fires that formerly influenced this forest community.

Specifically, longleaf pine seeds germinate after fires. When first emerging from the ground, longleafs are at the "grass" stage, just needles rising from the forest floor. Then a spindly "trunk" rises, topped with a single bulb-like expanse of needles emerging from the top of the plant. These pines are using all their energy to grow their trunk high

Pine wiregrass ecosystem is now rare along the Carolina coast.

enough to be able to withstand a low-intensity, lightning-caused ground fire, like those that naturally sweep through longleaf pine forests. Once they are tall enough, the longleaf branches out and continues to rise skyward, ultimately developing a very thick scaly bark to protect them from sporadic yet necessary fires upon maturity.

Longleaf pines really do have long needles. In fact they have the longest needles (10 to 15 inches) and largest cones (6 to 8 inches) of any pine east of the Mississippi River. They grow primarily in the eastern half of North Carolina, but their native habitat has been diminished in the Tar Heel State.

Longleaf pines are valued as naval stores—straight trunks are used for masts and sap is turned into turpentine. But standing longleaf forests offer regal beauty—where towering trunks contrast with the long green needles and tawny wiregrass sways between widely dispersed trees. The sound of the wind rustling through the pines is music unto its own.

You will see evergreens by the hundreds on this hike, as well as other plants that make up an ecosystem that also includes small ponds, of which Patsy Pond is the largest. These naturally occurring tarns are dependent on groundwater. Their darkish tint comes from decaying pine needles and other vegetation, leaving them highly acidic, which in turn limits the lifeforms contained within. Nevertheless, two carnivorous plants are found among the ponds. Bladderwort, identified by its yellow flowers growing 4 or 5 inches above the pond surface, contains tiny bladders that capture small invertebrate pond creatures after bladderwort's trigger hairs are set off. Bladderworts then digest the bugs using enzymes. Strange indeed.

Two views of Patsy Pond

Sundews, another carnivorous species, grow along the edges of these ponds, in the margin between the open water of the ponds and the high dry ground of the pines. Its nectar–like appearance attracts insects that get stuck onto sticky leaves, then hairs wrap around the bug. The inside of the bug is digested, leaving only the outer skeleton, which ultimately falls away from the plant. Occasional fires help the sundew by reducing ground litter and eliminating plant competition.

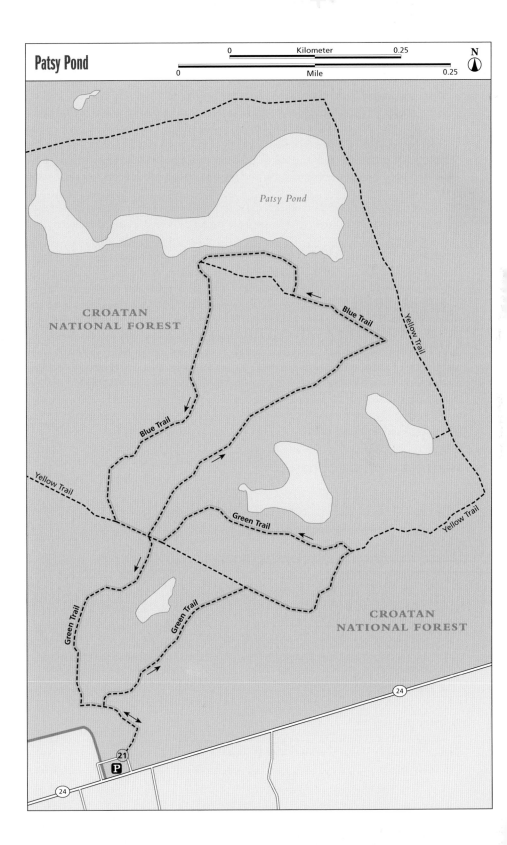

Patsy Pond

Patsy Pond

CROATAN
NATIONAL FOREST

Blue Trail

Yellow Trail

Blue Trail

Yellow Trail

Green Trail

Yellow Trail

Green Trail

Green Trail

CROATAN
NATIONAL FOREST

N

0   Kilometer   0.25
0   Mile   0.25

24

21

P

24

Both sundew and bladderwort play second fiddle to the two more famed carnivorous plants found in southeastern North Carolina—pitcher plants and the notorious Venus flytrap. The commonality among the "big four" carnivorous plants is that they all grow in nutrient-poor places and use insects to supplement their "diet."

A few things to consider before your walk: The official trail system is well marked with color-coded blazes. However, the trail system is built on old jeep roads that can be misleading, especially when other hikers get turned around often enough to keep the old jeep tracks alive. Stay with the blazes. The tree canopy is widely dispersed, so expect conditions open to the sky overhead. Parts of the trail bed are sandy, so expect slow going in those spots.

The hike leaves the NC 24 trailhead at a signed and often busy trailhead. (Local residents use the Patsy Pond trail system for daily exercise.) You will join the Green Trail and immediately enter longleaf forest, where the pines grow widely dispersed with an understory of wiregrass. The first water feature comes after just a few steps, "Bob's Sinkhole." This small circular ground depression is filled with water, the levels changing with the seasons, whether wet or dry. Ahead, the Green Trail splits and you begin a counterclockwise circuit, with the Yellow Trail leaving right. Another pond lies ahead and you come near it, especially after joining the Blue Trail. The hike eventually comes near Patsy Pond, 7 acres in size at full pool, but nothing but a glorified mud puddle during dry spells. The tarn does provide a scenic contrast to the pines. From there you work your way through rolling evergreen woods back to the trailhead, a near perfect daily exercise routine for those who live nearby. Although the recommended loop is 1.7 miles, you can add distance to the hike by tacking on the 1.9-mile Yellow Trail. It circles the perimeter of the hiking area, nearing both Patsy Pond and Lily Pond, while connecting to the Green Trail and the Blue Trail.

MILES AND DIRECTIONS

0.0   Leave the parking area on NC 24 on the Green Trail. Walk a short distance, then find Bob's Sinkhole. Continue beyond the water-filled sink.

0.1   Reach an intersection. Head right as the Green Trail begins its loop under widespread pines.

0.3   Come to a second intersection. Stay left with the Green Trail as the longer Yellow Trail leaves right. Walk an old jeep trail.

0.4   Reach a four-way intersection and head right on the Blue Trail. Low wooded hills rise to your left as you walk near a pond to your right. Turkey oaks are scattered among the pines.

0.7   The Blue Loop makes a hard left as it follows old jeep roads. Stay with the blazes.

0.8   Take the right spur going closer to Patsy Pond. Enjoy good looks at the 7-acre wetland. Soon rejoin the main Blue Trail and turn southwest, away from Patsy Pond.

1.2   Meet the Yellow Trail as it comes in on your right. Head left here, walk a few feet, then split right, rejoining the Green Trail. Resume southwest among the rolling longleaf wiregrass ecosystem.

1.6   Complete the loop portion of the Green Trail. Backtrack toward the trailhead.

1.7   Arrive back at the NC 24 trailhead, ending the hike.

22. CEDAR POINT TIDELAND TRAIL

Enjoy one of North Carolina's better interpretive coastal trails. Part of the Croatan National Forest, and enhanced with nearby additional recreation opportunities, you will wander through maritime woods, then begin crossing a series of picturesque hiker bridges spanning circuitous tidal streams. Absorb panoramas near and far before joining land and walking the freshwater-based environment contrasting with the coastal marsh.

THE RUNDOWN

Distance: 1.4-mile loop
Start: Cedar Point Picnic Area
Nearest town: Swansboro
Hiking time: 1.0 hour
Fees and permits: None
Conveniences: Picnic area, restrooms, campground with full amenities nearby
Beach access: No
Trail users: Hikers
Trail surface: Packed gravel, boardwalk, natural surface

Difficulty: Easy
Highlights: Bridges over tidal streams, interpretive information, views
Canine compatibility: Leashed dogs permitted
Schedule: Daily from sunrise to sunset
Managing agency: Croatan National Forest, 141 E. Fisher Ave., New Bern, NC 28560; (252) 638-5628; www.fs.usda.gov/nfsnc

FINDING THE TRAILHEAD

From the east side of Swansboro on NC 24 at the bridge over the White Oak River, drive east on NC 24 for 3.3 miles to NC 58. Turn left on NC 58 North for 0.6 mile to VFW Road. Turn left on VFW Road and follow it for 0.5 mile to a left turn onto Cedar Point Recreation Area. Follow the paved forest road 0.7 mile to a dead end at the trailhead. GPS trailhead coordinates: 34.691834, -77.086472

WHAT TO SEE

The alternate title of this hike could be "The Bridges of Cedar Point," for this trek features a series of gorgeous bridges spanning tidal creeks, each span delivering views afar and quaintness in the near. Luckily for us coastal hikers, both South Carolina and North Carolina offer national forest lands such as this to explore the coast. South Carolina has the Francis Marion National Forest, while here in North Carolina we have the Croatan, with its hiking, camping, fishing, boating, hunting, and more. The Cedar Point Tideland Trail takes you to the point where national forest land meets the salty sea.

Not only can you hike here at Cedar Point in the Croatan National Forest, but the greater Cedar Point Recreation Area boasts a worthy campground, open year-round, which can make your visit better. At the trailhead itself you can picnic on tables under evergreens with restrooms and water nearby. Also, a boat ramp avails paddlers, motor boaters, and anglers a place to set out on the nearby White Oak River.

The Cedar Point Tideland Trail, an officially designated national recreation trail, comprises two loops. The shorter loop is ADA accessible and is packed gravel its entire way. Enjoy the interpretive information and contemplation benches scattered throughout the

Top: Walkways lead over coastal tidelands.
Bottom: Looking over tidal White Oak River to Emerald Isle

hike. It isn't long before you reach the first bridge. These bridges are not only attractive but also sturdy, built to withstand tropical storms that periodically lash the coastal Carolinas. From the bridge, look down on the water. Are the waters of the tidal cycle going in or out? In the distance, the White Oak River stretches out to your left. The open Atlantic Ocean begins on the far side of Emerald Isle, gleaming in the yon. Salt pannes—flats where the ocean dries after storm surges leave standing seawater—stand in the fore, barren places where only high salt–tolerant plants can survive.

Ahead, a spur trail leads to another overlook on the banks of the water, toward a network of tidal creeks and the White Oak River. More views await from atop the next tidal creek bridge. Observe how the ecotones merge and change with elevation and proximity to salt water. This is also a good place to scan for shorebirds such as heron and egrets, raptors like hawks and osprey, or songbirds from the Carolina wren to the mockingbird. Below the bridge, look for fiddler crabs scurrying across the mud flats.

Drop to land and relish more views, then trek one more bridge of the bridges of Cedar Point. These elevated perches reveal the interrelationship between the grass-bordered tidal creeks within your vision. Beyond the bridge, the environment morphs to freshwater woods on a slope descending to the tidal marsh. Here laurel oak, pine, and holly rise overhead, while beard cane thickens the understory. Occasional freshwater streamlets

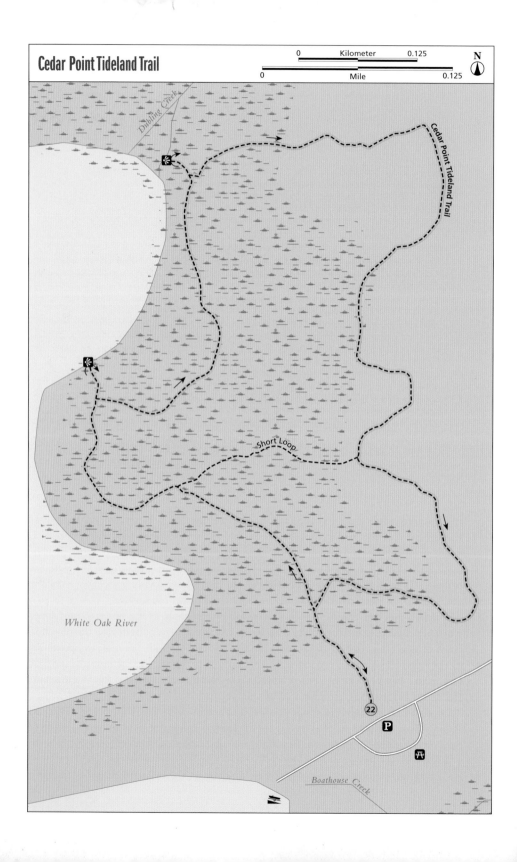

Cedar Point Tideland Trail

0 Kilometer 0.125

0 Mile 0.125

N

Dibbing Creek

Cedar Point Tideland Trail

Short Loop

White Oak River

22

P

Boathouse Creek

The bridges on this hike lend an artistic scene to the natural beauty of the Croatan National Forest.

flow across the trail, from the hills to the marsh, where mingling fresh and salt waters create a rich nursery of life. Boardwalks span these streamlets, taking you near the convergence of marsh and woodland. The final part of the hike stays along the marsh edge, all too soon completing the circuit portion of the hike. From there it is a simple backtrack to the trailhead. Consider a picnic or campout at Cedar Point, enjoying more of North Carolina's coastal national forest—the Croatan.

MILES AND DIRECTIONS

0.0 Leave the parking area on a packed gravel track to enter wind-pruned cedar, pines, wax myrtle, and live oaks. Storms, salt water, and winter winds keep the forest smaller than inland.

0.1 Reach an intersection. Head left and start your loop, rising on a bridge-like boardwalk spanning a Spartina grass–bordered tidal stream.

0.2 Come to a second intersection. Stay left as the short ADA-accessible loop leaves right.

0.3 Take the spur trail leading left to the White Oak River. Soak in a view from its marshy banks. Ahead, rise on another tidal stream bridge.

0.6 Reach a second waterside overlook, this one beside tidal Dubling Creek. A final scenic span takes you over more salt flats and streams.

0.7 Leave the tidal stream and enter piney freshwater forest.

1.1 The short loop comes in on your right. Our hike goes left, but you may want to walk out the short loop to yet another tidal bridge to view the tidelands from another perspective.

1.3 Complete the loop portion of the hike. Backtrack toward the trailhead.

1.4 Arrive back at the trailhead, completing the coastal trail.

23. LAKESHORE TRAIL

This gorgeous lakeside ramble leads beside big waters before returning via inland woods. Situated at alluring Lake Waccamaw State Park, you will first take one of two boardwalks reaching into Lake Waccamaw, where distant views delight. The Lakeshore Trail runs along the water's edge, often bordered by lush cypress trees. After enjoying the lakeside boardwalks and woods, turn back among rising pines and oaks in often sandy soil, fashioning a different environment through which to hike.

THE RUNDOWN

Distance: 4.5-mile loop
Start: Park visitor center
Nearest town: Lake Waccamaw
Hiking time: 2.2 hours
Fees and permits: None
Conveniences: None
Beach access: Yes
Trail users: Hikers
Trail surface: Natural
Difficulty: Moderate
Highlights: Copious lake views, vegetational variety

Canine compatibility: Leashed dogs permitted
Schedule: Dec, Jan, Feb from 7 a.m. to 7 p.m.; Mar, Apr, Oct from 7 a.m. to 9 p.m.; May, June, July, Aug, Sept from 7 a.m. to 10 p.m.; Nov from 7 a.m. to 8 p.m.; closed Christmas Day
Managing agency: Lake Waccamaw State Park, 1866 State Park Dr., Lake Waccamaw, NC 28450; (910) 646-4748; www.ncparks.gov/lake-waccamaw-state-park

FINDING THE TRAILHEAD

From the junction of NC 211 and US 74/US 76 near Bolton, take US 74W/US 76W for 4.6 miles, then turn left on Old Lake Road and follow it for 1.4 miles to a left turn on Lakeshore Drive. Follow Lakeshore Drive for 0.6 mile, then turn right on Bella Coola Road and follow it for 2.6 miles. Turn left into Lake Waccamaw State Park. Drive just a short distance farther, then turn right into the visitor center parking area. GPS trailhead coordinates: 34.278721, -78.465487

WHAT TO SEE

Lake Waccamaw is another one of the unusual bay lakes found in the eastern Carolinas. Although most of the bay lakes are smallish and filled with vegetation, Lake Waccamaw is one of the big ones, with an abundance of open water. Fourteen miles of shoreline ring the almost 9,000-acre oval-shaped lake. Lake Waccamaw is an unusual body of water even for a bay lake. Why you ask? First, the Friar Swamp flows into Lake Waccamaw, giving it an additional source of water other than rainfall. Second, the tannic, normally highly acidic bay lakes often lack richer aquatic life. However, Lake Waccamaw is blessed with limestone bluffs along its north shore. The limestone neutralizes the acids and results in Lake Waccamaw being richer in aquatic life that in turn makes for more robust plant and animal life all the way up the food chain, to the black bears and alligators that roam these parts.

Some claim Lake Waccamaw to be the largest of all the bay lakes, but others contend that Lake Mattamuskeet in far eastern North Carolina is the biggest. However, at one

Your hike starts in these inviting woods.

time Lake Mattamuskeet was drained and farmed before being restored to its former state and is now the centerpiece of the Lake Mattamuskeet National Wildlife Refuge. But Lake Waccamaw has been altered too, in a sense. Back in 1926, a dam was built where Lake Waccamaw drains out. It is from this dam that the coastal Waccamaw River begins. The dam was overhauled in 2007.

From Lake Waccamaw, the 140-mile long notoriously twisting Waccamaw River heads south through swamps, merging with other swamp streams until it reaches the Atlantic coastal ridge at the South Carolina state line after 50 miles. From here, the Waccamaw aims more southwesterly, still within a swampy floodplain. It widens near Conway and takes a tidally influenced course for the sea. Its lowermost portion becomes part of the

Looking into Lake Waccamaw

Intracoastal Waterway before finally emptying into the Atlantic near Georgetown, at Winyah Bay. Much of the river is fine for paddling and boating.

But at Lake Waccamaw State Park, we have a fine loop hike to explore. The hike presents a variety of hiking conditions, trails, and environments through which to walk. To best understand the rich park ecosystem, make sure to explore the visitor center here. The plethora of pathways in the immediate visitor center area can be confusing, but you will soon find yourself heading on a boardwalk that leads through swamp woods, then out to the water's edge and a pier that extends into the big freshwater tarn. What a view! A picnic shelter built into the boardwalk makes for a fine place to take in a meal.

The hike joins land and heads southwest along a wooded low sand berm just above the thickly vegetated shoreline, where cypress rise in thick ranks along with willow and bay trees. Waves lap the land just to your right. Loblolly pines rise tall overhead. Other parts of the Lakeshore Trail turn a little more inland, into sweetgums, oaks, and lesser pines. Contemplation benches are situated throughout the hike. Plank boardwalks negotiate some of the wetter locales.

The trail emerges at a boardwalk linking the main picnic area to a long pier and trailside picnic area. This can be a popular spot, with its rewarding views and water access. The expanse of Lake Waccamaw is guaranteed to impress. Beyond the long pier you will enter the cluster of group campsites. Be watchful here, as numerous sand roads and user-created trails can make the situation confusing. You'll cut back away from the lake near

Group Campground 4, as the Lakeshore Trail continues along the water to end after 4 miles at the Lake Waccamaw dam.

After navigating through the group camps, join the Sand Ridge Nature Trail. This path traverses sandy ground thick with turkey oaks and pines, on an elevated margin of land with Lake Waccamaw to the left and a swamp to the right. This path leads you to the park picnic area, another potentially confusing locale. After finding the Pine Woods Trail, you will meander among evergreens and sandy soils to reach State Park Drive. A short road walk leads right to more hiking in relaxing woodland dominated by evergreens. The final part of the trek uses the Loblolly Trail to escort you back to the visitor center, completing the adventure at this most unusual of Carolina bay lakes.

Notes: The Lakeshore Trail can be quite rooty in spots, as well as pocked with cypress knees—watch your feet. A host of spur trails and sand roads make the group camp cluster potentially confusing. When you get to the group camp cluster, it is time to head back toward the visitor center, northeasterly. Stay with the blazes on all trails, as unblazed side tracks can prove confusing.

Lake Waccamaw extends beyond the horizon.

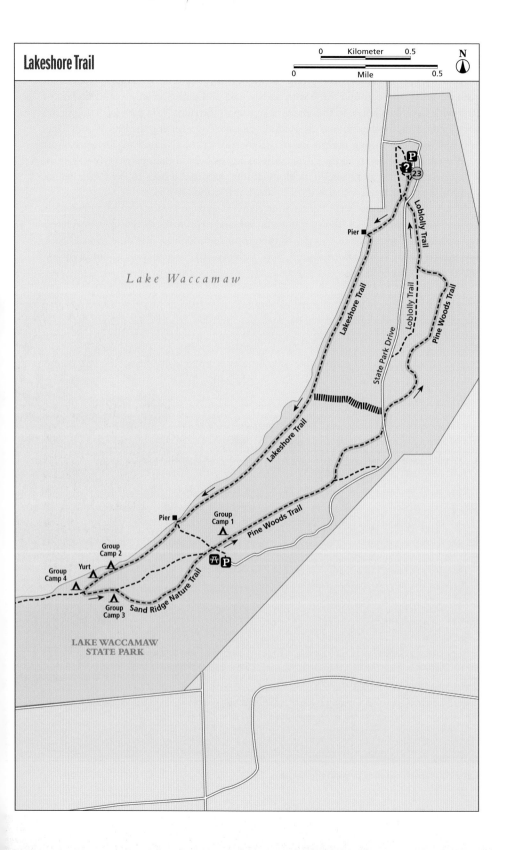

Lakeshore Trail

0   Kilometer   0.5

0   Mile   0.5

N

Lake Waccamaw

Pier

Lakeshore Trail

Lakeshore Trail

Lakeshore Trail

State Park Drive

Loblolly Trail

Loblolly Trail

Pine Woods Trail

Pine Woods Trail

P

?

23

Pier

Group
Camp 1

Group
Camp 2

Group
Camp 4

Yurt

Group
Camp 3

Sand Ridge Nature Trail

P

LAKE WACCAMAW
STATE PARK

MILES AND DIRECTIONS

0.0 As you face the park visitor center, walk around to the left-hand side of the building, then pick up a paved path leading toward Lake Waccamaw. Quickly split left as the very short Overlook Trail leads right. Join the Lakeshore Trail and a boardwalk leading through swamp woods of maple, bay, and willow; pass a covered shelter built into the boardwalk.

0.3 Reach an intersection and another covered shelter. Walk through the shelter out to an extensive panorama of Lake Waccamaw. Gaze for miles across the water and near along the wooded shore. Backtrack, then continue the Lakeshore Trail, heading southwest.

0.9 Reach a junction. Here the Boardwalk Connector Trail splits left, linking to State Park Drive and the Pine Woods Trail. The Boardwalk Connector offers a link in a shorter loop option. Continue straight on the Lakeshore Trail, traipsing underneath lush forest. Cross boardwalks ahead in wet areas.

1.6 Come to a trailside picnic area, picnic shelter, then the boardwalk connector to the main picnic area as well as a pier extending well out to shore. Walk out the wide pier to enjoy a superlative vista of Lake Waccamaw. Resume the Lakeshore Trail.

2.0 The Lakeshore Trail passes through Group Camp 2, then to Group Camp 5, a yurt. Continue ahead, then emerge into a confusing area as the Lakeshore Trail keeps along the shore. Find Group Camp 4, then cut northeast on a roadlike trail.

2.2 Pass Group Camp 3, then ahead split right onto the Sand Ridge Nature Trail, bordered by ferns and berry bushes under pines and oaks. Work along the edge of a swamp to your right as a longleaf pine restoration area rises to your left. A keen eye might spot a Venus flytrap plant hereabouts.

2.6 The Sand Ridge Nature Trail ends. Keep right, immediately reaching the picnic area restrooms. Continue northeast through the picnic area and join the signed Pine Woods Trail, where you will quickly pass Group Camp 1.

3.1 A spur leads right to State Park Drive, stay left with the blazes on the Pine Woods Trail.

3.4 Emerge at State Park Drive. Head left and walk the road for 0.1 mile, then turn right, rejoining the signed Pine Woods Trail, a pleasant grassy doubletrack, as the Boardwalk Connector Trail goes left. Listen to the wind rustle through the evergreens.

4.1 Head right upon meeting the Loblolly Trail.

4.4 Cross State Park Drive.

4.5 Arrive back at the visitor center, completing the hike.

Wildflowers brighten the woods at Lake Waccamaw State Park.

24. SUGARLOAF TRAIL

This coastal trek at a super scenic state park has it all. Start your hike by cruising along the Cape Fear River, where you will skirt a backwoods beach. Next, turn inland only to head riverward again, making a marsh overlook. After that, climb historic and huge Sugarloaf Dune. Wander among other forested sand hills before reaching the Flytrap Trail, where you can perhaps view one of the rare carnivorous plants. Finally, complete the loop hike with a walk through tall trees.

THE RUNDOWN

Distance: 5.6-mile loop
Start: Park marina
Nearest town: Carolina Beach
Hiking time: 3.0 hours
Fees and permits: None
Conveniences: Concession stand, picnic area, restrooms nearby
Beach access: Yes
Trail users: Hikers
Trail surface: Natural, slow sandy sections in places
Difficulty: Moderate
Highlights: Beach, views from Sugarloaf Dune, Venus flytrap, rolling terrain

Canine compatibility: Leashed dogs permitted
Schedule: Dec through Jan from 7:00 a.m. to 6:00 p.m.; Feb from 7:00 a.m. to 7:00 p.m.; Mar through Apr from 7:00 a.m. to 9:00 p.m.; May through Sept from 7:00 a.m. to 10:00 p.m.; Oct from 7:00 a.m. to 9:00 p.m.; Nov from 7:00 a.m. to 7:00 p.m.; closed Christmas Day
Managing agency: Carolina Beach State Park, 1010 State Park Rd., Carolina Beach, NC 28428; (910) 458-8206; www.ncparks.gov/carolina-beach-state-park

FINDING THE TRAILHEAD

From Wilmington, drive south on US 421 15 miles, crossing the Intracoastal Waterway. Turn right on Dow Road past the Intracoastal Waterway, shortly reaching the park, on your right. From there, follow the main park road to a dead end at the park marina. The trailhead is in the south corner of the marina parking area. GPS trailhead coordinates: 34.049033, -77.919131

WHAT TO SEE

This area of the Carolinas certainly has some remarkable natural attributes, but the most unusual of all may be the carnivorous plant known as the Venus flytrap. This is but one of many highlights you will experience here at Carolina Beach State Park. The preserve also features a fine campground as well as additional attractions nearby.

But hiking is what we're here for, and this trek is one of the best in this guide. The hike traverses a wide variety of habitats, additionally adding vertical variation. Even the trail bed changes, from grass to pine needles to open sand. Make sure to bring a trail map with you, because you will encounter many trail junctions. The hike first leads you from the trailhead to the shores of the Cape Fear River, where you will come alongside a small beach while hiking among scrubby sand live oaks. Soon enjoy freshwater pinewoods before turning out to a marsh overlook of the Cape Fear River. And soon the habitats change quickly yet again as you make your way to the top of Sugarloaf Dune, a massive mountain of sand that has been a marker for mariners for hundreds of years. And

Top: Find this trailside beach along the Cape Fear River
Bottom: Looking out from Sugarloaf Dune

Turkey oaks border the path.

to this day, as tourists have been doing for one hundred years or more before, you can climb this dune to enjoy an extensive panorama of the lands beyond the Cape Fear River. Beyond here you will cruise alongside the Cape Fear River, then turn inland, winding among regal longleaf pines and scads of turkey oaks. Much of the trail here is over open, blinding-white sand, offering yet another setting here at Carolina Beach State Park. The terrain remains hilly and gorgeous, then you enter an area of woods and freshwater ponds, adding another dimension to the hike. Next it is time to make a little loop on the Flytrap Trail to hopefully see this rare plant. The final part of the hike takes you through tall thick woods that seem extraordinarily dense after the sandy open pine and turkey oak woods. Make sure to snap plenty of pictures and take ample video, because it's impossible to capture the essence of this state park in just a single visual.

Consider overnighting here. The campground is situated in piney woods near Snows Cut, a waterway connecting the wide Cape Fear River to the Intracoastal Waterway. Pines, live oaks, and water oaks rise above the two campground loops with plenty of low brush to enhance campsite privacy. The large sites—some with electricity —are blessed with sand-and-pine-needle floors. Each of the two loops features a bathhouse. The campground fills most weekends from Memorial Day through Fourth of July week-end, though spring and fall are the best times to visit.

Anglers can enjoy the park's fishing pier located near this hike's trailhead. Vie for croaker, flounder, and striped bass. The marina store sells bait and tackle. Additionally, an on-site concessionaire offers kayak and paddleboard rentals as well as guided paddling tours during the warm season.

Beach accesses are plentiful on nearby Pleasure Island, as well as Fort Fisher State Rec-reation Area. You can also enjoy the North Carolina Aquarium at Fort Fisher or tour the USS *North Carolina* battleship, conspicuously located on the Cape Fear River near Wilm-ington. So maybe you should hike, paddle, fish, and camp here at Carolina Beach State Park. Don't forget to add a little time for boasting about your hike around the campfire.

THE STRANGE BUT TRUE VENUS FLYTRAP

The strangely named—and downright strange—Venus flytrap is a carnivorous plant that lays claim to being the most well-known carnivorous plant on the planet. The Venus flytrap grows in only fifteen counties in North Carolina and one county in South Carolina, all within a 75-mile radius of Wilmington, North Carolina. (Its range once extended down to Charleston County in South Carolina.) The plant catches insects—visualize ants, beetles, or spiders—by trapping them between two lobes of its leaf, when hairs of that leaf are stimulated by the landing and movement of insects (only 5 percent of the insect diet of a Venus flytrap is actually a fly). The closing of the trap is quick, a trick only a few plants worldwide can pull off. Although the Venus flytrap does grow through photosynthesis, the sandy, nutrient-poor soils in which the flytrap grows make it necessary for the plant to gain nutrients from the insects it digests to thrive. After prey is caught, digesting enzymes are released, breaking down the bug.

Habitat for the Venus flytrap, longleaf pine among the inland sand hills and the wet margins of sand pine savannas here at Carolina Beach State Park and other coastal places, is rare indeed these days. Fire suppression, development, and agriculture continue to shrink the habitat for this fascinating plant. On this hike you will walk Flytrap Trail. Perhaps you may see one of these rare species. Unfortunately bad guys still try to poach plants from this very state park, and other places as well, even though the flytrap has been successfully transplanted and grown elsewhere and is commercially available. While on this hike appreciate that this strange carnivorous plant is just one more exciting highlight you can enjoy while hiking the coast of the Carolinas.

Carnivorous pitcher plants grow in this park along with the Venus flytrap.

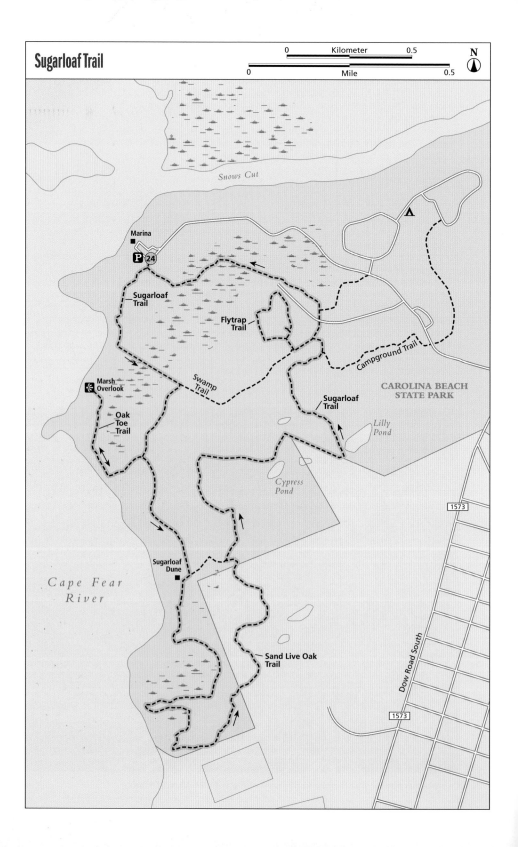

Sugarloaf Trail

0   Kilometer   0.5

0   Mile   0.5

N

Snows Cut

Marina

P 24

Sugarloaf
Trail

Flytrap
Trail

Campground Trail

Swamp
Trail

Marsh
Overlook

CAROLINA BEACH
STATE PARK

Oak
Toe
Trail

Sugarloaf
Trail

Lilly
Pond

Cypress
Pond

1573

Sugarloaf
Dune

Cape Fear
River

Dow Road South

Sand Live Oak
Trail

1573

White sand shows the route of the trail.

MILES AND DIRECTIONS

0.0   Leave the south corner of the marina parking area near a trailhead kiosk, joining the Sugarloaf Trail, heading right, southwest, among maritime woods of loblolly pines, wax myrtle, cedar, and oak. Marsh and the Cape Fear River extend through the trees to the right. The woods quickly morph into scrubby sand live oaks.

0.2   Pass a little beach on the Cape Fear River. Shortly turn away from the beach to bridge a marsh. Return to freshwater wetlands.

0.4   Reach a trail intersection. Stay right with the Sugarloaf Trail as the Swamp Trail keeps straight. Travel fire-managed pinewoods.

0.6   Come to another trail intersection. Here, turn right with the Oak Toe Trail. Head out through scant woods and abundant grasses, plus sandy sections.

0.9   Reach an overlook of the Cape Fear River. Backtrack.

1.2   Return to the Sugarloaf Trail. Head right.

1.7   Reach the top of Sugarloaf Dune. Grab a historic view to the west. After this, join the Sand Live Oak Trail, descending. Roll on lesser dunes parallel to the Cape Fear River, only to turn away, working around a wetland. The trail traverses sandy terrain vegetated with tall longleaf pines and turkey oaks galore. Old roads spur off here and there; stay with the trail blazes.

3.2   Climb some more wooded dunes.

3.4   Head right at an intersection, rejoining the Sugarloaf Trail. Hike piney, lesser-sloped terrain. Ahead, skirt along Cypress Pond.

4.1   The trail makes a hard left near Lilly Pond.

4.5   Intersect a leg of the Campground Trail. Stay left here, then quickly intersect the Swamp Trail and turn left, then immediately meet the Flytrap Trail and stay right, making a counterclockwise loop, passing the parking area of the Flytrap Trail.

5.1   Meet the Swamp Trail again after looping the Flytrap Trail. Follow it northeast, passing the Campground Trail again, then cross the Flytrap Trail access road.

5.2   Meet the Sugarloaf Trail a final time. Head left, westerly, as a leg of the Campground Trail leaves right, crossing a boardwalk through a freshwater wetland, at yet another habitat here.

5.6   Complete the coastal hike, arriving back at the marina trailhead.

25. **FORT FISHER HIKE**

This hike leaves the recreation area visitor center to follow a pathway south among scattered trees and marsh, past the site where a hermit lived in seclusion for a decade plus, then to an overlook on the tidal Cape Fear River. From there, it returns near the visitor center, then treks the high beach along the Atlantic Ocean, with additional history and walking opportunities nearby.

THE RUNDOWN

Distance: 2.8-mile there-and-back
Start: Visitor center
Nearest town: Kure Beach
Hiking time: 1.2 hours
Fees and permits: None
Conveniences: Picnic area, restrooms, information at visitor center
Beach access: Yes
Trail users: Hikers, beachcombers
Trail surface: Natural
Difficulty: Easy, some walking over potentially loose sand

Highlights: Views, military history, Atlantic Ocean
Canine compatibility: Leashed dogs permitted
Schedule: Nov, Dec, Jan, Feb from 8 a.m. to 6 p.m.; Mar and Oct from 8 a.m. to 7 p.m.; April, May, Sept from 8 a.m. to 8 p.m.; June, July, Aug from 8 a.m. to 9 p.m.; closed Christmas Day
Managing agency: Fort Fisher State Recreation Area, 1000 Loggerhead Rd., Kure Beach, NC 28449; (910) 458-5798; www.ncparks.gov/fort-fisher-state-recreation-area

FINDING THE TRAILHEAD

From the intersection of US 421 and NC 132 on the south side of Wilmington, take US 421 South and travel 6.6 miles to a right turn onto Dow Road. Follow Dow Road for 4 miles to a right turn onto Forest Fisher Boulevard in Kure Beach, still on US 421. Follow Fort Fisher Boulevard for 2.3 miles, then turn left onto Loggerhead Road and stay with it for 0.2 mile to reach the state recreation area visitor center on your left. GPS trailhead coordinates: 33.964444, -77.922599

WHAT TO SEE

Fort Fisher State Recreation Area is a place of beauty where visitors come to relax beside the ocean, perhaps beachcombing, fishing, swimming, or hiking. And maybe become a hermit (more about that later).

Back before Europeans ever came to the Carolinas, aboriginals hunted, farmed, and gathered on the Cape Fear Peninsula. Continental Europeans settled into what became Wilmington around 1730, where the fledgling town became a trading place where naval tar, pitch, and turpentine—tapped and modified from pine trees—were exported. These products were used to make wooden ships watertight and were the basis for North Carolina getting its official nickname as the Tar Heel State.

Strategically located near the tip of Cape Fear (at that time known as Federal Point), Fort Fisher was built in 1861 by the Confederate States of America to defend the important port of Wilmington, through which the CSA got essential supplies for food, uniforms, and other sundries. Throughout the war, the fort grew in importance as Confederate coastal forts—and supply routes—fell one by one. However, Fort Fisher was

Top: This was the home of the Fort Fisher Hermit.
Bottom: A roiling ocean crashes into the Atlantic coast.

A winter sky at Fort Fisher

a well-constructed and defended fort. The bastion was made of earth and sand, ideal for absorbing the shock of explosives hurled against it. A series of guns faced outward, protecting the Atlantic Ocean and the Cape Fear River, the access route to the ports of Wilmington. The Army of Northern Virginia, led by General Robert E. Lee, had to have the supplies from Wilmington, and the Rebels also exported Confederate farm products such as cotton and tobacco that were traded to British smugglers. The Union army decided to take Fort Fisher. On Christmas Eve 1864 the two armies clashed, but to no avail. The Union withdrew their forces, thinking Fort Fisher was too strong to take. However, the Yankees once again mustered their forces on January 12, 1865. A combination land and sea assault worked. Fort Fisher was lost to the Confederacy and is considered the most important battle fought in the Tar Heel State. The South was doomed with its last reliable supply line cut off. Just a few months later, the war was over.

During World War II Fort Fisher became a firing range of the larger Camp Davis. Here future fighters were honed into better soldiers. During this hike you will see a bunker remaining from the World War II base. However, even more interesting is the man who lived in that abandoned bunker from 1955 to 1972—Robert E. Harrill, known to thousands as the Fort Fisher Hermit. Harrill hailed from the mountains of Morganton, North Carolina, and was said to be a mental institute escapee. He was once removed from his bunker home here on Fort Fisher, but he returned and ended up staying here long enough to become an institution. Some said he was a wise man, and they sought to gain knowledge from him, while others derided and even harassed him. Harrill, who worked the angle of reclusive sage while getting thousands of visitors per year, lived off the bounty of nature—from vegetables in his own garden to fish, clams, and oysters. In retrospect it's hard to call him a true hermit, since he had his own guestbook for visitors to sign and also sought donations from those who sought him out. He actually became one of coastal North Carolina's biggest tourist attractions. Alas, in 1972 he was found dead at his bunker. Some say the would-be Thoreau was murdered, but his death certificate states heart attack. Yet he was bloodied when found. After your hike to the hermit's bunker, draw your own conclusions.

Start the coastal trail adventure by leaving the park visitor center to join the Basin Trail. It leaves south, winding through woods and wetlands, coming very near the North Carolina Aquarium at Fort Fisher, one of four official state aquariums. From there the Basin Trail leads you through an open sandy area. The path continues south among scattered cedars with marsh stretching out in all directions. Then you come upon the site where Robert E. Harrill spent the last seventeen years of his life. Today vegetation surrounds the humble concrete bunker. Walk inside—the darkness is broken only by a small opening in the back and the doorway opening in front. It's hard not to wonder what the bunker looked like when Harrill came upon it in 1955 looking for a place to live, perhaps a new way of life. Whether you agree with his way of existence, his squatting on other people's land, or his dropping out of society, you have to admire his pluck for creating a life here. A plaque on the concrete structure notes this as being the home of Mr. Harrill.

Continuing on, the Basin Trail leads farther and farther into the marsh with open views of the dunes of the Atlantic to your left and the waters of the Cape Fear River to

The Fort Fisher State Recreation Area office

Fort Fisher Hike

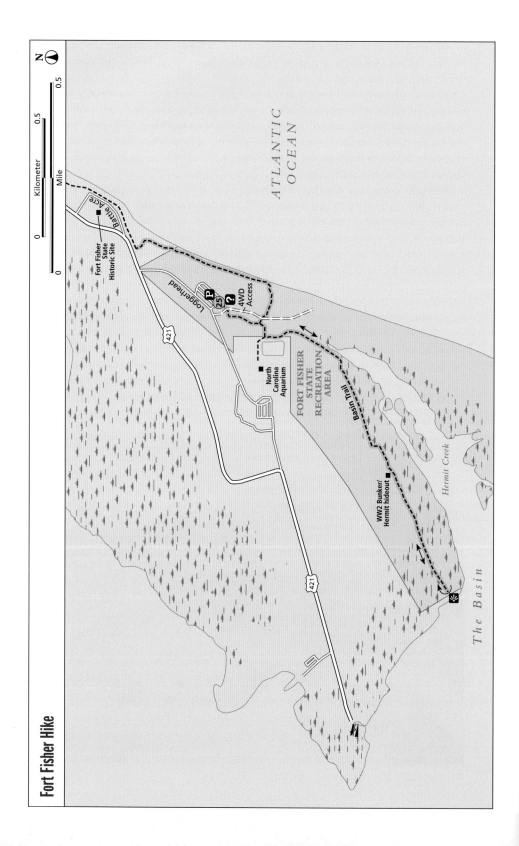

N

0   0.5   Kilometer
Kilometer

0   0.5   Mile
Mile

Battle Acre

Fort Fisher State Historic Site

Loggerhead

P

25

?

4WD Access

North Carolina Aquarium

FORT FISHER STATE RECREATION AREA

Basin Trail

WW2 Bunker/ Hermit hideout

421

421

ATLANTIC OCEAN

Hermit Creek

The Basin

your right. Then you reach an observation platform. Here, a view opens into The Basin, the other side of which stands Zekes Island, an important parcel of wild eastern North Carolina and an official state estuarine reserve.

From the observation point, backtrack to a trail junction just past the spur trail to the North Carolina Aquarium. Here follow a doubletrack east to the Atlantic Ocean. After reaching the beach you turn north (although if you head south you have nearly 5 miles of beach to explore) and head along the steep-sided sand, a popular area for beachcombers and folks who just want to relax oceanside. You will reach the north end of the state recreation area and then come to the official grounds of the state historic site. It has a half-mile asphalt path running along the ocean should you want to add mileage to your trek. From this point it is a simple backtrack to the state recreation area visitor center. While here you should also explore the Civil War Museum at the Fort Fisher state historic site. You will pass it on the way in before reaching the trailhead parking area.

MILES AND DIRECTIONS

0.0 While facing the state recreation area visitor center look right for the signed Basin Trail. Quickly cross the four-wheel-drive beach access road and continue on a foot-path in thick, low woods of yaupon, oak, and cedar.

0.1 Bridge a tiny canal. Note the spur left to the beach ahead, near a kiosk. You will return to it later.

0.2 Cross a second canal and come to the spur trail to the North Carolina Aquarium. Soon open onto sandy terrain with views of Atlantic beach dunes. Stay with the signs.

0.4 Return to scattered woods. The trail bed hardens. Angle away from the Atlantic dunes.

0.5 Pick up a long boardwalk with expansive views.

0.8 Come to the World War II bunker and home of hermit Robert E. Harrill. Continue down trail among wind-blown cedars.

1.1 Reach the observation point, with waters and lands extending to the horizon. Backtrack.

2.1 Head east to the pedestrian beach access, cutting across the four-wheel-drive access. Come to the beach, then head north along the Atlantic. Ahead, pass the access to the visitor center. Keep north along the steeper-than-average beach.

2.6 Reach a jetty and the beginning of the Fort Fisher State Historic Site. You can go north on a half-mile asphalt track for added mileage. Otherwise backtrack to the visitor center.

2.8 Arrive back at the state recreation area visitor center, completing the hike.

SOUTH CAROLINA
COASTAL TRAILS

Admiring the Atlantic Ocean beach
at Myrtle Beach State Park.

26. MYRTLE BEACH STATE PARK HIKE

Make a circuit through this venerated preserve, walking both woodland and oceanfront while at the same time visiting the state park facilities. Begin your hike near the nature center, traversing tall woods on the Sculptured Oak Nature Trail to circle a pond. Make your way to the Atlantic Ocean beach and its signature wind-sculpted forest. Crunch your feet on the shoreline, passing under the park's fishing pier. Enjoy more beach walking to the park's end, then backtrack a bit. On your return, cut through the park campground and stop by the nature center, finally returning to the trailhead.

THE RUNDOWN

Distance: 2.6-mile loop with spurs
Start: Nature Center trailhead
Nearest town: Myrtle Beach
Hiking time: 1.2 hours
Fees and permits: Entrance fee
Conveniences: Restrooms, water fountains, picnic shelters, campground
Beach access: Yes
Trail users: Hikers, beachcombers
Trail surface: Natural, a little pavement
Difficulty: Easy
Highlights: Tall woods, beachfront, pier

Canine compatibility: Dogs not allowed on the beaches from 10 a.m. to 5 p.m. (7 days a week) May 1 through Labor Day. This county ordinance is effective on all public Horry County beaches.
Schedule: Mar through Nov from 6 a.m. to 10 p.m.; Dec through Feb from 6 a.m. to 8 p.m.
Managing agency: Myrtle Beach State Park, 4401 South Kings Hwy., Myrtle Beach, SC 29575; (843)238-5325; southcarolinaparks.com/myrtle-beach

FINDING THE TRAILHEAD

From the interchange of US 17 and US 501 in Myrtle Beach, take US 501 South for 0.9 mile to turn right on Third Avenue South and follow it for 1.1 miles to a right turn onto US 17 Business South. Stay on US 17 for 3.6 miles to a left turn into Myrtle Beach State Park. Follow the main park road past the entrance booth and continue 0.8 mile from the park entrance to the Nature Center parking on the left. The Sculptured Oak Nature Trail begins on the right-hand side of the main park road. GPS trailhead coordinates: 33.651828, -78.929450

WHAT TO SEE

Myrtle Beach State Park is South Carolina's busiest—and first—state park. When it opened in the 1930s, the Grand Strand, the oceanside tourist haven of South Carolina, did not exist. However, Myrtle Beach grew as a tourist destination, and the Grand Strand expanded to entirely surround the state park. Yet the park shone, becoming a Palmetto State institution, a natural haven in Horry County, a coastal treasure still in its natural state, a place where you can hike coastal trails. Entering the park is an experience unto itself. You'll leave the busy vacation strip to discover a rich maritime forest at odds with the civilized world.

The Atlantic Ocean rolls in near the park pier.

The Sculptured Oak Nature Trail is your conduit to explore the preserve by foot. The path winds through tall oaks, pines, and yaupon, detouring past a small freshwater pond, where you can scan for alligators as well as winged wildlife. From there, join the Yaupon Nature Trail, aiming seaward in dense woods and freshwater swamps before emerging oceanside at a picnic shelter. A boardwalk leads to the unaltered beach offered here. High-rises, camping resorts, and houses line the shore elsewhere in this part of South Carolina, except for one place, and that is at Myrtle Beach State Park. A mile of beachfront is protected here. The wide beach gently rolls from dunes covered in sea oats down to the Atlantic Ocean. At this point, turn left, heading northeasterly up the state park beach. In the distance the park fishing pier extends far into the water. The pier and

Top: Sunbathers enjoy the shoreline at Myrtle Beach State Park.
Bottom: The state park pier

park store are attached, so anglers can make those emergency bait runs and other visitors can find drinks, sunscreen, and souvenirs. Ahead, four walkway beach accesses connect the sand to parking areas. Freshwater showers are available at all the walkways. You'll have to work around a tidal creek just before the pier. It can be a little hop, tide depending.

After passing under the pier, continue along the wide swath of sand with the Atlantic Ocean rolling shoreward in its ceaseless manner. To your left a large picnic area in a mix of shade and sun catches the ocean breezes. The sea breezes are evidenced by the wind-sculpted oaks by the picnic area. More picnic tables are adjacent to the parking areas, as are more covered picnic shelters. After making your way to the park boundary, shown by hotels where the park isn't, turn back. To make a loop, take the wide campground access, passing the ranger station in the campground.

The park campground is very large. With over 300 campsites, the immediate area can be bustling, especially on summer weekends. A wooded oasis of tall oaks and pines provides more than ample shade. The actual campsites are laid out in concentric loops. Hot showers, laundry, and a camp store are on-site. This park fills on weekends from mid-May through August and on some summer weekdays. Reservations are strongly recommended anytime in the summer.

Finish the hike by leaving the campground and making your way to the park's worth-a-visit nature center. The park presents daily interpretive programs during the summer, primarily based out of the park nature center. Learn a little bit more about the coastline here in South Carolina before emerging at the trailhead parking area.

When the Great Depression deepened in the early 1930s, President Roosevelt came up with the New Deal, and the Civilian Conservation Corps (CCC) was born. The men of the CCC were instrumental in developing Myrtle Beach State Park, as well as many other state and national parks throughout the country.

For their work the men received housing, meals, and $30 a month. This gave rise to the saying, "another day, another dollar." The CCC performed a variety of work throughout South Carolina, including soil conservation, reforestation, fire prevention, and the development of recreational areas. Thanks to the CCC, Myrtle Beach State Park opened in July 1936 and the South Carolina state park system was born. By 1938 fourteen South Carolina state parks were open. The CCC was disbanded in 1942, due to World War II. However, by then South Carolina had opened more state parks. Today the Palmetto State has forty-seven state parks ready for your visit.

In addition to hiking, other park activities center on the ocean. The facilities here are designed to handle loads of visitors. In high summer the park beach can become crowded with shoreline lovers engaging in every type of pastime. The large fishing pier draws in fishers galore, as they go for whiting, Spanish mackerel, flounder, and sea trout, among other finned fare. Furthermore, limited park size restricts park activities to camping and beach happenings.

Yet many others will be enjoying the attractions at nearby tourist destinations in Myrtle Beach, ranging from putt-putt to dinner shows to water slides. It claims over 17 million visitors per year and 60 miles of beaches along the Grand Strand. Tourist pursuits of every stripe can be undertaken. Shopping, amusement parks, go-kart rides, and eateries line US 17. It's a fun place to people-watch, too. Make Myrtle Beach State Park your coastal trail diversion while in the tourist haven that is the Grand Strand.

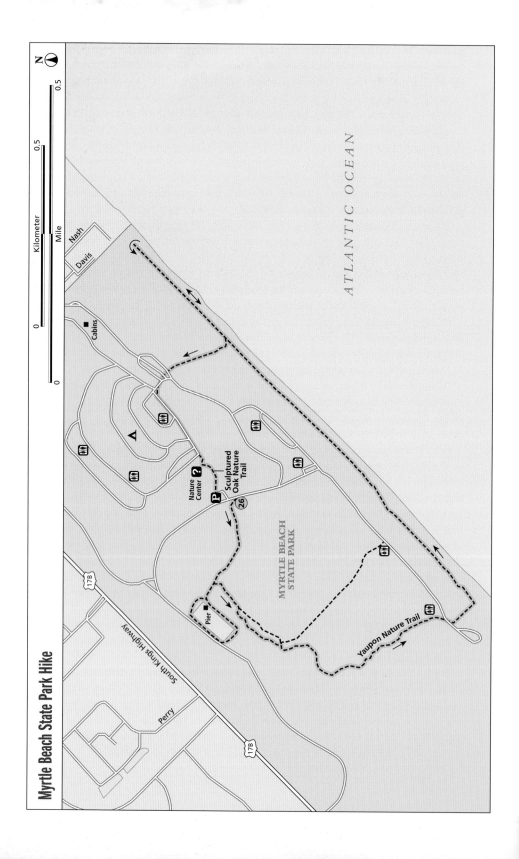

Myrtle Beach State Park Hike

Kilometer
0   0.5   0.5

Mile
0   0.5

N

Nash
Davis
Cabins

Nature
Center
P

Sculptured
Oak Nature
Trail

26

MYRTLE BEACH
STATE PARK

Pier

17B

South Kings Highway

Perry

17B

Yaupon Nature Trail

ATLANTIC OCEAN

Beach view from the state park pier

MILES AND DIRECTIONS

0.0 Pick up the Sculptured Oak Nature Trail across from the nature center parking area. Enter the last stand of forest left along the Grand Strand, the only undeveloped beach tract in Horry County. Magnolia, oaks, loblolly pine, and wax myrtle rise above. Ahead a short spur goes left to overflow camping; stay right. Bridge a small creek.

0.2 Come to an intersection. Here, stay straight, aiming to circle a small freshwater pond. Walk out to the pier and scan for gators, then circle the pond. Return to the Sculptured Oak Trail. Enjoy the interpretive information.

0.6 Split right on the Yaupon Nature Trail.

0.7 The Sculptured Oak and Yaupon Nature Trails reconnect. Stay right again, still with the Yaupon Nature Trail. More interpretive information enhances the experience. Begin turning toward the ocean.

1.0 Cross a wooded boardwalk with a freshwater swamp nearby.

1.1 Emerge at picnic shelter B6. Cross the park road, then take the boardwalk to the Atlantic Ocean beach. Turn left, with the surf to your right.

1.4 Hop over a tidal creek just before walking under the park's fishing pier. Keep along the beach, passing accesses linking each to parking.

1.8 Pass the campground access. You will return here later. For now, continue on the beach, passing the park cabins access.

2.0 Reach the park boundary and backtrack to enter the park campground access, crossing the dune line.

2.4 Pass the campground check-in building, then head left past the ranger station, leaving the campground via wide trail.

2.5 Reach the nature center. Pay a visit, then keep straight.

2.6 Arrive back at the nature center parking area, completing the coastal hike.

27. HUNTINGTON BEACH HIKE

Enjoy a combination woods and beach hike here at scenic Huntington Beach State Park, a preserve with more than just trails. Begin your hike in maritime woods on the Sandpiper Pond Nature Trail to come alongside an estuary separating you from the Atlantic Ocean and beachfront. Roll through undulating forest under windswept trees to emerge at an elevated deck where you can scan Sandpiper Pond for wildlife. Meet an alternate parking area, then hit the beach. Here you can walk betwixt ocean and dune to Murrells Inlet and its long jetty, where an asphalt track atop the jetty can lead you well out to water. On the backtrack, wander the beach, scanning for shells and doing a little people-watching.

THE RUNDOWN

Distance: 5.0-mile there-and-back
Start: Sandpiper Pond trailhead
Nearest town: Murrells Inlet
Hiking time: 2.6 hours
Fees and permits: Entrance fee
Conveniences: Restrooms, water fountain, picnic area, campground at state park
Beach access: Yes
Trail users: Hikers, beachcombers
Trail surface: Natural
Difficulty: Easy to moderate

Highlights: Sandpiper Pond, wildlife viewing, Atlantic Ocean beach, jetty walk
Canine compatibility: Leashed dogs permitted on trail only; no dogs allowed north of North Beach access
Schedule: Daily from 6 a.m. to 6 p.m. (extended to 10 p.m. during daylight saving time)
Managing agency: Huntington Beach State Park, 16148 Ocean Hwy., Murrells Inlet, SC 29576; (843)237-4440; www.southcarolinaparks.com/huntingtonbeach

FINDING THE TRAILHEAD

From Myrtle Beach, take US 17 South for 16 miles to the state park, on your left. Enter the park, passing the entrance station, and continue for 0.4 mile; turn left onto the road leading toward the North Beach access. Follow it for 0.2 mile, parking on the right just after passing the marsh boardwalk on your left. This parking area is labeled "Sandpiper Pond Nature Trail, Overflow Parking." (The overflow parking is for the marsh boardwalk and the former nature center.) GPS trailhead coordinates: 33.510164, -79.061696

WHAT TO SEE

Huntington Beach State Park boasts 3 miles of Atlantic Ocean beach as the centerpiece of its 2,500 acres situated between Murrells Inlet and Litchfield Beach. The land was once the winter home of Mr. and Mrs. Archer and Anna Hyatt Huntington. Nearly a century ago, in 1930, the Huntingtons were floating the Intracoastal Waterway when they noticed this scenic swath of South Carolina and fell in love with it. The wealthy New Yorkers bought the land right then and there, enthusiastically conjuring up plans for the property. They wanted to build a house in which to spend the winters, while simultaneously preserving the property's beauty, ranging from the tidal streams to maritime forests

Walking the beach on a foggy day

to Atlantic beach. They began building an intriguing brick house, expanding the plans as they went along, always remembering to keep it strong for the hurricanes that occasionally made their way to the Carolina coast. Today you can tour their home, viewing the tower-centered courtyard, and explore Mrs. Huntington's sculpture studios. The couple enjoyed the property for a decade and a half, making their last stay in 1947. Ultimately, Mrs. Huntington leased the property to the State of South Carolina for the state park we enjoy today, and they also lent their property to what has become Brookgreen Gardens.

Brookgreen Gardens stands across from the state park, divided by US 17. If the Huntingtons could see how their property has become an icon of the Carolina coast! The mission of 9,000-acre Brookgreen Gardens is

> *To collect, conserve and exhibit figurative sculpture by American artists; To cultivate a display garden and exhibit sculpture therein; To collect, conserve and exhibit the plants, animals and cultural materials of the South Carolina Lowcountry; To educate a diverse audience about sculpture, horticulture and the ecology and history of the Lowcountry; To provide additional artists and cultural opportunities for members, guests and the community; and To sustain the institution and all of its assets with visionary leadership, sound management and prudent fiscal policies.*

They do it all well at Brookgreen Gardens. The artist in Mrs. Huntington would be proud. Add a tour here to your state park visit. Special events take place throughout the year. For more information, visit www.brookgreen.org.

Your hike at Huntington Beach State Park can be special, too. Your blood will start pumping as you listen to the Atlantic breaking against the shoreline. The Sandpiper Pond Nature Trail leads under pines and live oaks to shortly reach a spur trail, on your right, turning to the marsh boardwalk trailhead. Our hike heads left under cedars and pines and yaupon growing from rolling former dunes.

Top: Even gulls like hiking at Huntington Beach State Park.
Bottom: This jetty is popular with anglers.

The trail remains in thick woods but comes along Sandpiper Pond, a tarn that through the years has been opened and closed to the ocean during storms. In places, short spurs will open to the edge of Sandpiper Pond, where you can look over the estuary beyond to the sandy partly vegetated beach facing the Atlantic. Overhead the tree branches take unusual configurations formed by continual breezes blowing in from the Atlantic. In places, especially where the path is open to the sun overhead, the sandy trail bed can make for slow travel.

Staying roughly along Sandpiper Pond, the view changes moment to moment. One minute you are under dark widespread cedars, and the next minute along an open sun-burnished path bordered by waterside thickets. Other times live oaks form a woodland roof. Finally you open onto an elevated wooden platform, good for wildlife and land-scape viewing.

Then comes the beach walk, after crossing the dunes via a path. Once out here, head left toward Murrells Inlet. As with any beach, weather and time of year dictate whether it is crowded or not. You can see your goal in the distance—the Murrells Inlet jetty, curving seaward. This part of the beach is a park-declared bird sanctuary, therefore dogs are not allowed. You will likely be watching for gulls and doing a little people-watching, too, a time-honored tradition on beaches.

Upon reaching the jetty you will be looking for underwater wildlife. Murrells Inlet and the jetty are often heavily populated with anglers vying for saltwater species including flounder, redfish, mackerel, and more. Walk to the end of the jetty for fun if you desire a little more mileage. Otherwise, return down the beach and the Sandpiper Pond Nature Trail.

The historic home known as Atalaya

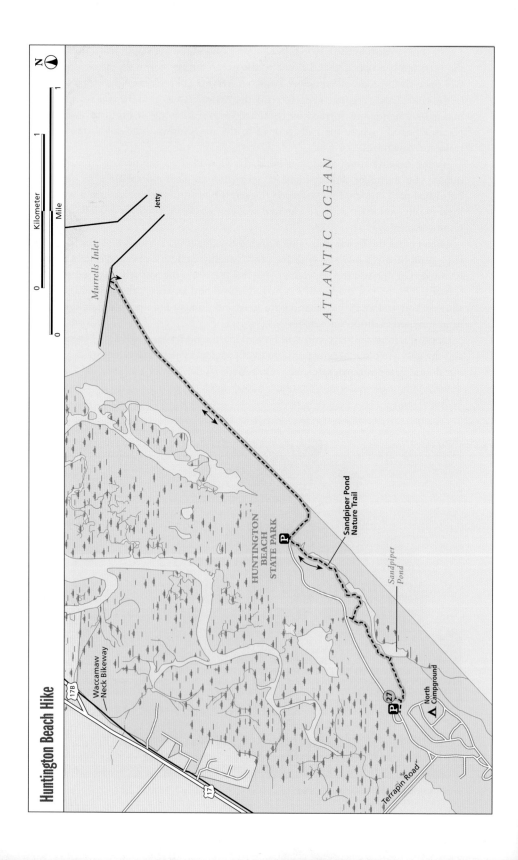

Huntington Beach Hike

N

Kilometer
Mile

ATLANTIC OCEAN

Murrells Inlet

Jetty

HUNTINGTON
BEACH
STATE PARK

Waccamaw
Neck Bikeway

Sandpiper Pond
Nature Trail

Sandpiper
Pond

North
Campground

Terrapin Road

P

P 27

17B

17

Beachcombers at Huntington Beach

There's even more to do here at Huntington Beach State Park. Consider camping and historical study, among other pursuits. You've got to check out the Huntington's home, Atalaya. Ranger-led tours are most informative. The home is shockingly different than what most visitors expect. Weddings and other special events are held regularly at Atalaya.

Campers can enjoy two distinct camping areas, with nearly 180 sites. Most have electricity and water, though some also have sewer. Tent campers will enjoy six special walk-in sites shaded by live oaks and pines. This campground is hopping during the warm season, full nearly every weekend from March through September, and in mid-summer. However, reservations can be made to quell concerns. Winter can be a good time to see this park; there are fewer visitors, less heat, and fewer bugs, and hiking here when it's colder can be invigorating.

MILES AND DIRECTIONS

0.0 Join the Sandpiper Pond Nature Trail under pines and live oaks. Stay left as a trail comes in from the right, leading to the marsh boardwalk. Roll among ancient dunes.

0.2 Sandpiper Pond comes into the view through the trees. Ahead, spurs open to the pond and you can view the pond and the ocean beyond.

0.5 Cross a small tidal creek connecting to Sandpiper Pond. Just beyond there, a user-created trail leads left and connects to a park road, while the nature trail turns right. Other boardwalks lead you across wet areas.

1.0 Come to the elevated platform overlooking Sandpiper Pond. Climb 20 feet up and see what lies in the yon, from alligators to herons and plovers to seagulls. The Atlantic crashes in the distance. Leave the platform, then immediately come to an alternate parking area and the North Beach access. This is a potentially busy area, but it has a picnic area and restrooms. Follow the wide path leading to the Atlantic beach.

1.1 Come to the Atlantic Ocean. Head left, northeasterly, for the jetty. Enjoy the wide sands with the Atlantic to your right and sea oat–covered dunes to your left.

2.5 Come to the Murrells Inlet jetty. Note it is overlain in asphalt, allowing visitors to walk atop it. From here you can head left toward the marsh or right into the Atlantic. This is a popular fishing area. See what's biting. Backtrack.

5.0 Arrive back at the trailhead, completing the woodland and oceanic coastal hike.

28. SANTEE COASTAL RESERVE

This coastal loop hike tours a large tract astride the lower South Santee River as the waterway transitions from freshwater to brackish to tidal waters. The 24,000-acre reserve presents multiple habitats centered by the Washo Reserve, home to the oldest continuously used bird rookery in the United States. Our hike mostly traces the Ormand Hall Trail as it first comes near Washo Reserve, where you can see nesting birds among other wildlife. Next the loop wanders deep into remote woods before coming along coastal marsh, where you can gaze across wetlands to the Intracoastal Waterway. Finally you return to forest and more marsh before completing the hike.

THE RUNDOWN

Distance: 6.5-mile loop with boardwalk spur
Start: Wildlife Management Area campground
Nearest town: McClellanville
Hiking time: 3.5 hours
Fees and permits: Free permit required
Conveniences: Campground near trailhead
Beach access: No
Trail users: Hikers, birders
Trail surface: Natural

Difficulty: Moderate
Highlights: Bird rookery, varied habitats, marsh views
Canine compatibility: Leashed dogs permitted
Schedule: Daily from sunrise to sunset; closed during managed hunts
Managing agency: Santee Coastal Reserve, 210 Santee Gun Club Rd., McClellanville, SC 29458; (843) 546-6062; www.dnr.sc.gov

FINDING THE TRAILHEAD

From the intersection of SC 45 and US 17 in McClellanville, take US 17 North for 3 miles to the signed right turn for Santee Coastal Reserve on Santee Coastal Road. Stay on Santee Coastal Road for 2.6 miles to reach Santee Gun Club Road. Turn right onto Santee Gun Club Road, shortly entering Santee Coastal Reserve, driving a total of 2.7 miles to reach a parking area on the left and a gate. Alternate directions from Georgetown: From the intersection of US 17 and US 17A in Georgetown, take US 17 South for 16.3 miles to South Santee Road. Turn left onto South Santee Road and follow it for 1.4 miles to Santee Gun Club Road. Turn left on Santee Gun Club Road, shortly entering Santee Coastal Reserve, driving a total of 2.7 miles to reach a parking area on the left and a gate. GPS trailhead coordinates: 33.153750, -79.366763

WHAT TO SEE

If you are looking for a quiet coastal hike in the back of beyond, come to Santee Coastal Wildlife Management Area. Formerly home to Santee Indians, the land became a plantation during the colonial period and after the United States became a country, established by one Joseph Blake. On this property Blake grew indigo, cotton, and rice. To grow rice, a planter needs a reliable source of water. Blake dammed a tributary of the Santee River to flood his rice lands when they needed it. Blake liked his new pond, but wildlife liked it

Forests tower over wetlands in this rich environmental preserve.

even more. Unbeknownst to Blake he also established a bird rookery, a freshwater cypress lake and cypress-gum swamp that has been used by egrets, wood storks, and other nesting birds for over two centuries.

Time moved on and the Civil War just about did in the Blake Plantation. The farm limped along until the 1898 Hurricane truly did it in. About that time the Santee Gun Club was established and bought the land. They realized the marshes of the plantation were rich with waterfowl. The Santee Gun Club acquired still more land for their private hunting retreat. Then, in 1974, the gun club donated over 24,000 acres to the Nature Conservancy, ranging from freshwater to saltwater to coastal islands and beaches (only accessible by boat). The Nature Conservancy in turn deeded most of the land to

Blooms add color to a cloudy day.

the South Carolina Department of Natural Resources (DNR), keeping back the area around the Washo Reserve pond. The South Carolina DNR manages the former plantation, enhancing the flora and fauna, from the wood storks of Washo Reserve to the waterfowl of the marshes to the loggerhead turtles on the beaches. The reserve boasts the largest concentrations of nesting ospreys in the country.

The Ormand Hall Trail is marked with red-tipped posts its entire length. The path uses a series of closed doubletrack roads that lead you throughout the reserve. Fall through spring is the best time to visit the preserve. Mosquitoes can be rough when the weather warms up.

The reserve is open from 8 a.m. to 5 p.m. daily but is closed the first full week in October, the first two full weeks of November, the first full week in December, and Wednesday and Saturday between January 21 and March 1. Hunts go on at the reserve during these times. If you want to confirm that the reserve will be open, call (843) 546-8665. By the way, Santee Coastal Reserve has a beautiful campground shaded by regal live oaks. Applications must be submitted and approved in advance. The application is found on the Santee Coastal Reserve DNR website.

To improve habitat in the Washo Reserve rookery, the Nature Conservancy and the South Carolina DNR have been planting new cypress trees to replace dying ones and attempting to rid the pond of excessive waterweeds by altering water levels and chemically treating the weeds. This has increased open water, making it better for wood storks. On this hike you will go by the dam installed in 2013 to better manage water levels in Washo Reserve.

It can be difficult to figure out exactly where to begin your hike. After parking on the campground side of Santee Gun Club Road very near the campground, you will find an informative kiosk with a map in a grassy area. From the kiosk head southwest into woods to pick up a doubletrack that is both the Marshland Trail and the Ormand Hall Trail. Note the yellow- and red-tipped posts. (The yellow-tipped posts indicate the Marshland Trail.) Join a doubletrack entering swamp woods with live oaks to soon reach the Washo Reserve Boardwalk. This boardwalk leads southwest above wooded swamp. Look for birds and alligators.

After backtracking the boardwalk, continue the Ormand Hall Trail, heading southwest among fern-floored swamp trees, pines, hollies, and live oaks before opening onto Washo Reserve. Clear vistas open of the pond and the cypress trees around and in it. Beyond the water, rise into pines broken with fields. Note the white-banded pine trees, nesting areas for red cockaded woodpeckers. Ahead the trail changes roads and continues its grand loop. (By the way, all these doubletracks are open to vehicular travel only by management personnel.) After turning back east, the hike comes along dikes, traveling atop them, with freshwater marshes to the left and tidal brackish marshes to the right, seaward. Ahead the Cape Trail leaves to your right and makes a 7-mile loop. This is a favorable bicycling

Wetlands here attract coastal bird life.

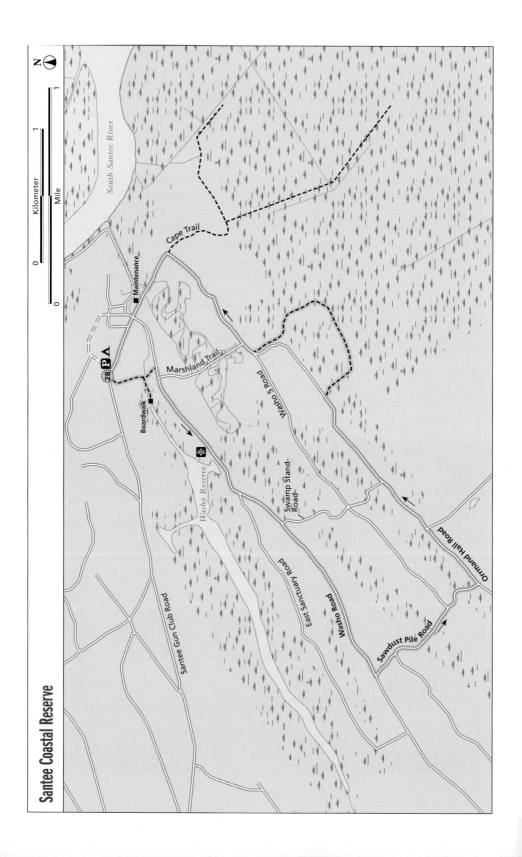

Santee Coastal Reserve

N

0   1   Kilometer
0   1   Mile

South Santee River

Cape Trail

Maintenance

28 P

Marshland Trail

Boardwalk

Washo Reserve

Washo S Road

Swamp Stand Road

Santee Gun Club Road

East Sanctuary Road

Washo Road

Ormand Hall Road

Sawdust Pile Road

option, but be sure you have sunscreen, as much of the circuit traverses shadeless dikes. The bike route travels alongside the Intracoastal Waterway at points. The Ormand Hall Trail turns left at its junction with the Cape Trail, joining a dike crossing open marsh to pass through the DNR maintenance area. Walk among the management tools of the trade—boats, tractors, farm implements, and the people to run them, working to maximize the wildlife management area for the birds, beasts, and flora within.

Beyond the maintenance area the hike passes the reserve office and other buildings as you walk among fields. Return to the trailhead, recollecting the variety of habitats encountered on this preserved coastal swath of the Palmetto State.

MILES AND DIRECTIONS

0.0 Leave southwest from the trailhead kiosk in a grassy area. Enter forest and join a doubletrack heading through swamp woods.

0.2 Come to an intersection. Here, head right on the Washo Reserve boardwalk, going a long way above wooded swamp to end at a partial view of the reserve. The water levels may be lowered to discourage waterweeds. Backtrack, then resume the Ormand Hall Trail.

0.6 Turn right at a three-way intersection. Head southwest in woods. Just ahead the Marshland Trail splits left. Keep straight.

1.1 Come to a stellar view of Washo Reserve at the dam and water control structure. Scan for egrets, anhingas, night herons, ospreys, bald eagles, and, of course, wood storks in the 200-acre freshwater pond once known as Blake's Reserve. Enjoy the solitude of the piney woods ahead.

1.3 Split left on Washo Road as the East Sanctuary Road splits right. Traverse a variety of environments from fields to upland woods, maximizing wildlife.

1.5 Swamp Stand Road heads left. Stay straight.

2.4 The Ormand Hall Trail turns left on Sawdust Pile Road. Look for the old huge tree-covered sawdust pile to the right of the road. Look for wildlife clearings dotted with fruit trees. Just ahead Sundew Road leaves right; stay straight on Sawdust Pile Road. The terrain turns swampy.

2.9 Washo 5 Road leaves left. Stay straight.

3.1 Turn left, joining Ormand Hall Road, now heading east–northeast. Marshy flats begin opening to your right.

3.5 Long Island Road leaves right. Keep straight.

3.8 Pass the other end of Swamp Stand Road. Keep straight, pass open food plots.

4.3 Turn right onto Fish Pond Road. Open onto marshy terrain, traversing dikes.

4.5 Curve left with open marsh to your right.

5.1 Reenter woods and rejoin Ormand Hall Road.

5.2 Head right on Washo 5 Road.

5.3 The Marshland Trail comes in on your left. Keep straight.

5.9 Intersect the Cape Trail leaving right. Our hike heads left on a sturdy gravel road, opening onto a dike with marsh views in both directions.

6.1 Bisect the DNR maintenance area. Ahead, stay left on a gravel road. Pass a parking area for the Cape Trail. Continue on the gravel road with buildings to your right.

6.5 Arrive back at the trailhead, completing the coastal hike.

29. TRAILS OF SOUTH TIBWIN

This hike offers some of the finest views in the Lowcountry. The terrain through which you walk is the former Tibwin Plantation, now part of the Francis Marion National Forest. Traverse thick woods and then come upon a freshwater impoundment, advantageous for birding. Work your way along dikes to the edge of Tibwin Creek, where marshes and woodlands stretch to the horizon, presenting natural vistas seldom seen in this part of the country. The views get even better when you come within sight of the Intracoastal Waterway, opening to the Atlantic Ocean and beyond, sans civilization. Other panoramas are of wildlife that call this parcel home.

THE RUNDOWN

Distance: 3.5-mile loop
Start: US 17 trailhead
Nearest town: McClellanville
Hiking time: 1.7 hours
Fees and permits: None
Conveniences: None
Beach access: No
Trail users: Hikers, bicyclists, birders
Trail surface: Natural
Difficulty: Easy to moderate

Highlights: Views, birding opportunities
Canine compatibility: Leashed dogs permitted
Schedule: 24/7/365
Managing agency: Francis Marion National Forest, 2967 Steed Creek Rd., Huger, SC 29450; (843) 336-3248; www.fs.usda.gov/main/scnfs/

FINDING THE TRAILHEAD

From exit 30 on I-526 in Mount Pleasant, follow US 17 North for 27 miles to the South Tibwin entrance, FR 245, on your right. This is 3.1 miles beyond Buck Hall Recreation Area. Parking is immediately after the turn. Alternate directions: From the intersection of SC 45 and US 17 in McClellanville, take US 17 South for 3.1 miles to the trailhead on your left. GPS trailhead coordinates: 33.070648, -79.520136

WHAT TO SEE

The land that once was South Tibwin Plantation is now a large tract of transitional terrain, where the tall pine forests of the inland Lowcountry morph to freshwater and brackish wetlands, ultimately linking to the Atlantic Ocean. The US Forest Service acquired South Tibwin in 1996 as part of its efforts to create a natural transition area from land to sea.

And the plan has worked. South Tibwin is now an important birding habitat on the Atlantic Flyway. Not only is it an important wildlife corridor, the tract also houses the most significant historic building on the entire 260,000-acre Francis Marion National Forest, the South Tibwin Plantation manor. This two-story wooden building was built in 1803. South Tibwin Plantation came to be in 1705 when an English land grant was given to one Captain John Collins. In the 1700s it continued to pass through his family, but it was ultimately acquired by William Matthews, who built the historic house and land. Originally the manor was closer to the ocean, but it was later moved back from the

Gates like this are used to control water levels at South Tibwin.

waterfront after a hurricane threatened the home. South Tibwin continued to be inhabited and the land worked in rice, Sea Island cotton, and potatoes.

By the late 1930s, South Tibwin seems to have been abandoned, and the home fell into disrepair, with a hunt club established on the property interested in hunting South Tibwin, rather than living there. Interestingly, Henry Ford purchased a rice mill from South Tibwin Plantation, and it is still on display in Dearborn, Michigan. The rice days are long gone, but wildlife thrives on the big tract. Furthermore, interest has grown in preserving the plantation house, partly due to its significance to the area and the certainty that the South Carolina Lowcountry is being developed at a rate that is surprising everyone. And once a historic building is lost, it is gone forever. Hurricane Hugo tore the roof

Flowering buckeye along the trail

off the house but the US Forest Service replaced the roof and stabilized the building. In 2014, the house was stabilized again, as the front porch was pulling away from the front of the structure. More funds are being sought to complete a restoration of the house, which is estimated to cost around $500,000.

You will not see the plantation house on your hike. It is across Tibwin Creek. However, you will view a variety of woods, waters, marshes, and even the Intracoastal Waterway and Cape Romain National Wildlife Refuge. Take note: The trails are not named but are merely a network of tracks. The hike joins a closed forest road then loops past a Forest Service dwelling, before curving along a freshwater impoundment. Walk along the pond, then turn alongside tidal Tibwin Creek, where cordgrass marshes and natural coastal scenes please the eye. The trails are doubletrack, allowing you to absorb the scenery, as well as scan for birds, rather than watching every footfall.

Year-round resident birds include a wide variety, from songbirds to seaside species: king rail, pileated woodpecker, anhinga, white ibis, red-shouldered hawk, brown-headed nuthatch, and seaside sparrow. Ducks and eagles come to South Tibwin in winter, while summer finds the indigo bunting, swallow-tailed kite, Mississippi kite, whippoorwills, and more. The best birding is March through June. And of course other species use the Atlantic Flyway, the bird migratory route stretching from Greenland in the north, down the east coasts of Canada and the United States, down to the Caribbean, and beyond to South America. The route is favorable for migratory wildlife because it offers food and cover the whole route (that is why places like South Tibwin are so important). Think of raptors such as bald eagles, geese and other waterfowl, and songbirds such as American goldfinch and black-capped junco. Understand that not all species travel the entire length of the flyway—most don't. Crossing oceans can be arduous. Some species move just 300 or 400 miles in search of a better climate and food sources.

More views open as you come closer to the coast and are walking atop elevated open dikes that avail views in all directions, including seaward. These are some of the best panoramas in the Lowcountry. More ponds lie out here and are important bird nesting areas. For this reason, some trails are closed seasonally. The last part of the hike leads

Coastal lands here are bordered by grassy estuaries.

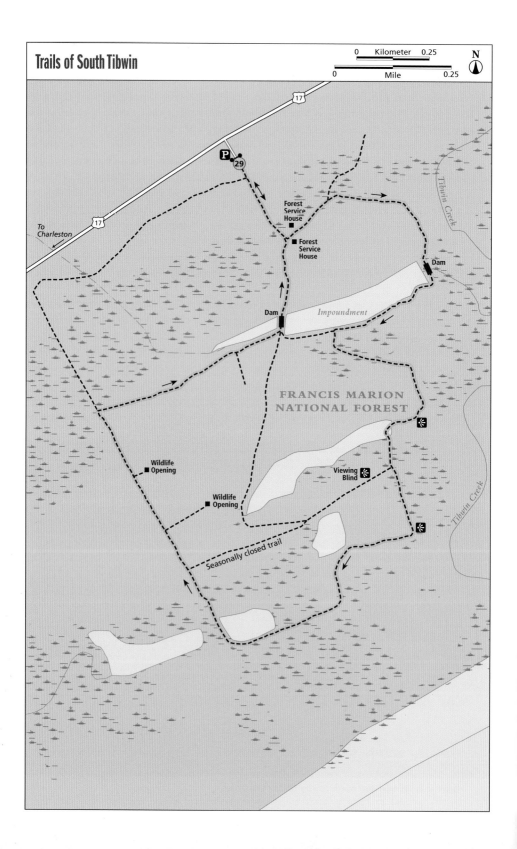

Trails of South Tibwin

0 Kilometer 0.25

0 Mile 0.25

N

17

P

29

To Charleston

17

Forest Service House

Forest Service House

Dam

Impoundment

Dam

Tibwin Creek

FRANCIS MARION NATIONAL FOREST

Wildlife Opening

Wildlife Opening

Viewing Blind

Tibwin Creek

Seasonally closed trail

through freshwater swamps and back to upland forest and the trailhead. After your hike you'll appreciate this parcel of the Lowcountry that is fast being developed as the South Carolina coast continues to grow in popularity. And the birds that call South Tibwin home—and those passing through the Atlantic Flyway—appreciate it too.

MILES AND DIRECTIONS

0.0   Leave the parking area on US 17, heading south on gated FR 245. Just ahead, a trail enters on the right. Keep straight on the forest road.

0.2   Reach an intersection in woods near a house and other national forest buildings. Head left, passing between a house on your right and a screened shelter on your left, northeasterly.

0.3   A lesser-used doubletrack heads left, but you stay right.

0.6   Curve near Tibwin Creek, then cross the dam over an impoundment. You are looking out on tidal brackish marsh to your left and freshwater pond to your right. Ahead, turn along the impoundment.

0.9   Turn left, away from the impoundment, southbound.

1.1   Stay right as a dead-end trail goes left. Ahead, pass wild views to the southeast.

1.4   Keep straight as a seasonally closed trail leaves right. Open onto a dike with wide-open marsh vistas.

1.6   The dike turns right. Look for the Intracoastal Waterway and Cape Romain in the distance. Wilderness views abound.

2.7   Turn right, northeasterly, as the trail you have been on heads north toward US 17.

3.1   Turn left at a four-way intersection, crossing a dam separating two impoundments. Keep north.

3.3   Return to the forest service dwelling, completing the loop. Backtrack north on gated FR 245.

3.5   Arrive back at the trailhead, completing the hike.

30. SWAMP FOX PASSAGE OF THE PALMETTO TRAIL

This lengthy trek stretches for almost 50 miles through Lowcountry forests, where blackwater swamps, regal pinewoods, biologically diverse shrub bogs, and wilderness reign. Part of South Carolina's 500-plus mile Palmetto Trail, the Swamp Fox Passage presents a chance for an extended coastal backpacking opportunity where you can immerse yourself in untamed lands.

THE RUNDOWN

Distance: 47.6 miles end to end
Start: US 52 Swamp Fox Passage trailhead
Nearest town: Bonneau
Hiking time: 23 hours
Fees and permits: None
Conveniences: None
Beach access: No
Trail users: Backpackers, hikers, and mountain bikers
Trail surface: Natural

Difficulty: Difficult due to distance
Highlights: Spring wildflowers, autumn colors, long distance hike
Canine compatibility: Leashed dogs permitted
Schedule: 24/7/365
Managing agency: Francis Marion National Forest, Francis Marion Ranger District Office, 2967 Steed Creek Rd., Huger, SC 29450; (843) 336-2200; www.fs.usda.gov/scnfs/

FINDING THE TRAILHEAD

From the intersection of US 17 and I-526 in Mount Pleasant, take US 17 North for 21.3 miles to the signed Swamp Fox Passage of the Palmetto trailhead on your left. US 17 trailhead GPS: 33.037510, -79.617581. To reach the hike's beginning, backtrack on US 17 South for 0.2 mile, then turn right onto Steed Creek Road and follow it 12 miles to the intersection with SC 41 in Huger. Here, cross SC 41 and join SC 402 West and follow it for 16 miles to the intersection with US 52. Turn right on US 52 West and follow it for 4.2 miles to the signed trailhead on your right. US 52 trailhead GPS: 33.277978, -79.962553

WHAT TO SEE

The Swamp Fox Passage of the Palmetto Trail extends east–west across the breadth of coastal Francis Marion National Forest. The forest was named for South Carolina's Revolutionary War hero whom the English named the "Swamp Fox" for his penchant to attack then disappear into the watery backwoods, before harassing the Redcoats again and again, all the while using fighting techniques he learned from aboriginal South Carolinians. Francis Marion is a bona fide South Carolina hero whose name graces places all over the state.

Built when the 1960s outdoor craze swept the country, what was originally called Swamp Fox Trail was later incorporated into part of South Carolina's master path, the Palmetto Trail. Today the Swamp Fox Passage offers the longest coastal backpacking opportunity in the Carolinas. Designated primitive campsites are scattered in convenient distances along the trail. The camps offer a fire ring and nearby water access. The sites are first come, first served. Although the Swamp Fox Passage of the Palmetto Trail

Fall colors near Harleston Dam

crosses remote forest roads and occasional paved roads, a backwoods aura prevails as it winds through the 250,000-plus acres that compose the Francis Marion National Forest. Almost all streams are bridged. Plank boardwalks extend over most wetlands. Much of the hike traces old logging railroad trams, elevated passages through otherwise impenetrable, often wet terrain. Do not hike this trail in the summer; the heat will wilt you and the mosquitoes will eat you alive. Autumn offers fall colors and dry conditions, while in spring wetland expanses and wildflowers will be highlights. Winter offers maximum solitude.

A few more points: Watch for foot-eating potholes in the trail, left by eroded pines. The plank boardwalks can be slippery, and some are in varied states of disrepair. Use the plank boardwalks with caution, especially after rains. The trail is generally 4 feet wide

Crossing a narrow plank walkway

and mown through the pines. Sections using old logging trams can be arrow straight and are elevated above the surrounding wetlands, allowing you intimate glimpses into otherwise inaccessible terrain. Here, watch for the roots of cypress trees extending into the path. The detailed maps of Swamp Fox Passage of the Palmetto Trail, found at palmetto conservation.org, are very useful. The entire track is well signed and well blazed, so you shouldn't get lost. However, be watchful where the path goes off and on or crosses dirt forest roads.

The adventure starts at the US 52 trailhead near Lake Moultrie. After initiating yourself in intermittent wetlands using plank boardwalks, you bridge beautiful Wadboo Swamp on a long boardwalk and elevated bridge. From there you rise to pinelands and cross the newer bridge over Cane Gully to make Witherbee Ranger Station, where additional

Pitcher plants thrive in wetlands along the hike.

trailhead parking is available. From there the Swamp Fox Passage of the Palmetto Trail wanders upland to pick up an old logging tram to find swamp hardwoods of beech and maple, providing abundant color in autumn. Logging trams and standard trails lead you among magnificent evergreens of live oak and pine, passing through the strange phenomena that are Carolina bay lakes. Eventually bridge freshwater but tidal Steed Creek, ending at the US 17 trailhead on the east end of the national forest, very near the Intracoastal Waterway and the Atlantic Ocean. Note: In the Miles and Directions segment, only paved road crossings are noted. The Swamp Fox Passage of the Palmetto Trail crosses numerous dirt national forest roads in the course of its journey from Lake Moultrie to US 17.

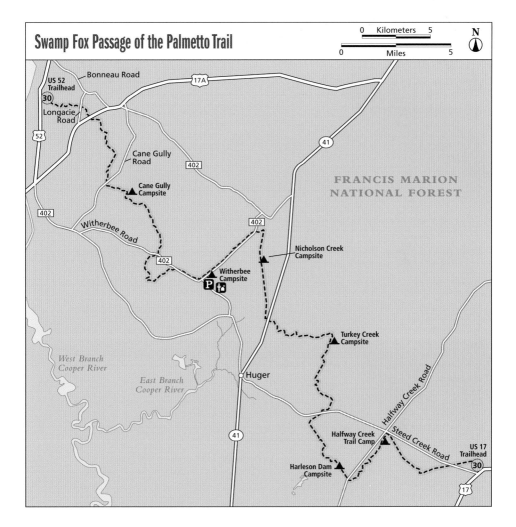

Swamp Fox Passage of the Palmetto Trail

FRANCIS MARION
NATIONAL FOREST

US 52 Trailhead
Bonneau Road
Longacie Road
Cane Gully Road
Cane Gully Campsite
Witherbee Road
Witherbee Campsite
Nicholson Creek Campsite
Turkey Creek Campsite
West Branch Cooper River
East Branch Cooper River
Huger
Halfway Creek Road
Steed Creek Road
Halfway Creek Trail Camp
US 17 Trailhead
Harleson Dam Campsite

MILES AND DIRECTIONS

0.0 Leave east from the US 52 trailhead on the signed Swamp Fox Passage of the Palmetto Trail. It isn't long before you experience plank boardwalks over wetlands flowing among pine/oak woods.

2.2 Cross paved Longacie Road.

3.0 Cross US 17A to enter longleaf wiregrass woods, bordered by wetlands of beard cane and wax myrtle.

4.2 Enter big Wadboo Swamp and bottomland hardwoods. Bridge Wadboo Creek, then come to a centuries-old rice cultivation area. Walk grid pattern slave-built dikes bordered with hand-dug canals. This is a super scenic area, take your time.

6.4 Cross Callum Branch after rising into pines from Wadboo Swamp.

7.2 Bisect paved Cane Gully Road, then keep along the uplands above Cane Gully Branch. The stream and bordering swamps fall away to your right.

8.5 Span the swamps around Cane Gully Branch on a dike, bridging the actual stream on an iron truss bridge erected in 2019. Come to pine-shaded Cane Gully primitive camp on your left just after the bridge. Hike southeast in pines broken by sporadic wetlands, crossing occasional dirt forest roads.

12.6 Cross paved Witherbee Road. Look for pitcher plants in the wetter margins. Wander among occasional pine plantations.

14.5 Span Alligator Creek. Rise to walk among longleaf pines then cross Witherbee Road again in 1.2 miles.

16.3 Walk across Little Hellhole Reserve Dam, an important waterfowl area in the Francis Marion National Forest. Briefly join Witherbee Road to cross the Seaboard Coast railroad tracks, then reenter woods.

17.0 Reach attractive, oak-shaded Witherbee campsite. A nearby man-made ditch provides water.

17.7 Pass the Witherbee Ranger Station with trailhead parking. Continue in evergreens, running parallel to Witherbee Road.

20.8 Cross Witherbee Road a final time, then join a long, straight southbound logging tram through wooded swamps. This tram is part of a 300-mile, century-plus-old logging tram network that timbered these coastal woods prior to their becoming national forest. Enjoy being dry footed in a hardwood swamp.

22.5 Come to pine-shaded Nicholson Creek campsite just before Nicholson Creek, then span the stream on dikes and bridges.

25.4 Cross paved SC 41 then begin walking the hardwood forests along Turkey Creek. This section traverses the margins above the creek as well as through bottomlands. Span small tributaries of Turkey Creek.

28.5 The Jericho Horse Trail leaves left.

29.5 Bridge Turkey Creek in scenic swampy hardwood bottoms. Rise to pines and sweetgums to soon meet the Turkey Creek campsite, with a fire ring. Turn south in high pines before making a dogleg around Dog Swamp. You can see the swamp's hardwood forest on your right for some distance.

34.1 Cross paved Steed Creek Road. Enter dense forest with pond pines. Ahead, join a southeast-bound logging tram, jumping off it to span Harleston Dam Creek on a forest road before rejoining the tram.

38.1 Reach Harleston Dam campsite, shaded in younger pines and oaks. Water is available from Southampton Creek to the southwest. Avoid water from the nearby small pond. Cross paved Halfway Creek Road in 0.6 mile. Walk among mature pines and live oaks in a scenic section.

41.6 Come to auto-accessible Halfway Creek Campground, with many campsites about, but no water. Shortly turn southeast on a railroad grade bisecting the unusual Carolina bay lakes, wooded wetlands mixed with evergreen shrub bogs. In places you can spot old rail ties in the grade. This is another superlatively scenic stretch of trail.

44.6 After leaving the railroad grade, go on and off a forest road in swamp on a well-signed and blazed trail, then join yet another railroad grade, eastbound.

46.0 Cross Steed Creek Road again, quickly picking up the logging grade again. Walk among tall trees and regal swamp woods surrounding Steed Creek.

46.8 Span Steed Creek on a sturdy iron bridge. Continue east.

47.1 Reach a trail intersection. Here the Awendaw Passage of the Palmetto Trail keeps straight, but we turn right, southbound, staying with the Swamp Fox Passage of the Palmetto Trail in live oaks.

47.6 Reach the Swamp Fox Passage trailhead on US 17, ending the extended coastal hiking adventure.

31. AWENDAW PASSAGE OF THE PALMETTO TRAIL

The Awendaw Passage of the Palmetto Trail is South Carolina's 500-plus mile trail's official eastern terminus. And it is a fitting endpoint, for it is generally acclaimed as the most beautiful passage of the entire path. This stellar coastal hike begins on the Intracoastal Waterway at Buck Hall Recreation Area, part of the Francis Marion National Forest. The Awendaw Passage works through piney woods and freshwater marshes before opening onto a bluff overlooking Awendaw Creek, a tidal stream wandering through saltwater marsh. Hike 'neath maritime forest of palm and live oak, often bridging tributaries of Awendaw Creek on wide boardwalks that open to extensive marshy panoramas. End at a canoe launch on Awendaw Creek with an alternative trailhead that avails an opportunity to make a one-way hike.

THE RUNDOWN

Distance: 4.4-mile end-to-end, 8.8-mile there-and-back
Start: US 52 Swamp Fox Passage trailhead
Nearest town: Awendaw
Hiking time: 2.2 or 4.4 hours
Fees and permits: Parking fee at Buck Hall Recreation Area
Conveniences: Picnic area, flush toilets, picnic shelter, campground, boat ramp
Beach access: No
Trail users: Hikers, bicyclists, backpackers

Trail surface: Natural
Difficulty: Moderate
Highlights: Views of tidal creek, Intracoastal Waterway
Canine compatibility: Leashed dogs permitted
Schedule: 24/7/365
Managing agency: Francis Marion National Forest, Francis Marion Ranger District Office, 2967 Steed Creek Rd., Huger, SC 29450; (843) 336-2200; www.fs.usda.gov/scnfs/

FINDING THE TRAILHEAD

 From the intersection of US 17 and US 17A in Georgetown, take US 17 South for 29 miles to the Buck Hall Recreation Area on your left. Turn into the recreation area; the trail begins on your left just before the recreation area boat ramp. There is a parking fee. Alternative directions from Charleston: Follow US 17 north for 30 miles to Buck Hall Recreation Area, on your right. Trailhead GPS: 33.039823, -79.560622

WHAT TO SEE

Raise your expectations on this coastal trail. Remember: The hike is every bit of 8.8 miles going out and back. The hike offers fine scenery in all seasons, but bring bug dope when making this hike during summer. If you want to make a shorter trek, you can turn around at any point or set up a shuttle to make it a one-way adventure. Either way, the scenery will not fail to please the eye.

Awendaw Creek

You could even make a combination hike/paddle here, using a canoe or kayak on Awendaw Creek and the Intracoastal Waterway, where hiking trailheads on either end are also both endowed with boat ramps. Thus, you can incorporate the 3.8-mile Awendaw Creek Canoe Trail through cordgrass marshes bordered by a maritime woodland standing atop resplendent bluffs. The waterway makes a serpentine course southeasterly as it follows the daily fluctuations of the tide, for the mouth of this creek is less than a mile from the Atlantic Ocean. Awendaw Creek opens onto the Intracoastal Waterway. There you will join boaters of all stripes, from anglers to sailors to hikers and paddlers like us. On one side you will have the national forest and the other will be Cape Romain National Wildlife Refuge. The paddle concludes with a trip northeasterly on

The trail travels bluffs above Awendaw Creek.

Morning view of Awendaw Creek

You can hike along Awendaw Creek, then paddle back to the trailhead.

the Intracoastal Waterway, where the boat ramp of Buck Hall Recreation Area awaits. No matter your preference, factor in the tides. The tides here are about two and a half hours behind that of Charleston Harbor.

Awendaw Creek has its origins in the Francis Marion National Forest. Its headwaters drain parts of Little Wambaw Swamp and Wambaw Swamp. Cooter Creek and Steed Creek flow from these wetlands, and along with Bell Creek all come together to form Awendaw Creek. Here the upper waters of Awendaw Creek briefly course through private land then reenter the national forest near the Awendaw Creek canoe launch. By this juncture the stream is tidal and brackish. A wide cordgrass marsh forms a wide wetland bordered by bluffs. The creek wanders through this wetland until it opens to the Intracoastal Waterway. Here the Intracoastal Waterway forms a wide channel heading southwest to northeast. You will be hiking atop the creekside bluffs above the marsh.

Buck Hall Recreation Area makes for a fine starting point; not only is it the eastern terminus of the entire Palmetto Trail, but Buck Hall also presents an intimate campground with fourteen RV sites that include electricity as well as five tent-only sites. The whole affair overlooks the Intracoastal Waterway. The campground features running water and hot showers. The busy boat ramp is frequented by day users and campers. The shaded picnic shelter at the trailhead comes in handy before or after your hike.

Being the eastern terminus of the Palmetto Trail, consider thru hiking the entire path and ending here at Buck Hall. The trail is slated to be around 500 miles long. Over 350 trail miles are completed. The project began in 1994. Just so you know, it took decades to complete the entire Appalachian Trail, and even today minor reroutes occur on the granddaddy of all long trails. Here in South Carolina, visualize starting the Palmetto Trail

Awendaw Passage of the Palmetto Trail

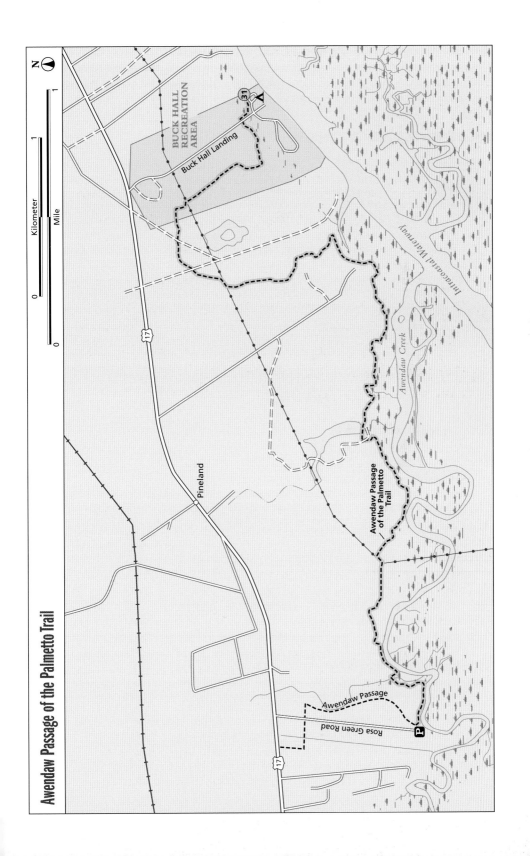

in the mountains of the Upstate, working your way through the Midlands (where most of the trail work is yet to be completed), and into the Lowcountry, the coastal lands, and finally here to Buck Hall. Ah, we can dream can't we? To learn more about the Palmetto Trail, go to www.palmettoconservation.org.

MILES AND DIRECTIONS

0.0 The Awendaw Passage of the Palmetto Trail leaves the day-use parking area near a picnic shelter. Immediately join a boardwalk that circles a palm tree commemorating both the Palmetto State and the Palmetto Trail. The boardwalk cuts through vegetated wetland before reaching dry land to cross the Buck Hall access road. Continue before curving right and nearing a large grassy overflow parking area.

0.6 Hike under a transmission line. Ahead, the trail makes a left, while the grassy track you've been following keeps straight. Stay with the blazes. Span a canal to cross a sand forest road.

1.1 Pass under the transmission line for the second time. You are working around a parcel of private property in mostly pines, increasing in oaks as you turn back toward the saltwater. Gently descend toward Awendaw Creek.

1.8 The Awendaw Passage comes to a boardwalk with handrails. Before you opens Awendaw Creek and the massive Intracoastal Waterway at a place known as Walnut Grove. Peer into the yon where the tidal marsh merges with open water. Spyglass for boats of all stripes, enjoying the aquatic portion of the setting. You have now reached the best—and extensive—portion of the coastal trail, with overhanging Spanish moss–draped oaks framing the panoramas. Ahead, tromp over small boardwalks in the wetter portions of the marsh.

2.3 Hike into a dense palm grove. The palms continue along Awendaw Creek, complemented by stately live oaks.

2.6 Cross a wide-open boardwalk.

2.8 Cross the largest tidal tributary of the hike using an extravagant iron-railed hiker bridge. Look down to determine the direction of the tide and outward to absorb broad marsh vistas. See if you can find where Awendaw Creek meets the Intracoastal Waterway. Boat-only accessible Cape Romain National Wildlife Refuge lies beyond the Intracoastal Waterway. Beyond the bridge fewer palm trees are found as the Awendaw Passage of the Palmetto Trail winds along the fringe where saltwater marsh and maritime woods converge. Views continue to open between live oaks.

3.3 The hike turns away from Awendaw Creek, entering oak woods after crossing a boardwalk.

3.6 Walk beneath a transmission line, still hiking through forest away from the salt marsh. Look for sweetgum trees in the forest. Turn back toward the bluffs overlooking the marsh.

4.0 Return to the bluff and walk along its edge. The bluff is highest here and is enhanced with contemplation benches overlooking the scene. See if you can spot the bluff on the far side of Awendaw Creek.

4.4 Come to the elaborate all-access canoe/kayak launch. It offers a chance for paddlers to access Awendaw Creek and for nonpaddlers to get close to the water. Walk down to the water and check the speed and direction of the tides. Just beyond here you reach the alternate trailhead for this hike. At this point you either have a bike, boat, or car shuttle, or you backtrack toward Buck Hall.

8.8 Arrive back at Buck Hall Recreation Area.

32. INTERPRETIVE TRAILS OF AWENDAW

Enjoy three interpretive trails near one another that you can easily hike in a day. First enjoy the 4,000-year-old Sewee Shell Ring and a 600-year-old clamshell midden, both vestiges of a previous culture, while walking woods and salt marsh. Next visit the Sewee Visitor and Environmental Center and the Nebo Nature Trail to learn about the Lowcountry. The third interpretive trail loops through I'on Swamp, where you walk dikes above dark waters, while birds call and other creatures lurk in the distance. Finally, walk what was once a working rice plantation from the 1700s, left to time and the elements.

THE RUNDOWN

Distance: 1.0 mile, 1.6 miles, 2.1 miles, respectively
Start: Sewee Shell Ring trailhead
Nearest town: Awendaw
Hiking time: 0.6, 0.9, 1.0 hour, respectively
Fees and permits: None
Conveniences: Sewee Visitor and Environmental Center offers restrooms, water fountain, picnic shelter
Beach access: No
Trail users: Families, naturalists, history buffs
Trail surface: Mostly natural, some boardwalk
Difficulty: Easy

Highlights: Ancient shell mound, interpretive information, historic canals
Canine compatibility: Leashed dogs not permitted on Nebo Nature Trail at Sewee Visitor and Environmental Center; leashed dogs otherwise permitted
Schedule: Sewee Shell Ring Trail, I'on Swamp Trail 24/7/365; Nebo Trail at Sewee Visitor and Environmental Center, Wed through Sat from 9 a.m. to 5 p.m.
Managing agency: Francis Marion National Forest, Francis Marion Ranger District Office, 2967 Steed Creek Rd., Huger, SC 29450; (843) 336-2200; www.fs.usda.gov/scnfs/

FINDING THE TRAILHEAD

To reach the first hike, Sewee Shell Ring Trail, from exit 30 on I-526 in Mount Pleasant, take US 17 North for 17.1 miles to a right turn on Doar Road. Pass the Awendaw water tower and Awendaw town hall, following Doar Road for 2.1 miles to Salt Pond Road, FR 243. Turn right on FR 243 and follow it 0.3 mile to the trailhead on your right. GPS trailhead coordinates: 33.001281, -79.609030. After that, backtrack to US 17, then turn left and follow US 17 South for 1.8 miles to reach the Sewee Visitor and Environmental Center. To reach I'on Swamp Trail, from the visitor center head south on US 17 for 0.3 mile, then turn right I'on Swamp Road and follow it for 2.5 miles to reach the trailhead on your left.

WHAT TO SEE

Bag three short and scenic hikes all close to one another, with each offering its own special attributes. Enjoy the ancient Sewee Shell Ring; learn a lot at the Sewee Visitor and Environmental Center, even seeing red wolves; then trek the dikes and canals of what once was a rice plantation from the 1700s.

Imagine exploring South Carolina's coastline and coming upon a circular shell ring approximately 3 to 10 feet high and 225 feet in diameter. If you are like early colonial South Carolinians, you might think it was constructed by the coastal Sewee Indians. After all, the Sewee utilized the resources of the coastline, eating shellfish such as clams and oysters, as well as finny fish. Additionally, there is a clamshell midden in close proximity to the strange, circular shell ring with the flat center. Why wouldn't it be the Sewee? However, the nearby clamshell midden is just that—an unsystematic, haphazard pile of shells, rather than the specific circular form of the nearby Sewee Shell Ring.

Archaeologists learned the Sewee Shell Ring is over 4,000 years old, preceding the Sewee Indians by thousands of years! No one knows the name of the aboriginals who left the Sewee Shell Ring, but we do know a bit about them. It seems their shell ring evolved from a simple shell midden piled up from their nearby dwellings. This ring was then used in feasts and ceremonies and as an everyday gathering place.

The Sewee Shell Ring is the northernmost of these ceremonial rings that stretch along the coastline from Florida to South Carolina. At the shell ring, join a boardwalk to walk along a portion of the ring, hollow in the center. Look for unusual plants growing along heaps of shells. The calcium seeped from the shells into the ground, altering

Walking along the canals of I'on Swamp

the soil, changing its composition, and allowing rare and unusual plants to thrive, such as shell-mound buckthorn, Spanish bayonet, and coral bean. Beyond the Sewee Shell Ring, the hike leads along the edge of cordgrass marsh through maritime woods to visit the relatively new Sewee shell midden. After all, it is only 600 years old.

The Sewee Visitor and Environmental Center is the site of the Nebo Nature Trail. Jointly operated by Francis Marion National Forest and Cape Romain National Wildlife Refuge, the visitor center not only has the Nebo Nature Trail but also presents exhibits detailing the ecosystems of the wildlife refuge and national forest and primary habitats of the Lowcountry.

The Nebo Trail first cruises behind a pond where you might see an alligator. It then heads to the red wolf habitat, where these fascinating canines live. Continue on a boardwalk through swamp forest before reaching Old Nebo Pit Road, a now-closed auto access to former phosphate mines now filled with water, presenting fishing and waterfowl viewing opportunities. After circling the ponds, return toward the visitor center. On the third walk, when you explore I'on Swamp, the thick forests belie its previous incarnation as a rice plantation, a place cleared in the 1700s, to plant what became South Carolina's "white gold." The swamp was named for Colonel Jacob I'on, who owned the land in the early 1800s. Later, when official US Geological Survey maps were made, the name was mistakenly changed to Iron Swamp and eventually back to I'on Swamp. Name aside, the swamp became part of Wytheywood and Clayfield Plantations. A trailside interpretive sign states it all, giving the recipe for a 1700s South Carolina rice plantation:

Traditional Rice Dish

1. *Clear swamp of all trees by hand*

2. *Dig ditches and build banks with hand tools*

3. *Build wooden floodgates to control drainage and water flow to rice fields*

4. *Cultivate rice by hand using mules wearing special rawhide boots to keep them from sinking in the mud.*

5. *Perform the above tasks in extreme heat and humidity and periods of heavy rain, thick clouds of mosquitoes and possibly with swamp fever, a.k.a. malaria.*

The hike turns along Wytheywood Canal. The canal was used to irrigate the rice fields and to move push pole–driven boats loaded with rice down the 7-mile hand-dug canal to the Wando River and on down the Wando to Charleston to be sold. Slaves dug the canals, cleared the land, and built the levees upon which you walk today. Consider the physical toils that have taken place here, in a place now reverted to the howling wilderness, where time and the healing hand of nature has turned this from a sun-scorched level field, laced with dikes, to a wooded wetland where nature's beasts from the reptilian alligator to singing warblers now thrive.

Nowadays, trees line the canal and grow in the middle of it. Alligators may be seen during warmer weather. Tupelo trees, also known as gum trees, complement the cypress. Maples, sweetgum, and oaks occupy higher ground. The last part of the walk traces the Wytheywood Canal a final time before completing the loop portion of the hike. From there backtrack to the trailhead.

Interpretive Trails of Awendaw

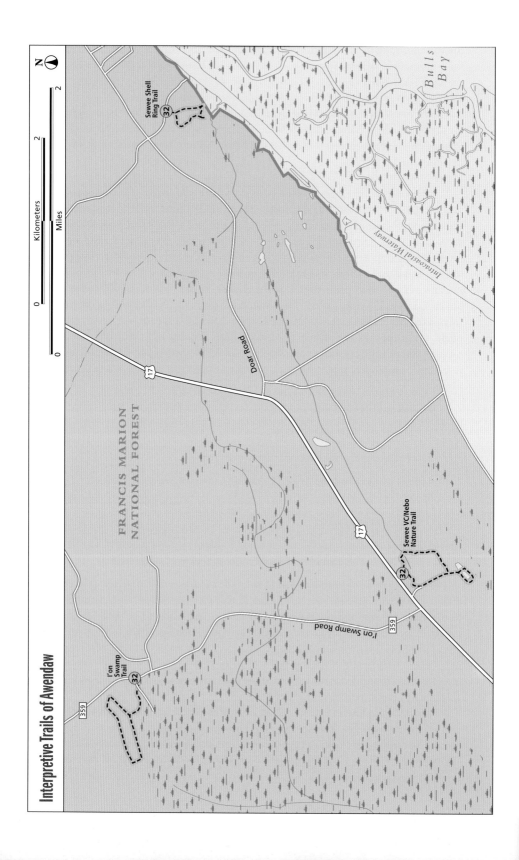

MILES AND DIRECTIONS

0.0 At the Sewee Ring Trail leave the wooded Salt Pond Road trailhead, heading south into thick, cool forest of live and willow oak, pignut hickory, and magnolia.

0.1 Come to the loop portion of the walk. Note the interpretive signage detailing natural and human history of the locale.

0.4 Reach a trail junction. The path going left shortcuts the loop and misses the historical sites. Instead, stay right and shortly come to a second intersection. Here, stay right and join the boardwalk circling around the south side of the Sewee Shell Ring. The boardwalk was damaged in 2016 by Hurricane Matthew. Note views near and far and the circular ceremonial site, plus unusual plants. Backtrack from the boardwalk's end and continue the loop.

0.7 Come to another intersection after passing a monstrous live oak and plentiful palms. Here, take the spur right to the 600-year-old clamshell midden. Backtrack to the main loop.

0.8 Pass the shortcut and keep straight, traversing young woods again.

0.9 Complete the loop portion of the hike. Backtrack.

1.0 Arrive back at the trailhead, completing the hike. Drive to the Sewee Visitor and Environmental Center.

0.0 Now on the Nebo Nature Trail, leave left from the back door of the visitor center. Pick up a boardwalk and the Nebo Nature Trail. Cruise along a pond, absorbing interpretive information.

0.1 A spur trail leads left to the parking area. Stay right here.

View wolves at Sewee Visitor Center

0.2 Come to the spur leading left to the red wolf habitat. Walk to the viewing area overlooking the enclosure. Return to the main loop, traversing a wetland on boardwalk.

0.4 The boardwalk ends. Veer right on a wide, natural surface track under pines.

0.6 Come to Old Nebo Pit Road. Head left toward the Nebo Ponds.

0.7 Reach the Nebo Ponds and a wildlife viewing blind. Stay left here, splitting between two popular fishing ponds. Begin circling clockwise along the shore of the ponds.

0.8 A shortcut between two ponds leaves right. Stay left, circling around the outermost pond.

1.0 Complete the loop of the Nebo Ponds. Head north, backtracking on Old Nebo Pit Road.

1.1 Keep straight, passing the earlier hiked segment of the Nebo Nature Trail.

1.3 Curve right near the Cape Romain National Wildlife Refuge headquarters.

1.4 A spur leads left to a large parking area. Stay right here, curving past a small pond. Join a sidewalk heading toward the front of the visitor center.

1.6 Arrive back at the visitor center, completing the walk. Drive to I'on Swamp Trail.

0.0 Leave the I'on Swamp trailhead on a narrow foot trail beneath sweetgum, oak, pine, and bay trees. Cross a short boardwalk to join a doubletrack path leaving right.

0.4 Pass a spring on trail left, then reach the loop portion of the hike and the Wytheywood Canal. Turn left here.

0.8 The trail reaches a metal water control structure. Here, the loop crosses the canal and turns right, leaving the Wytheywood Canal to parallel a newer canal.

0.9 The trail turns again and passes through nearly pure-red maple stands. While walking the wooded wetlands, search out the grid pattern of the rice fields.

1.3 The trail turns again, then crosses a boardwalk over a particularly wet section.

1.4 Cross the old Wytheywood Canal for the second time on a bridge. The trail then parallels the Wytheywood Canal again. Wood duck nesting boxes are scattered in the woods in great numbers.

1.6 Span another boardwalk just before completing the loop portion of the hike. Backtrack to the trailhead.

2.0 Arrive back at the trailhead, completing the hike.

33. PALMETTO ISLANDS HIKE

Situated on a mix of wooded islands and cordgrass marshes bordered by tidal streams amid fast-growing Mount Pleasant, a suburb of Charleston, Palmetto Islands County Park presents a series of interconnected natural surface and asphalt trails exploring what once was an aboriginal seasonal camp, plantation, and brick-making area and is now a county park. Today you can hike amid maritime woods and along cordgrass marsh and visit Nature Island. The walk continues to an elevated observation tower where you can gaze over the Wando River basin and other tidal waterways. Beyond that the trek passes near picnic areas, fishing docks, and the balance of park offerings.

THE RUNDOWN

Distance: 3.5-miles multi-loop
Start: Dog park parking lot
Nearest town: Mount Pleasant
Hiking time: 2.0 hours
Fees and permits: Entrance fee required
Conveniences: Restrooms, water fountain, picnic area, playground
Beach access: No
Trail users: Families, bicyclists in some areas, joggers, anglers
Trail surface: Natural, some asphalt
Difficulty: Easy

Highlights: Marsh-bordered islands, viewing tower
Canine compatibility: Leashed dogs permitted
Schedule: Jan through Apr from 8 a.m. to sunset; May through Labor Day from 8 a.m. to 8 p.m.; Sept through Dec from 8 a.m. to sunset
Managing agency: Palmetto Islands County Park, 444 Needlerush Pkwy., Mount Pleasant, SC 29464; (843) 884-0832; www.ccprc.com

FINDING THE TRAILHEAD

From exit 28 on I-526 north of Mount Pleasant, take Long Point Road east for 1.7 miles to Needlerush Parkway. Turn left on Needlerush Parkway and follow it 1.3 miles to enter Palmetto Islands County Park. Upon entering the park, pass the entrance gate, take your first right, and then take a second immediate right into the dog park parking area. GPS trailhead coordinates: 32.861996, -79.831863

WHAT TO SEE

Palmetto Islands County Park is a happening place. In fact the first time you visit, you may be overwhelmed at the outdoor offerings—boating, fishing, picnicking, sliding waterslides at a water park, bicycling, learning through nature programs, and even hiking! Furthermore, the park trail system and facilities are inextricably intertwined underneath an attractive forest cover, making the numerous roads, trails, and facilities seem confusing upon your first visit here. This is understandable, since there is an abundance of both trails and amenities at this park situated along Horlbeck Creek and its tidal tributaries, marshes, and smaller islands. Despite the beautiful nature of this 943-acre park, the biggest draw is Splash Island, a water park with a body flume, sprays and geysers, and a water ride and pool, all supervised by lifeguards. Maybe you can go swimming after your hike . . .

This long hiker bridge leads to Nature Island.

Looking down on wetlands from the park observation tower.

Palms border the trail here

The park also has boat and bike rentals, a large playground, multiple fishing docks, kayak launches, and numerous picnic areas and shelters. The dog park is also a big draw, and you start the hike there. The hike winds past facilities, then settles alongside a cordgrass marsh in surprisingly attractive woods of live oak, palm, cedar, and yaupon. Extensive views stretch out across the marsh, dotted with the Palmetto Islands, for which the park is named. Ahead, you will visit one of these Palmetto Islands, now named Nature Island. A long boardwalk with good views spans the marsh, linking wild Nature Island to the more developed side of the preserve. The name is appropriate, as this isle has been left in its natural state, overlain only with trails. The trip out to Nature Island allows you to visit uninterrupted forest and features an extensive westerly view to the Wando River.

Aboriginals used to stay on islands such as this during the summer, harvesting shellfish and other foods from the nearby waterways. They also enjoyed sea breezes that kept things relatively cool and made the mosquitoes more bearable. They left in the fall to not only get away from the worst of the hurricane season, but also reap the bounty of lands away from the salty sea, from meaty mammals to succulent berries.

After leaving Nature Island, the hike skirts around the north side of the park, presenting more views of the cordgrass marshes and tidal creeks. The park observation tower—a must visit—allows an elevated vista of the Palmetto Islands that stretches to the horizon and is a true highlight of the hike. The second part of the trek heads over to Horlbeck Creek, a large tidal waterway. You cruise along the edge of this stream, passing fishing docks, kayak launches, and even a crabbing dock while circling around a peninsula. (They also have canoe and kayak slips for rent hereabouts.) The hike curves out to a peninsula and then makes a series of mini-loops linked by the Marsh Trail and the Bicycle Trail.

Palmetto Islands Hike

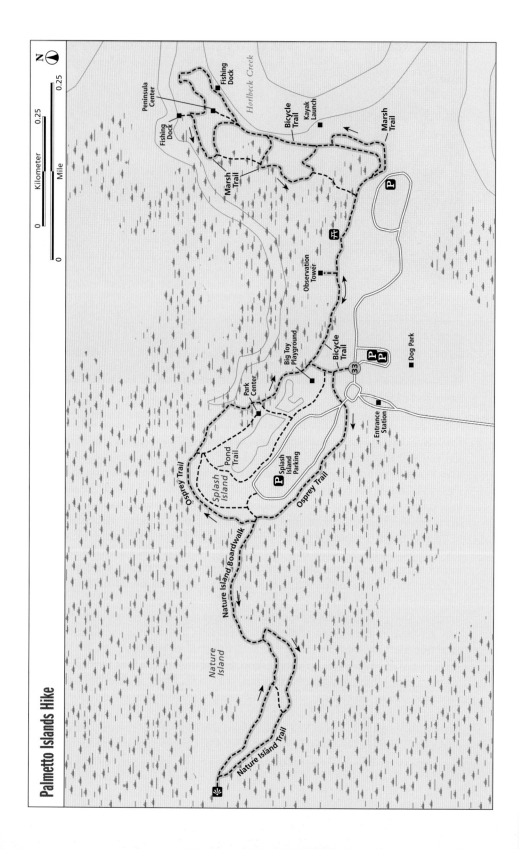

The final part of the hike returns you to the trailhead, where one of the friendly park employees will help you figure out what to do next at this park that offers so much more than hiking.

MILES AND DIRECTIONS

0.0 After parking in the dog park lot, join the paved Bicycle Trail, leaving north from the parking area. Go just a short distance, then turn left onto the yellow-blazed Osprey Trail. The first part is paved, then it crosses the road to the Splash Island parking area, then becomes a natural surface trail, sometimes overlain with gravel. Pass a ranger residence on your left, then come alongside marsh. Hike through maritime hardwoods of palm, live oak, and cedar with the marsh to your left and the parking area to your right. The woods are alluring.

0.3 Reach a trail intersection. Head left onto a boardwalk toward Nature Island. Cross a cordgrass marsh. The open boardwalk and low marsh present open looks at Nature Island ahead.

0.4 Head left on the loop portion of the Nature Island Trail. Walk under pines, palms, and wax myrtle. Stay left, passing a shortcut.

0.8 Stay left again to join the spur with a westerly view of the Wando River. Continue the loop, passing the other end of a shortcut.

1.1 Complete the loop on Nature Island. Backtrack over the boardwalk toward the main park.

1.2 Head left on natural surface Osprey Trail. Walk the margin of wood and marsh, with the paved Bicycle Trail and Splash Island to your right.

1.5 Open onto a view and connector to the Pond Trail. Keep straight on the Osprey Trail. Pass near the park office, joining the Bicycle Trail.

1.7 Pass the trail leading right to the dog park. Keep straight, walking under a transmission line.

1.8 Come to the observation tower. Climb the steps to grab a top-down view of the marsh, islands, and civilization beyond, then keep east on the Bicycle Trail.

2.0 Pass the Marsh Trail leaving left. Stay right, then join another part of the Marsh Trail. Curve north along Horlbeck Creek.

2.2 Come near the kayak launch. Head out to the launch for a good look at Horlbeck Creek, changing directions with the tides. Stay right, briefly joining the Bicycle Trail only to spur away.

2.4 Pass near the Peninsula Center and fishing dock, complemented by restrooms and drink machines if you are thirsty. Curve around the peninsula, passing another fishing dock.

2.7 Stay left as a branch of the Marsh Trail splits right as a boardwalk. Rejoin the Bicycle Trail.

2.8 Split right, making a second loop on the Marsh Trail. Rejoin the Bicycle Trail, backtracking.

3.5 Arrive back at the trailhead after backtracking on the Bicycle Trail.

34. CHARLES TOWNE LANDING STATE HISTORIC SITE

Come see where South Carolina was born and where the first Charleston colonists set up in 1670, at a preserved state historic site. The hike leads you first from the worthwhile visitor center to the Animal Forest, where a variety of creatures from bears to bison to bobcats are ensconced in habitats, along with farm animals. From there you will head out to Albemarle Point, the site of Charleston's original settlement, viewing historic sites and absorbing interpretive information. See the ship *Adventure* on Old Towne Creek. On your way back, view the Legare Waring House and the scenic gardens framed in incredible live oaks.

THE RUNDOWN

Distance: 3.5-mile loop with spur
Start: Visitor center
Nearest town: Charleston
Hiking time: 1.5 hours
Fees and permits: Entrance fee
Conveniences: Restrooms, picnic area, visitor center
Beach access: No
Trail users: History buffs, hikers
Trail surface: Paved and natural
Difficulty: Easy

Highlights: Historic site of Charleston's founding, Animal Forest
Canine compatibility: Leashed dogs permitted, except in Animal Forest
Schedule: Daily from 9 a.m. to 5 p.m.; closed Christmas Eve and Christmas Day
Managing agency: Charles Towne Landing State Historic Site, 1500 Old Towne Rd., Charleston, SC, 29407; 843-852-420; www.southcarolinaparks.com

FINDING THE TRAILHEAD

From exit 216A on I-26 north of downtown Charleston, take SC 7 South for 1.8 miles to veer left onto SC 171, Old Towne Road, at a traffic light. Stay on SC 171 for 0.5 mile and then turn left into the state historic site. The hike starts from the rear of the visitor center. GPS trailhead coordinates: 32.807574, -79.986480

WHAT TO SEE

Imagine embarking on the ultimate move—across the Atlantic Ocean to a little-known continent, to settle in untamed lands inhabited by natives about whom you know nothing (or else heard wildly erroneous tales), not to mention knowing little of the land upon which you are to settle (about which more wild tales abounded). That's exactly what a group of 120 English colonists did when they settled Albemarle Point, near the confluence of what became known as Old Towne Creek and the Ashley River. Though this spot was hampered by a lack of a deepwater port, the locale was more defensible than what became the town of Charleston we see today across the Ashley River. Nevertheless, for nine years the colonists of Charles Towne Landing carved out a life on this spot before moving to today's Charleston. And you can come here and tour this special site.

Regal live oaks add a sophisticated air to the hike.

This first European settlement in South Carolina is today one of just a few preserved original settlement sites that exist in the United States. (Most sites simply grew and changed over time and are now modern towns and cities.) The 634-acre state historic site, complemented with 80 acres of gardens, presents a picture of the past that covers not only the time of the colonists, but also of aboriginal South Carolinians, African slaves, the antebellum plantation, and the later residents of the peninsula who occupied what is known as the Legare Waring House.

This coastal hike with a historical bent starts at the visitor center and museum. Explore the visitor center; you can gain a comprehensive overview of what took place at Charles Towne Landing. This is no ordinary visitor center. Its twelve rooms house a

A re-created structure at Charles Towne Landing

comprehensive recollection of the place and times. Alternatively, you could learn about the past through guided tours that delve deeper into varied aspects of the state historic site, from cannon firing to daily life at the settlement and more. Check the park's website if you desire a guided tour.

The hike then cruises by an aboriginal ceremonial site and a slave cemetery before delving into natural history at the 22-acre Animal Forest. Here, check out red wolves, bears, bison, and otters in outdoor habitats. You can view domestic livestock as well. Kids of all ages love to see the animals up close. When encountering nature's beasts in the wild, we often see nothing but a fleeting blur disappearing into the woods; here we can take long looks at bobcats, otters, skunks, bison, and other creatures, studying them in detail.

After leaving the Animal Forest, you pass by the noble statue of Cassique, an Indian who helped the colonists, even going so far as suggesting their place of settlement. Pass by the Horry-Lucas House ruins, where a pre–Civil War plantation once stood. Next enter the original settlement area. Though little remains from the actual settlement, archaeologists have figured out the basic layout and lifeways of Charles Towne. See the Common House, the defensive cannons, and "the stocks," where those who ran afoul of the law were sent. It is a rite of passage here at Charles Towne Landing to have your picture taken in the stocks.

Next visit the historic garden. Here colonists systematically tried to grow cash crops such as sugar cane, indigo, and cotton, as well as foods for sustenance like beans, potatoes,

The author is put in the stocks for tripping during the hike.

and corn. Stop by the water, gaining long looks into the Ashely River and south toward the Atlantic Ocean. See the ship *Adventure*, a 1700s era transport vessel. When rangers are present, they will take you for a tour of the boat. They sometimes fire off the cannons, a sight to see. Check out the re-created shipbuilding area. The archaeology exhibits explain how the area was systematically dug for clues to the past on this peninsula along the Ashely River.

The trail takes you through gorgeous maritime forest to another place and period and the Legare Waring House. Originally an overseer's dwelling during the plantation period of what is now Charles Towne, the home was later enlarged and made into the primary residence after the plantation house was burned during the Civil War. The Legare Waring house fell into disrepair but was restored by Ferdi Waring. She also established the 80 acres of gorgeous gardens around the home, including the Avenue of Oaks, the whole of which enhances and complements the balance of the park. In spring the gardens of the Legare Waring House, a popular site for weddings and special events, color the grounds in pink, purple, and red.

The final part of the trek leads past a 700-year-old oak, long established when the Charles Towne colonists arrived. Finish your journey in the shade of more widespread hardwoods before returning to the visitor center. If you want to walk more, the park boasts a total of 7 miles of walking trails. Bicycles are welcome on the paths and you can rent them by the hour or the day.

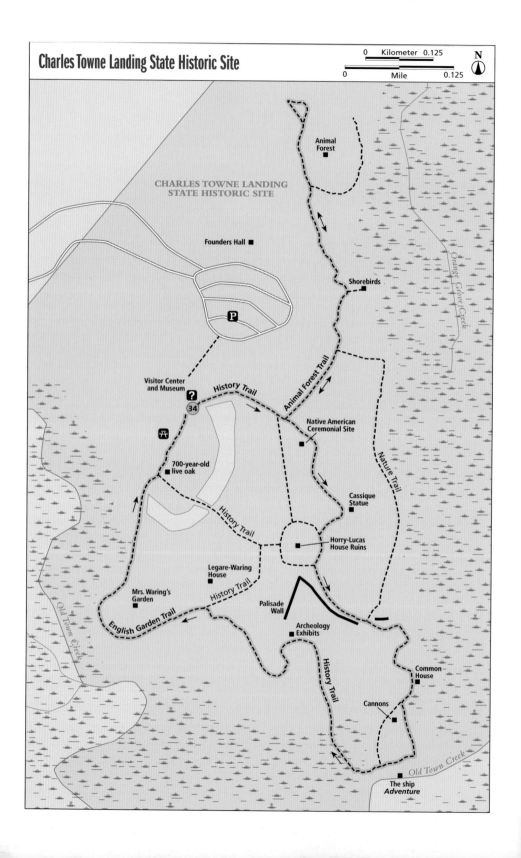

Charles Towne Landing State Historic Site

0   Kilometer 0.125

0   Mile   0.125

N

CHARLES TOWNE LANDING
STATE HISTORIC SITE

Animal Forest

Founders Hall

Shorebirds

P

Visitor Center and Museum

History Trail

Animal Forest Trail

Native American Ceremonial Site

700-year-old live oak

History Trail

Cassique Statue

Nature Trail

Horry-Lucas House Ruins

Legare-Waring House

Mrs. Waring's Garden

History Trail

English Garden Trail

Palisade Wall

Archeology Exhibits

History Trail

Common House

Cannons

The ship *Adventure*

Old Town Creek

Orange Grove Creek

MILES AND DIRECTIONS

0.0 After passing through the visitor center, leave east, crossing a boardwalk above the nearby pond. Join the signed History Trail, an asphalt track.

0.1 Reach a trail intersection. Head left on the Animal Forest Trail. Pass by the African American Cemetery, then come to the concentration of animals. The paths split, heading to the various exhibits of the animals in natural habitats. Backtrack after viewing the critters.

1.2 Rejoin the History Trail after leaving the Animal Forest. Pass by the statue of Cassique, then come to the circular walk around the Horry-Lucas homesite ruins, a former plantation burned during the Civil War. From here, stay left with the History Trail as it cuts through the Palisade Wall and enters the Original Settlement, with multiple exhibits, including the fabled stocks, where many visitors have their pictures taken.

1.8 Come to the ship *Adventure*, a replica 1700s sailing vessel, docked in Old Towne Creek. The History Trail turns back north, bridging a wetland on a boardwalk. Ahead, pass the archeology exhibits, by a line of live oaks.

2.2 Reach a trail intersection. The Legare Waring House is to your right. Go check it out up close and then head left on the English Garden Trail, passing under widespread live oaks and azaleas, hibiscus, and camellia. Walk through first-rate Lowcountry scenery.

2.5 Meet the other end of the History Trail after passing by a pond. Look right for the 700-year-old live oak, which was here when Charles Towne was settled. Keep straight toward the visitor center, nearing a picnic area.

3.5 Arrive back at the visitor center, completing the hike.

35. CAW CAW INTERPRETIVE CENTER

Explore Caw Caw Interpretive Center via the Habitat Loop. It uses a network of trails traversing a variety of ecosystems to deliver an all-encompassing overview of Lowcountry flora and fauna. The sheer number of trails will ensure repeat visits to this preserve. Even the trails are as varied as the terrain, using boardwalks over swamps, narrow natural surface paths in deep woods, and open grassy tracks atop dikes. Make time to enjoy the interpretive center before or after your hike.

THE RUNDOWN

Distance: 3.8-mile loop
Start: Caw Caw Interpretive Center
Nearest town: Ravenel
Hiking time: 2.0 hours
Fees and permits: Entrance fee
Conveniences: Restrooms, water fountain, picnic area
Beach access: No
Trail users: Hikers, birders
Trail surface: Natural
Difficulty: Easy to moderate

Highlights: Marsh views, boardwalk, colonial history, wildlife
Canine compatibility: Dogs not permitted
Schedule: Tues through Sun from 9 a.m. to 5 p.m.; closed Mon
Managing agency: Caw Caw Interpretive Center, 5200 Savannah Hwy., Highway 17 South, Ravenel, SC 29470; (843) 889-8898; www.ccprc .com

FINDING THE TRAILHEAD

From Exit 212B on I-526 West near Charleston (the end of I-526 West), take Sam Rittenburg Boulevard a short distance to US 17. Turn right on US 17 South and follow it for 10 miles. The park entrance will be on your right. Continue on the park road to end at the visitor center. GPS trailhead coordinates: 32.782935, -80.193738

WHAT TO SEE

Caw Caw Interpretive Center boasts a total of 6 miles of hiking trails spidering over 654 acres. The preserve was once part of a 5,000–plus acre rice plantation from two centuries ago. Officially a low-impact wildlife preserve, the Charleston County park presents extensive environmental education programs covering habitats, plants, rice cultivation, Gullah culture, and natural resource management, among other subjects. The visitor center is manned during park hours, and the staff can answer other questions you may have. Water and restrooms are also available. Beyond that it is just you, nature, and a trail map. By the way, no bicycles are allowed.

The best way to experience Caw Caw is to follow the Habitat Loop, which incorporates the varied trails into one grand circuit and is detailed on the park map. Interpretive kiosks are spread out along the trail system, adding an educational component to your hike.

The marshes and swamps of Caw Caw are managed to maximize conditions for wildlife. Water levels at the preserve are maintained by water control structures. On the

The entryway to Caw Caw Interpretive Center

Habitat Loop you will become very familiar with wetlands while taking the Georgia Pacific Swamp Boardwalk through cypress, maple, and gum trees of this seasonally inundated floodplain where cypress knees and palmetto grow in the shadow of the swamp giants.

The boardwalk ends and you trace a wide grassy road to the Laurel Hill Slave Settlement amid large live oaks. Nothing remains of the actual settlement, but the high ground under live oaks was home to African slaves while they worked the adjacent rice fields. And it makes the most sense, as the ground is the highest around and the oaks provide needed shade after working in the open rice fields. Restrooms are located near the settlement site.

Laurel Hill is a good place to contemplate the Stono Rebellion, in which the plantation here became embroiled. Back in 1739, when America was an English colony and South Carolina was but one of the American colonies, a group of slaves in nearby coastal Carolina met in secret near the Stono River, plotting to gain their freedom. They raided a store, getting guns and powder, hoping to make their way south to St. Augustine, where the Spaniards ruled Florida and offered freedom and free land to escaped slaves. (The Spaniards believed encouraging slaves to escape would destabilize the colonies and any slave-based agriculture system.) The slave owners chased down the insurgents to the Edisto River, and a bloody and deadly battle ensued, thus ending colonial America's largest slave rebellion, after a second splinter group was captured a week later. Following

Early blooms bring hope for spring.

this came South Carolina's Negro Act of 1740, resulting in even rougher times for Palmetto State slaves, including barring assembly and education for blacks. It is believed that slaves from the plantation here at Caw Caw were caught up in the rebellion. If so, they would've lived right here on Laurel Hill.

Beyond Laurel Hill, join a dike and open area on a grassy track heading toward the waterfowl area, now on the Waterfowl Trail. Swamp forest stands to your left, while open waters mixed with aquatic vegetation lie off to your right. The open wetlands are now managed for ducks instead of rice. Waterfowl are seen here, in what were once agricultural fields. Open watery expanses of tidally influenced and brackish water border the left side of the trail. The right side is fresh water. The aforementioned water control structures also divide the freshwater and saltwater areas. The tides push up nearby Wallace Creek.

A gate opens to flood wetlands at Caw Caw Interpretive Center.

The Maritime Forest Trail skirts a marsh in woods. Here you will walk among cedar, live oak, and palm, along with ever-present pines. Your next part of the aptly named Habitat Loop is the Bottomland Hardwood Forest Trail. Here the path snakes through thick woods of hickory and oak. Pass some wild tea plants, leftover from when the area was a tea plantation. Interestingly, the only tea plantation currently operating in North America is nearby. Known as the Charleston Tea Plantation, it is actually on Wadmalaw Island, about 10 miles southwest of the historic port city. You can view the fields on a trolley tour and even visit the tea factory. At Caw Caw, vegetables were later raised where tea once was grown. You can still see the crop rows and shallow ditches made to drain the vegetable fields. The rest of the walk uses wide paths to loop you back to the visitor center.

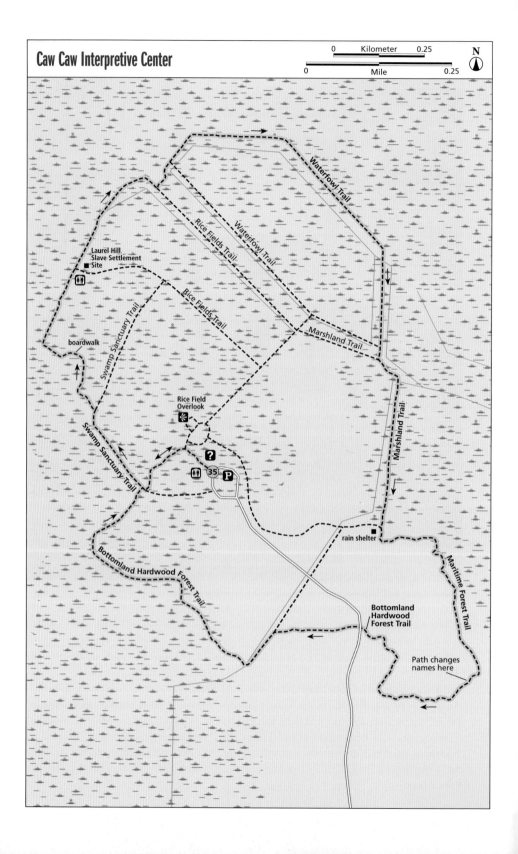

Caw Caw Interpretive Center

0   Kilometer   0.25

0   Mile   0.25

N

Waterfowl Trail

Rice Fields Trail

Waterfowl Trail

Laurel Hill
Slave Settlement
■ Site

Swamp Sanctuary Trail

Rice Fields Trail

Marshland Trail

boardwalk

Marshland Trail

Rice Field
Overlook

Swamp Sanctuary Trail

?

35   P

rain shelter

Bottomland Hardwood Forest Trail

Maritime Forest Trail

Bottomland
Hardwood
Forest Trail

Path changes
names here

MILES AND DIRECTIONS

0.0 Leave the walkway between the two buildings of the interpretive center, shortly reaching a trail junction. A trail leads to the right, reaching the rice field overlook-boardwalk, which is worth a look. Imagine this open swamp once having been irrigated straight-lined rice fields. Leave the junction left, shortly intersecting the Swamp Sanctuary Trail and the Bottomland Hardwood Forest Trail. Begin the Habitat Loop by leaving right to cross a bridge over a strand of Caw Caw Swamp.

0.4 Head left on the Georgia Pacific Boardwalk, traversing a wooded swamp.

0.6 Leave right from the boardwalk toward Laurel Hill Settlement.

0.8 Pass the slave settlement site and keep straight, joining the Rice Fields Trail. Open onto dikes bordered by wetlands.

0.9 Leave left on the Waterfowl Trail, crossing a canal. Begin circling around marsh to your right.

1.6 Intersect the other end of the Waterfowl Trail coming in on your right. Stay left, atop a dike separating fresh and salt marshes. Pass a couple of water control structures, staying left, to join the wide Marshland Trail.

2.0 Come near a rain shelter, then head left on the singletrack Maritime Forest Trail. It enters woods that border a canal. Cedars are prevalent here, as the trail winds through palmetto. Views extend across the canal.

2.2 Join a doubletrack path leaving left.

2.3 Split right at a kiosk, back on a singletrack path, joining the Bottomland Hardwood Forest Trail. This section can be mucky after rains, true bottomland.

2.8 Cross the park entrance road. The Bottomland Hardwood Forest Trail becomes doubletrack.

3.0 Stay left as a pink-blazed trail leaves right for the Marshland Trail. Continue in superlative rich woodlands.

3.6 Complete the loop portion of the hike. Backtrack right toward the visitor center.

3.8 Arrive back at the trailhead, completing the hike.

36. **BOTANY BAY**

Botany Bay Plantation Wildlife Management Area is one of South Carolina's finest coastal treasures. Here a large swath of rich maritime woods, marshy creeks, and 2 miles of wild beaches await your footfalls. A trail leads from the mainland across a marsh to the edge of the Atlantic, where you can walk unspoiled beach bordered on one side by the Atlantic Ocean and the other by an open marsh with views extending in all directions as far as the eye can see.

THE RUNDOWN

Distance: 5.2-mile there-and-back
Start: Botany Bay beach access
Nearest town: Ravenel
Hiking time: 2.8 hours
Fees and permits: Free registration required
Conveniences: None
Beach access: Yes
Trail users: Hikers, beachcombers
Trail surface: Natural
Difficulty: Moderate

Highlights: Wild beach, views
Canine compatibility: Leashed dogs permitted
Schedule: Sunrise to 30 minutes after sunset; closed Tues
Managing agency: Botany Bay Plantation Wildlife Management Area, 10666 Botany Bay Rd., Edisto Island, SC 29438; (843) 869-2713; dnr.sc.gov/

FINDING THE TRAILHEAD

From Exit 212B on I-526 West near Charleston (the end of I-526 West), take Sam Rittenburg Boulevard a short distance to US 17. Turn right on US 17 South and follow it for 19.1 miles to SC 174. Turn left, south on SC 174, and follow it 17.7 miles to the left turn onto Botany Bay Road. Follow Botany Bay Road 1.6 miles to the left turn into the wildlife management area. Register just beyond the gate and continue straight for 1.7 miles to the signed right turn for the beach. Follow the unnamed road to the beach a short distance to a dead end at a parking area. GPS trailhead coordinates: 32.549408, -80.233479

WHAT TO SEE

Botany Bay Plantation is a fascinating place, chock-full of human and natural history. The site of two pre–Civil War plantations, one of which grew the long and fine Sea Island cotton, Botany Bay contains multiple sites listed on the National Register of Historic Places, including an old plantation site as well as a shell midden thousands of years old. The two plantations, Bleak Hall and Sea Cloud, were later bought and put together as one by a man named Jason Meyer, who established Botany Bay Plantation in the 1930s. He willed the property to the State of South Carolina upon his wife's death. She passed away in 2007, and the Department of Natural Resources opened Botany Bay to the public in 2008. Today visitors can drive the live oak shaded lanes and enjoy a 6.5-mile auto tour that visits over a dozen significant sites along the route. Botany Bay has increased in popularity just as sure as the greater Charleston area has grown. Nice weather weekends see big crowds and an overfilled parking area at the trailhead for this hike.

Make sure to add the auto tour to your hike. Along the way you can see the Meyers's residence, still in use as the Department of Natural Resource property manager's

Top: A sunken tree trunk stands bare on the beach.
Bottom: Previous hikers lined up shells on this fallen palm.

A conch shell rises among lesser shells.

residence. Next visit the grounds of the Bleak Hall Plantation. Though the main house was burned after the Civil War, you can still see two remaining buildings from the 1800s: the icehouse and the gardener hut. Interestingly, the remains of a slave cabin chimney still stand as well. Next, pass a barn that was used during World War II to store hay for the US Coast Guard, who patrolled the shores of Edisto Island on horseback, looking for offshore German boats. Ahead, view fields and other lands managed for wildlife that once grew the Sea Island cotton sought to fashion the finest lace by European weavers.

Next stop by Picnic Pond and Jason's Lake. Both bodies of water are rich in wildlife, including wood ducks, alligators, fish, shorebirds, osprey, and eagles. You are now on the property of the other plantation, known as Sea Cloud. This plantation had its origin as Revolutionary War land grants. The main plantation building, bordered by elaborate gardens, stood three stories high, with a ballroom occupying the entire third floor. All that remain are brick ruins. Beyond Jason's Lake, a beehive-shaped well from the 1820s can be seen from the auto tour.

By this point you are probably excited to take the trail to the beach, where natural preserved coastal beauty awaits. The wildlife management area features 2 miles of pristine beachfront. It is a completely different experience exploring a pure natural ocean environment without having cottages and high-rises stretching behind you. However, before reaching the beach, enjoy the trail leading out to it. You first follow an elevated roadbed across a tidal, cordgrass marsh. Then you join a small island, one of 3,500 of these South Carolina islands located landward of the barrier islands facing the Atlantic and seaward of the mainland. These relatively undisturbed isles provide isolated habitats for flora and fauna such as the painted bunting, which nests on these hammock islands during the spring and summer.

After passing through the small hammock island, the elevated track heads for the Atlantic. Emerge at the ocean, now on Pockoy Island. You will notice an abundance of fallen live oaks and palms, many embedded into the sands fronting the ceaseless crashing waves of the Atlantic Ocean. In 2016 Hurricane Matthew swept away a lot of beach. Therefore it is important to time your visit with the tides. To successfully undertake this hike, try to reach the beach on a falling tide, then make your way northeast to the plantation property boundary. You should have ample time to return before the tides overtake the surface upon which you walk. In times of spring tides, also known as king tides, when the tides are especially high, the waters go to the line of trees at the beginning of the beach and overwash the beach where the Atlantic Ocean and the marsh behind it are separated by only a thin line of sand, shell, sea oats, and salt cedar. This warning is not to scare you from coming, but to encourage you to be smart and use caution. The Botany Bay Plantation website advises the same.

This is a gorgeous beach. Find shells galore and sun-bleached trees embedded into the shore, giving way to wide-open terrain where you can look in one direction at the

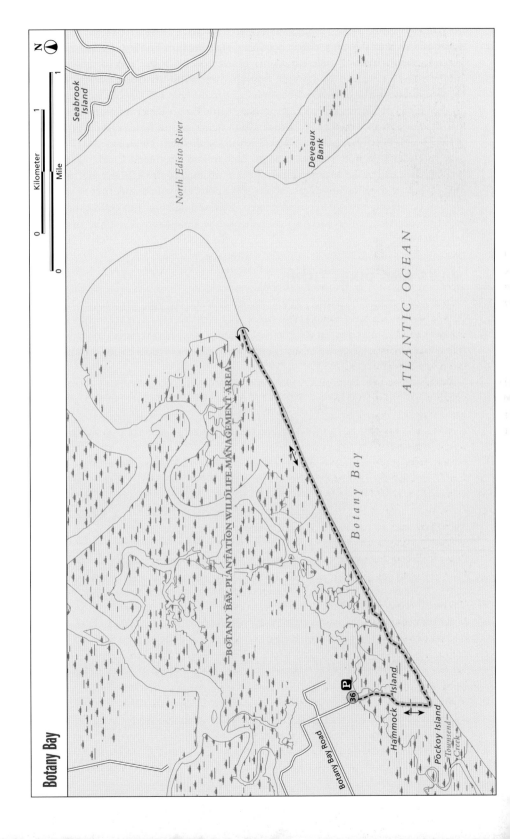

Botany Bay

Atlantic and in the other direction at marsh. It's a place to appreciate the melding of water and land at the edge of the continent, right here in South Carolina. The walk extends easterly. After 2 miles along the beach, you reach the end of the plantation property and a return to woods back from the beach. You may see a boundary marker or perhaps one of the boat-accessible-only habitations here. Off to your right stands the low shoreline of Deveaux Bank. Ahead, the North Edisto River makes its tidal run to the Atlantic Ocean. Populated Seabrook Island stands on the far shore of North Edisto River. This is beach hiking at its finest. You will see shells in abundance.

If you head west from the beach access trail, toward Townsend Creek, you can't go too far, since Hurricane Matthew opened a new channel to the Atlantic, effectively cutting off part of the beach from easy access. Take note: On your free permit to access the Botany Bay Plantation wildlife management area, you agree not to collect shells. This regulation is strictly enforced. Don't do it, despite the temptation. A stiff fine awaits those who break the law.

MILES AND DIRECTIONS

0.0   Pass around the pole gate heading south on the Pockoy Island Trail toward the beach. Enjoy wide views of the marsh.

0.3   Reach Hammock Island, an isolated hammock island. Pass through the small wooded isle, then emerge south, cruising through marsh on a causeway. Crabs inhabit the marsh by the thousands.

0.5   Reach the beach of Pockoy Island and the Atlantic Ocean after passing through more forest. Now you can leave left or right along the beach. Our hike heads left, northeast along the edge of the Atlantic Ocean. At first expect to work around embedded skeletal live oaks and palms, with little tidal pools created among them with streams running toward the Atlantic on a falling tide. Work your way among the trees.

0.8   Leave the trees and vegetation of Pockoy Island. Continue northeast along a wide beach that rises to a slender treeless sand spit covered in shells that drop to marsh on the landward side. You can look back at the parking area and trailhead. More important, views open of ocean to the horizon and nearby marsh dotted with isles. Marvel at the shells underneath your feet, with superlative ones placed together by previous visitors for admiration, including scads of conch shells.

2.4   Come near a piney hammock.

2.6   You may see a boundary marker delineating the boundary of the Botany Bay wildlife management area, but you will surely spot a water-accessible dwelling back from the beach. Turn around here, though the mouth of the North Edisto River is another 0.5-mile distant by foot.

5.2   Arrive back at the trailhead, completing the ocean hike.

37. EDISTO BEACH STATE PARK HIKE

This coastal hike travels to an ancient shell mound known as the Spanish Mount, situated on the banks of tidal Scott Creek. First, explore maritime hardwoods, coming along Scott Creek, where marsh views await. Continue under live oaks, cedars, and palms to the stabilized shell midden, where you can see layers of shells piled over time and rewarding panoramas of the surrounding estuary. The Forest Loop adds new trail on your return. After the hike, you can hit the state park beach, where 1.5 miles of Atlantic Ocean beachfront await your bare feet.

THE RUNDOWN

Distance: 3.7-mile balloon loop, plus 3-mile there-and-back beach walk
Start: State Cabin Road trailhead
Nearest town: Ravenel
Hiking time: 2.0 hours
Fees and permits: Entrance fee
Conveniences: Restrooms, water fountain, picnic area, campground
Beach access: Yes
Trail users: Hikers, bicyclists
Trail surface: Natural
Difficulty: Easy

Highlights: Big woods, tidal creek, ancient shell mound, beach nearby
Canine compatibility: Leashed dogs permitted
Schedule: Daily from 8 a.m. to 6 p.m. (extended during daylight saving time)
Managing agency: Edisto Beach State Park, 8377 State Cabin Rd., Edisto Island, SC 29438; (843) 869-2156; southcarolinaparks.com

FINDING THE TRAILHEAD

From Exit 212B on I-526 West near Charleston (the end of I-526 West), take Sam Rittenburg Boulevard a short distance to US 17. Turn right on US 17 South and follow it for 19.1 miles to SC 174. Turn left (south on SC 174) and follow it 20.8 miles to a right turn onto State Cabin Road, before you reach the main beach entrance on your left. Follow State Cabin Road 0.5 mile to the parking area on your right, near the Live Oak Campground. GPS trailhead coordinates: 32.511719, -80.302666

WHAT TO SEE

A trip to Edisto Beach State Park is a trip to yesteryear. This quaint park lies next to a small vacation village, with no high-rises and very few chain stores. In fact, Edisto Beach has been dubbed "Mayberry by the Sea." Edisto Beach, 20 miles off South Carolina's main coastal drag—US 17—is at the end of a dead-end road. Despite the location, this park and community are a place where families return year after year and bring their kids, who in turn bring their kids.

The beach here is a big draw. Edisto Beach is on the northern tip of St. Helena Sound, a large bay where the Ashepoo, Combahee, and Edisto Rivers converge to meet the Atlantic Ocean. Being an island that directly fronts the Atlantic allows beach formation on Edisto Island and beaches are what draw people in. Edisto Beach State Park boasts 1.5

Looking out on Scott Creek

miles of beachfront. The beach allows plenty of sunbathers and beachcombers to roam around. The sandy stretch extends north from the point where the town of Edisto Beach and the park meet. The park beach is backed by low dunes at the park entrance. Grassy picnic areas, back from the beach, are shaded by palms and oaks. Picnic shelters are also available for hot or rainy days. The historic park office and gift shop are nearby. Down the beach, sea oat–topped dunes give way to wind-sculpted maritime vegetation, which grows atop dunes. The Edisto Beach State Park campground lies behind these dunes and is connected to the beach by accesses. The park's land ends and private property begins at Edingsville Beach.

You will find the hiking trails at Edisto Beach State Park an added bonus. Our hike leads to the Spanish Mount, an ancient Indian midden. This shell mound, built up in a circle and filled in the middle, though known as the Spanish Mount, has nothing to do with the Spaniards. The midden, mostly of shells, dates back around 4,000 years. Mounds of shells at rich estuarine areas are not uncommon in the Southeast, but the ringed shape of this mound and name "Spanish Mount" remain a mystery, though the circular nature of the midden lends credence to it being a ceremonial site. The Spanish Mount is, how-ever, purportedly the second-oldest pottery site in South Carolina. Deer, rabbit, turkey, and bones of fourteen types of fish have been found here, as well as potshards. A viewing platform has been installed where you can look out on Scotts Creek below and into a cut in the mound, showing layer upon layer of shells. This platform also serves to check

Edisto Beach

the erosion of the site, as has happened over time by the ceaseless tides of Scott Creek. In 1809 it was reported to be 20 feet high and half an acre in size. Today it is one-tenth that size.

The Spanish Mount Trail leaves the trailhead into a tall shady forest of live oak and loblolly pine with a dense understory of yaupon. Magnolia, cedar, and palm add biodiversity to the trek. The doubletrack path makes for easy hiking. Handy maps are posted at all trail intersections. Pass both ends of the Forest Loop, your return route, then meet the Scott Creek Trail. It heads for the main part of the park, but our hike keeps west, coming along the edge of Scotts Creek marsh. Enjoy walking in woods and peering into the Scott Creek estuary. The maritime woods are a joy through which to travel.

You are almost to the Spanish Mount after meeting the Big Bay Trail, which leads to an alternate trailhead. Soon emerge at a bluff above Scott Creek. Views open in the far. In the near, you can see the layers of shells deposited over time by aboriginal South Carolinians. The shell midden has been stabilized by the wooden structure along the shore of Scott Creek. Soak in the interpretive information, then backtrack toward the trailhead, walking the Forest Loop for variety.

Consider camping here at Edisto Beach State Park. Edisto Beach has two camping areas offering different atmospheres. The Main Camping Area is the most popular. It is just a dune away from the Atlantic Ocean, with a creek on the mainland side of the campground. The campsites are spread far apart from one another and are banked against

Top: Lone beachcomber on Edisto Beach
Bottom: Wooden fences protect the dunes of Edisto Beach.

Shells on
Edisto Beach

tall dunes. Live oaks shade many of these sites. Other campsites overlook the marsh creek away from the beach.

The Live Oak Camping Area is less popular, simply because it is farther from the beach, and you must drive to the ocean. However, it is near the trailhead of this hike. It has fifty shaded campsites beneath live oaks and five walk-in tent campsites. These sites are generally larger and more widely separated from one another. Solitude seekers will camp back here. The five walk-in tent sites are even more remote and are very shady. They overlook the marshes of Scott Creek.

The park campgrounds will fill anytime during the summer, and reservations are highly recommended from June through August. The campground also sees an upsurge in business during spring break, but since alcohol is not allowed, a family atmosphere reigns then and throughout the year. This is part of the reason families return year after year.

After your hike, stroll the 1.5-mile-long park beach overlooking the Atlantic Ocean. Perhaps after hiking, beachcombing, and camping here at Edisto Beach State Park, you too will return here year after year.

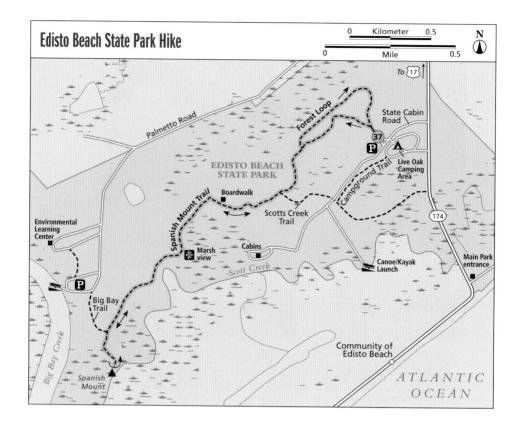

Edisto Beach State Park Hike

MILES AND DIRECTIONS

0.0 Leave the parking area off Cabin Road and head north on a doubletrack path, the Spanish Mount Trail, in rich woods of live oak, palm, pine, and cedar.

0.1 Stay left on the Spanish Mount Trail as the Forest Loop, your return route, leaves right.

0.4 Pass the other end of the Forest Loop.

0.6 Keep straight on the Spanish Mount Trail as the Scott Creek Trail heads left.

0.9 Cross a boardwalk over a marshy creek.

1.2 A short track leads left to a view of the Scott Creek marsh.

1.7 The Big Bay Trail leaves right.

1.8 Reach the Spanish Mount. Enjoy the views and interpretive information. Backtrack.

3.2 Head left on the Forest Loop.

3.6 Rejoin the Spanish Mount Trail.

3.7 Arrive back at the trailhead, completing the woods hike. Head to the park beach to enjoy a 1.5-mile each way walk on the Atlantic Ocean beach.

38. HUNTING ISLAND STATE PARK BEACH HIKE

Hunting Island State Park, one of South Carolina's most beloved preserves, is the setting for this trek. Facing the Atlantic Ocean and graced with its famed lighthouse, Hunting Island also features rolling maritime forests and a beautiful beach, as well as other amenities that enhance this state park. This particular adventure starts near the historic black-and-white lighthouse and its adjacent buildings and grounds. Here you can explore the lighthouse, even climb into it, before hitting the beach. At this point you walk south along the shoreline until reaching a channel cut by Hurricane Matthew back in 2016. From here, backtrack, enjoying this beautiful beach one more time and perhaps having a picnic in the shadow of the lighthouse.

THE RUNDOWN

Distance: 4.8-mile there-and-back
Start: Hunting Island Lighthouse parking area
Nearest town: Beaufort
Hiking time: 2.2 hours
Fees and permits: Entrance fee required
Conveniences: Restroom, picnic area, water, beach/gift shop
Beach access: Yes
Trail users: Hikers, lighthouse lovers, beachcombers
Trail surface: Natural

Difficulty: Moderate
Highlights: Hunting Island Lighthouse, Atlantic coast beach
Canine compatibility: Leashed dogs permitted
Schedule: Daily from 6 a.m to 6 p.m. (extended to 9 p.m. during daylight saving time)
Managing agency: Hunting Island State Park, 2555 Sea Island Pkwy., Hunting Island, SC 29920; (843) 838-2011; www.southcarolinastateparks.com/huntingisland

FINDING THE TRAILHEAD

From Exit 33 off I-95, take US 21 South for 42 miles through the town of Beaufort; stay with this road to Hunting Island. Once there, pass the left turn to Hunting Island State Park Campground and continue to a left turn into the main park. At this time follow all signs to the lighthouse and the north beach to reach Parking Area C. GPS trailhead coordinates: 32.390305, -80.438438

WHAT TO SEE

Hunting Island Lighthouse is one of South Carolina's iconic coastal structures. The top third of the beacon is painted black, while the lower two-thirds are coated white. Surrounded by historic satellite buildings circa 1900, the lighthouse stands tall, exciting your blood upon approach. Enhanced with interpretive historical highlights, you can tour the grounds around the beacon and even walk to the top of the tower for a small fee. This is the only lighthouse in South Carolina that visitors can enter, so don't pass up the chance.

From the top, visitors can see for miles in all directions, quite a panorama that rivals vistas in South Carolina's Appalachians far to the west. The 5,000-acre state park boasts 4 miles of scenic Atlantic Ocean frontage, a wide sandy beach in a natural state, which

Morning sun colors Hunting Island Lighthouse.

is hard to find along the coast these days. Behind it stand rolling maritime woods of live oak, cedar, palm, and pine, rising and falling along ancient dunes that were once coastline. Tidal creeks run behind the beach, adding an estuarine component to the park.

Overlooking Helena Sound at the mouth of the Coosaw River, the original brick lighthouse at Hunting Island was constructed in 1859. During the Civil War the Confederates dismantled the beacon to prevent the Union from using the lighthouse to navigate the treacherous shoals between Charleston and Savannah. In 1873 the lighthouse was rebuilt, this time ingeniously using metal plates (each weighing 1,200 pounds) then lined with brick in case the beacon would need to be relocated. How prescient, since the shifting shore of this barrier island undermined the structure. Thus it was moved in

1889, 1 mile away from its original location. After that, the lightkeeper's house, oil storage hut, and whole kit and caboodle were moved to the new lighthouse site. The beacon remained in use until 1933, when it was deactivated. The light cast out 18 miles to sea. During World War II the beacon was used as a radio tower, and the park, developed by the Civilian Conservation Corps in the late 1930s and early 1940s, was turned into a military post.

For those who climb the lighthouse, 167 steps await, taking you 132 feet above the beach. Imagine carrying oil to the light up the stairs, day after day after day, to keep the beacon lit. Of course that was after the oil was brought here by boat to a deepwater dock 0.5-mile distant, then moved barrel by barrel on a hand-cranked rail line from the dock to the lighthouse. It was a lonely job with little contact between the folks who lived on this once-remote barrier island and the rest of the world. Supply boats brought the mail and news of the world and were a highlight of the lighthouse keeper's life.

You can learn a lot more about the lighthouse—listed on the National Register of Historic Places—and the lives of those who kept it going while here at the park. The stories are fascinating. Plan to spend some time at the lighthouse before beginning the hike.

The grounds of Hunting Island Lighthouse

Left: You can hike Hunting Island Lighthouse.
Right: Hunting Island Lighthouse

Your hike leads from the lighthouse area down the coast following the narrowing strip of land between the Atlantic Ocean and the tidal creek behind it, until you are forced to turn back due to a tidal channel cutting you off from the balance of the park's shoreline. Hurricane Matthew struck the South Carolina coastline on October 8, 2016, and worked over Hunting Island State Park, including destroying the beachfront cabins, altering the beach and beachfront forest itself. Much of the park was closed for several months. The storm's effects can still be seen in a new tidal creek outlet, skeletal trees, crumbled asphalt, and a regenerating shore. Nevertheless, the park remains a jewel and continues to recover on Mother Nature's schedule.

The hike is best done at low tide, when you can enjoy more of what is revealed when the water is down, from shells to seaweed. Also, in areas where fallen trees are scattered along the shore, it is easier to work around them.

The beachfront trailhead includes not only the historic lighthouse area but also a shaded picnic area, restrooms, and beach/gift shop, making for a pretty and noncommercialized coastline, one ideal for a coastal hiking adventure.

MILES AND DIRECTIONS

0.0 Leave Parking Area C, near the lighthouse. You may want to inspect the beacon first. Nearby stand the beacon and other structures around it, as well as restrooms, a picnic area, and a gift shop. A path leads you past the facilities straight for the Atlantic Ocean, pounding beyond the palms. To your left, northbound, the park coastline is more littered with fallen trees embedded in the sand. Head right once on the beach, southbound. The wide-sloping beach is colored with gray sands from which rise palms and oaks, many of which were damaged in the storm.

0.5 A low bluff rises on your right. Note the jetties designed to capture sand to refurbish the beach. You will also see embedded fallen oaks and palms rising from the sand.

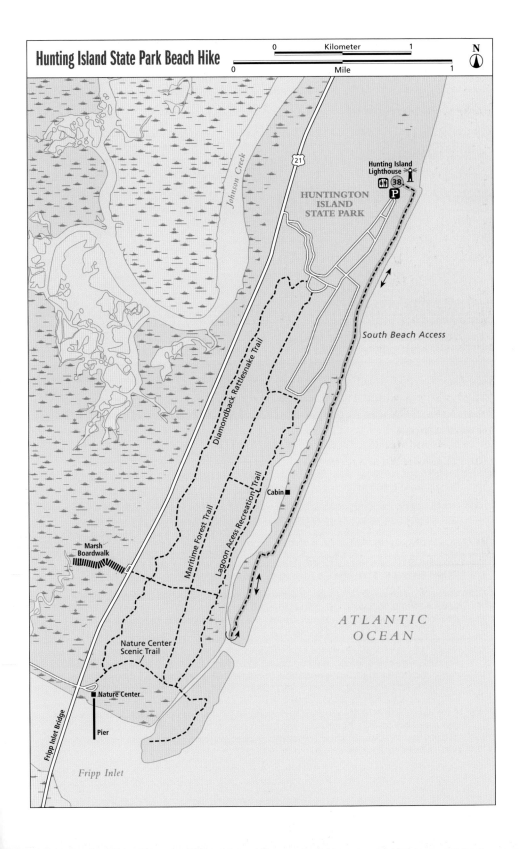

Hunting Island State Park Beach Hike

0 Kilometer 1
0 Mile 1

N

Johnson Creek

21

HUNTINGTON
ISLAND
STATE PARK

Hunting Island
Lighthouse

P 38

South Beach Access

Diamondback Rattlesnake Trail

Maritime Forest Trail

Lagoon Acess Recreation Trail

Cabin ■

Marsh
Boardwalk

ATLANTIC
OCEAN

Nature Center
Scenic Trail

Nature Center ■

Pier

Fripp Inlet Bridge

Fripp Inlet

The beach at low tide

0.6 Come to triangular concrete bases of a water tower from the 1950s. These triangular concrete pieces were exposed during Hurricane Andrew, after being buried for a period. Rolling surf resounds in your ears.

0.8 Reach the park's south beach access. Look south beyond Hunting Island and you can see the habitations of Fripp Island, across watery Fripp Inlet. The tidal creek begins to form on the landward side of the park. Notice how the cabin access road is now closed and impassable.

1.5 Pass the remains of the one park rental cabin that survived Hurricane Matthew. The others are gone. Gaze upward for osprey nests in the trees.

2.0 Come to an area with less sand and more fallen trees. If the tide is up, you may have to work inland, following the old cabin road. Here you will find huge piles of logs that look like matchsticks, demonstrating the incredible power of hurricanes. The tidal inlet is much wider to your right.

2.4 Reach the newer cut linking the tidal creek to the Atlantic Ocean, created in 2016. Formerly you could continue along the beach, then take a trail bridge over the tidal creek and return to the mainland. Now you have to backtrack along the beach.

4.0 Pass the south beach access. Keep north.

4.8 Arrive back at the north beach access, completing the coastal hiking adventure. However, on a falling tide you can work your way to the northern tip of the island, passing the campground and campground beach access, about a mile north, potentially extending your hike.

39. HUNTING ISLAND STATE PARK NATURE CENTER HIKE

This is a highlight-packed hike. Start at the park nature center, where you can enjoy interpretive displays as well as walk the fishing pier, then take off hiking. First, head out to a small barrier island linked by a trail bridge. Here you can enjoy a little beach overlooking Fripp Inlet and the Atlantic Ocean. From there backtrack and join a path cruising through woods bordering a tidal lagoon. Here you can absorb watery views of the estuary as well as the beach across the water. Turn inland to join the Maritime Forest Trail. You will be walking atop ancient wooded dunes overlooking surprisingly hilly woods before returning to the nature center. You also can add the park's Marsh Boardwalk to the multifaceted adventure.

THE RUNDOWN

Distance: 4.7-mile loop with spur
Start: Hunting Island State Park nature center
Nearest town: Beaufort
Hiking time: 2.3 hours
Fees and permits: Entrance fee required
Conveniences: Restroom, fishing pier, water, nature center, picnic area
Beach access: Yes
Trail users: Hikers, mountain bikers in spots
Trail surface: Natural
Difficulty: Moderate

Highlights: Small barrier island, beach, rolling maritime woods, tidal lagoon
Canine compatibility: Leashed dogs permitted
Schedule: Daily from 6 a.m. to 6 p.m. (extended to 9 p.m. during daylight saving time)
Managing agency: Hunting Island State Park, 2555 Sea Island Pkwy., Hunting Island, SC 29920; (843) 838-2011; www.southcarolinastateparks.com/huntingisland

FINDING THE TRAILHEAD

From exit 33 off I-95, take US 21 South for 42 miles through the town of Beaufort; stay with this road to Hunting Island. Once there, pass the left turn to Hunting Island State Park Campground as well as the main park entrance, continuing toward Fripp Island to turn left at the park nature center immediately before the bridge over Fripp Inlet. GPS trailhead coordinates: 32.342838, -80.461784

WHAT TO SEE

Hunting Island forms the southernmost rampart fronting the Coosaw River as it flows into the Atlantic Ocean. The open water of St. Helena Sound lies to the north. To the east runs the vast Atlantic Ocean. Four miles of park beachfront reach from Hunting Island's northern tip south to Fripp Island, which also fronts the Atlantic Ocean.

The park also boasts some of South Carolina's most gorgeous woodlands, through which much of this hike travels. Visitors can turn this hike into an all-day affair simply by enjoying the added amenities of the state park. Start your extended tour by first heading to the nature center, where you can learn all about the park's flora and fauna and

A palm cathedral covers the trail.

ask questions of the on-site naturalist. After this, stroll out to the fishing pier extending into Fripp Inlet. Even if you aren't tossing a line, you can see what's biting and also look outward to fine views in all directions, including easterly toward the barrier island you are fixing to visit. After enjoying your time around the visitor center, strike out on the Nature Center Scenic Trail, a wide track leading easterly through tall maritime woods of live oak, pine, and palm, as well as sweetgum and other species. After passing a couple of trail intersections, you reach a tidal lagoon and a bridge spanning this estuary. Here walk over the bridge, then reach a small barrier island. This isle was once connected to the mainland, but a channel formed during the storm surge of Hurricane Matthew back in the fall of 2016, cutting it off from the mainland. (The storm also downed trees and heavily impacted the park.) While hiking here, I once ran into a man who grew up on what is now this barrier island. He said it was paradise for a young boy, with the beach, ocean, tidal stream, and woods in which to play. Of course, the houses are all gone now and this parcel is part of the state park. Nowadays you can work your way through woods to the southern tip of the isle and explore a beach skirting Fripp Inlet. Much of the Atlantic Beach frontage here was washed away during Hurricane Andrew. Such is the ever-changing nature of barrier islands.

After returning to the mainland, our hike joins the Lagoon Access Recreation Trail as it leads along the tidal lagoon under shady forest. This track is quite level and offers views into the lagoon and beyond to the east. The trail comes near the park's south beach

Looking toward the Atlantic from a tidal lagoon

access area before joining the Maritime Forest Trail. This path will truly surprise you as it rambles through one of the most beautiful woodlands along the East Coast, amid ancient, now wooded, parallel dunes that give surprising vertical variation to the coastal hike. Much of the trail runs atop an old dune, allowing you to look down on the lands beside you, shrouded in cedars, live oaks, and palm trees. This is one place where you want to walk slowly, lingering to enjoy the preserve. If you want to extend your hike, a connector leads to the Marsh Boardwalk Trail. This additional track stretches west to a tidal marshland, adding another component to the adventure. Otherwise, just stick with the Maritime Forest Trail as it leads you back to the trailhead and the nature center.

Don't rush through a visit to Hunting Island. Give it at least a day, perhaps longer if pitching your tent or RV at the campground. Hunting Island State Park, one of South Carolina's largest preserves, is a superlative coastal destination. Left mostly in a wild state, the preserve is developed just enough to where you can enjoy the beach and the forest, yet not feel like you are in a place neither too busy nor too remote. It's just right.

Hunting Island is a destination in and of itself. However, nearby Beaufort is a small and historic town, established well before this country was founded. Take a buggy tour, see antebellum homes, and learn about the Gullah culture, where residents of Lowcountry, as the coastal area of South Carolina is known, have a culture of their own. Visit the Beaufort History Museum, learn about the Marines at the Parris Island Museum, or examine the John Mark Verdier House. Explore many other structures from the late 1700s and

Hiking through gorgeous maritime woods

early 1800s while learning about the history of this coastal town. It will enhance your Hunting Island experience.

MILES AND DIRECTIONS

0.0 Leave from the nature center parking area, across from the nature center, between two park houses. Pass around a gate and join the Nature Center Scenic Trail, on a gravel doubletrack through pine, palm, live oak, and yaupon.

0.1 The rolling Diamondback Rattlesnake Trail leaves left. Stay straight under a tall forest canopy. Pass freshwater wooded marshes ahead.

0.3 Partial views open to the right, south, of the salt marshes and Fripp Island beyond. Cut through some ancient dunes.

0.4 The Maritime Forest Trail leaves left and is your return route. At this point, keep straight, soon passing the trail intersection with the Lagoon Access Recreation Trail. For now keep straight and walk over the arched tidal creek bridge, reaching the small barrier island created in 2016.

0.6 After the bridge, head right on a well-worn path leading south toward Fripp Inlet.

0.8 Reach the sandy point overlooking Fripp Inlet. Explore the beach and then backtrack across the arched bridge.

1.0 Head right, northbound on the Lagoon Access Recreation Trail, weaving its way among the palms and oaks. Enjoy looks across the lagoon.

1.5 A spur trail leads left to link to the Marsh Boardwalk Trail. Keep straight, still cruising along the tidal creek. Look for deer tracks in the woods, as well as blackened tree trunks from prescribed fires. Sporadic views open to the Atlantic Ocean.

Hunting Island State Park Nature Center Hike

Kilometer 0 — 1

Mile 0 — 1

N

South Beach Access

Diamondback Rattlesnake Trail

Maritime Forest Trail

21

Lagoon Acess Recreation Trail

Cabin ■

HUNTINGTON ISLAND STATE PARK

Marsh Boardwalk

ATLANTIC OCEAN

Nature Center Scenic Trail

39 P
■ Nature Center

Fripp Inlet Bridge

Pier   Beach

Fripp Inlet

2.0 The Palmetto Pines Pass shortcuts the circuit. Stay straight with the Lagoon Access Recreation Trail.

2.7 A spur trail leads right to an alternate trailhead. Stay left here, now heading westerly, away from the ocean. Roll over old wooded dunes.

2.9 Turn left, joining the Maritime Woods Trail. Head south atop a wooded dune under a canopy of ultragorgeous woods. Soak in the elevated woodland looks.

3.3 Pass the other end of Palmetto Pines Pass. Continue south.

3.8 Reach the Marsh Boardwalk connector. It is about 0.25 miles to the road and alternate parking for the boardwalk. Otherwise, keep straight, still southbound on the Maritime Forest Trail.

4.3 Meet the Nature Center Scenic Trail. You've been here before. Head right, returning to the nature center.

4.7 Arrive back at the nature center, completing the eye-pleasing coastal hike.

40. PINCKNEY ISLAND NATIONAL WILDLIFE REFUGE

This coastal hike in the shadow of Hilton Head offers a lot of everything, from wildlife viewing to varied forests and even a beach you can walk. Historic Pinckney Island, now managed by the US Fish and Wildlife Service, presents a chance to enjoy a South Carolina coastal island in its natural state. The hike takes you the length of the isle, then loops back. First, walk amid forests bordered by salt marsh, allowing aquatic panoramas. Stop by wildlife-rich Ibis Pond. Continue to the north tip of the island and White Point, where a beach area allows you to walk the sands beside expansive, tidal Chechessee River. Your return trip takes you near the big Intracoastal Waterway while viewing small trailside ponds. The trails are level, wide, and easy to hike, but if the distance is more than what you bargained for, simply cut the loop short using shortcut cross trails.

THE RUNDOWN

Distance: 8.8-mile loop with spur
Start: Parking area on loop
Nearest town: Hilton Head
Hiking time: 4.0 hours
Fees and permits: None
Conveniences: None
Beach access: Yes
Trail users: Hikers, bicyclists, birders
Trail surface: Natural
Difficulty: Moderate despite the distance

Highlights: Wildlife at Ibis Pond, beach at White Point, marsh views
Canine compatibility: Dogs not permitted
Schedule: Daily during daylight hours only
Managing agency: Savannah Coastal Refuges Complex, 694 Beech Hill Lane, Hardeeville, SC, 29927; (843) 784-2468; www.fws.gov/refuge/Pinckney_Island/

FINDING THE TRAILHEAD

From exit 8 on I-95 near Hardeeville, take US 278 East for 19 miles to reach the left turn into the refuge just after bridging large Mackay Creek. Follow the entrance road for 0.6 mile to reach the shaded parking circle and the trailhead. GPS trailhead coordinates: 32.233719, -80.779182

WHAT TO SEE

Located just a half a mile west of busy Hilton Head Island, Pinckney Island National Wildlife Refuge protects 4,053 acres of South Carolina coastal islands, of which Pinckney Island is by far the largest and only one accessible to visitors; the rest are left to wildlife. Long used as a seasonal camp by aboriginals seeking shellfish and other easy to obtain edibles, it was visited by European explorers in the 1500s and 1600s but wasn't permanently settled until the early 1700s, when Indian trader Alexander Mackay used it as his home base. Mackay Creek, running along the west side of the isle, still bears the family name. Later the Mackay family sold the island to Charles Pinckney, father of South Carolina Revolutionary War legend and signer of the US Constitution, Charles

Wildlife here ranges from birds to reptiles.

Cotesworth Pinckney, a major force in South Carolina and American politics in the early days of our country. The Pinckney family established a plantation on the island, growing cotton using slave labor. During the Civil War, Union troops used Pinckney Island as a base. After the national conflict, the Pinckney plantation underwent decades of decline until it was sold off in the 1930s to a man named James Bruce. He transformed the former farm into a hunting preserve, digging freshwater ponds to attract waterfowl, planting trees, and cultivating some parts of the isle. Despite being passed through different hands, Pinckney Island remained a hunting preserve until it was donated to the US Fish and Wildlife Service in 1975.

Beach at the tip of Pinkney Island

For a half a century since being taken over by the US Fish and Wildlife Service, Pinck-ney Island, Corn Island, Big Harry Island, Little Harry Island, and Buzzard Island have been managed not only for game, but also for plants and nongame wildlife from nesting birds to butterflies. The adjacent tidal waterways and salt marsh also are preserved and managed to maximize their natural attributes.

You can often see alligators among the freshwater ponds, as well as migratory birds and waterfowl. In fact, the refuge is an important stopping point on the Atlantic Flyway, the path taken by migratory birds heading south for winter and north for summer. The refuge also provides nesting habitats for herons and egrets as well as smaller songbirds. It can be said that the refuge is a regular cacophony of birdsong throughout the year.

Much of the hike traverses maritime forest where Spanish moss–covered live oaks mingle with palms, pines, and cedars. Here you may see deer, armadillos, bobcats, and, more commonly, squirrels. Biodiversity is the accurate buzzword for this hike from start to finish. You leave the parking area following a doubletrack north along a narrow line of forest bordered by salt marsh with views. Trailside interpretive information enhances your experience. Your first major stop is Ibis Pond, a first-rate birding and alligator view-ing area. Many visitors turn around at Ibis Pond, but this hike takes you through more woodlands, offering marsh views in the distance and freshwater ponds in the near. Keep-ing north, you follow the full expanse of the coastal landmass, getting plenty of exercise while making your way to White Point. Here, the tidal Chechessee River runs past the

Hikers walk among salt pannes.

north tip of the island into Port Royal Sound and the nearby Atlantic Ocean, creating a beach curving around the point. Here you can leave the trail system and explore the shoreline to the west a bit and more so to the east. After getting your fill of salty sand while exploring the shoreline, backtrack from White Point, then pick up new trail, passing Clubhouse Pond before turning south in more maritime woods, cruising the eastern shore of the island where Skull Creek forms part of the Intracoastal Waterway dividing Pinckney Island from Hilton Head Island.

The final bit of the hike is a backtrack. During this last segment you will be reflecting on the multitude of ecosystems contained within this one coastal refuge. And more habitats mean more wildlife. Since the trails are wide and easy, well maintained, and decently marked, you can focus on learning about the finer points of this valuable South Carolina refuge laced with coastal trails we can enjoy.

MILES AND DIRECTIONS

0.0 Leave the signed trailhead on the west side of the circular parking road. A short trail leads west to a closed doubletrack. Head right, northeasterly, under tall pines, widespread live oaks, and palmetto, all draped in Spanish moss. Open onto salt marsh as you follow the road, an elevated causeway above the marl and needlerush where crabs are stepping lively. Views open to adjacent islands.

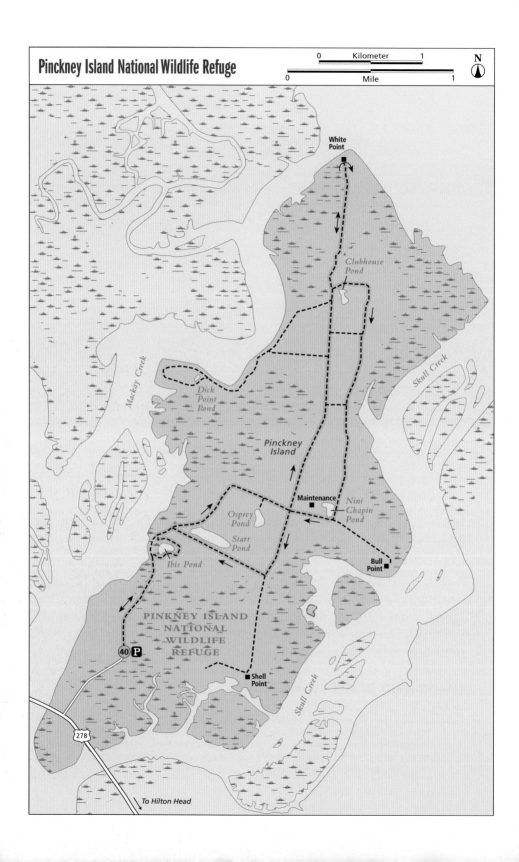

Kilometer
0   1

Mile
0   1

N

White
Point

Clubhouse
Pond

Mackay Creek

Skull Creek

Dick
Point
Pond

Pinckney
Island

Maintenance

Nini
Chapin
Pond

Osprey
Pond

Starr
Pond

Bull
Point

Ibis Pond

PINCKNEY ISLAND
NATIONAL
WILDLIFE
REFUGE

40 P

Shell
Point

Skull Creek

278

To Hilton Head

0.6 Join the spur leading right to Ibis Pond. Circle around the wildlife-rich freshwater habitation. Scan for alligator, ibis, egrets, and a host of birdlife while tracing the trail around the water. View birds from a telescope.

1.0 Return to the main track stretching from one end of the island to the other. Head right, continuing northeasterly.

1.1 Intersect the track coming in from your right heading toward Shell Point. This is your return route. For now keep straight on the main refuge track, passing Starr Pond. You alternate between sun and shade, depending on tree cover.

1.8 A spur trail leads right to Osprey Pond. Keep straight.

2.0 Reach a four-way intersection. You will be here again later. For now, turn left, heading northbound on the main refuge track. Pure woods rise around you, shading the path. Note the natural freshwater wooded marshes mixed in with the adjacent woodlands, adding yet another ecotone to the island ecosystem.

2.6 A spur trail leads east, shortcutting the loop.

3.0 A track leads left to Dick Point Pond. Stay straight on the main track, northbound.

3.1 Another spur trail leads east, shortcutting the loop.

3.3 A second track leads left to Dick Point Pond. Stay straight on the main track, northbound.

Live oaks and palmetto border the trail.

3.4 Come to Clubhouse Pond. Pay close attention, as the main track curves right. Here pick up the grassy trail leading left. Look for the sign indicating "White Point." Head north through a tree-bordered meadow. Dip across a neck of marsh, then walk under imperial live oaks.

4.2 Come to a turnaround at the island's north end. Here descend from the woods to the beach curving around White Point. After exploring the shoreline, backtrack from White Point, southbound.

5.0 Head left, easterly, with Clubhouse Pond to your right, now on new trail.

5.2 Curve south, avoiding closed and signed roads. Enjoy deep woods while walking with marsh and Skull Creek to the east.

5.5 Keep straight as a cross trail leads right. The track comes closer to the marsh.

6.0 Keep straight, southbound, as another cross trail leads right.

6.3 Nini Chapin Pond comes into view on your right, along with refuge maintenance facilities.

6.5 Turn right at an intersection as a spur trail leads left to Bull Point. Join the maintenance area access road.

6.8 Reach a four-way intersection. You have been here before. Head left, southbound, bisecting marsh on an elevated track. Views open to the east.

7.2 Turn right as a trail leads straight to Shell Point. Hike westerly, passing Starr Pond.

7.8 Return to the main track. You have been here before. Head left, southbound, backtracking.

8.8 Arrive back at the trailhead, completing the coastal hiking adventure.

HIKE INDEX